*Theories and Works
of Contemporary Architects*

James Stirling
Writings on Architecture

edited by
Robert Maxwell

*A special thank to the James Stirling
Foundation and Michael Wilford
and Partners*

Editor
Luca Molinari

Design
Marcello Francone

Layout
Sabina Brucoli

Distributed outside the United States
and Canada by Thames and Hudson Ltd.,
30 Bloomsbury Street, London WC1B 3QP,
United Kingdom

This book is subject to the condition that
no part of it shall be reproduced or otherwise
circulate in any form or by any electronic,
mechanic or other means without the prior
consent in writing of the right holders
and the publisher

© 1998 Skira editore, Milan
All Rights Reserved

Printed in May 1998
on behalf of Skira, Geneva - Milan

Contents

7 James Stirling: Writings
   Robert Maxwell

29 Garches to Jaoul.
   Le Corbusier as Domestic
   Architect in 1927 and 1953

41 Ronchamp. Le Corbusier's
   Chapel and the Crisis
   of Rationalism

51 Regionalism and Modern
   Architecture

61 A Personal View
   of the Present Situation

65 Packaged Deal
   and Prefabrication

73 Afterthoughts
   on the Flats at Ham
   Common

79 The Functional Tradition
   and Expression

89 An Architect's Approach
   to Architecture

111 Anti-Structure

125 Methods of Expression
    and Materials

133 James Stirling:
    Architectural Aims and
    Influences

151 The Monumentally
    Informal

161 Architecture and Politics

167 Restructuring
    of the Palazzo Citterio

173 Acceptance Address
    for the Pritzker Prize

179 Speech at the Opening
    Ceremony of the
    Braun Headquarters
    at Melsungen

183 Opening Speech
    for the Clore Gallery

187 Inauguration of Berlin
    Science Centre

195 James Stirling in Tokyo
    Interviewed by Arata
    Isozaki

211 James Stirling and Michael
    Dennis. Notes from
    an Informal Discussion

225 Stirling Stuff.
    Conversation
    with Sunand Prasad
    and Satish Grover

245 The Clore Gallery.
    Interview with
    Charles Jencks

263 Seven Keys to Good
    Architecture

265 This is Tomorrow

267 Three Loggias

275 Master Class: Comments
    on Teaching at Düsseldorf

279 Building into Landscape.
    Content into Form

James Stirling: Writings
Robert Maxwell

If the writings of James Stirling have any interest for us today, it's not because he was a great writer, but because he was quite possibly a great architect. Since he is no longer with us, since he was an architect of a certain quality, we would like to question him further about his work and his ideas. By collecting his writings together, it is possible to hear his voice again, and to gain some insights into his creative personality.

    The writings brought together here are of four kinds: articles, speeches, conversations and marginalia. The speeches were written before being spoken, the conversations were spoken before being transcribed. The writing is uneven, but the character is robust. This is someone who has given his life to architecture, who accepts it as a discipline encompassed by a matter-of-fact reality, yet lives it with passion.

    If his opinions are forthright, this is an aspect of his character. They are indeed often brusque, sometimes intemperate. However, they do not have to be right for them to be interesting. What they reveal to us is the strength of his beliefs and the courage of his convictions. They are the counterpart to the assurance proclaimed in his designs, and it is that assurance for which we are grateful, for it has added to the world.

James Frazer Stirling was born in Glasgow in 1923. After fighting in the Normandy landings, he was demobilised with a service grant, which paid for him to study architecture at Liverpool University. The school was by then under the direction of Lionel B. Budden, the successor to Charles Reilly, who had made it the leading architecture school in the country. If the Beaux-Arts influence was by 1945 virtually dead, the academic method was still studiously eclectic. Stirling began by doing renderings of the classical orders, and went on to design a house in the manner of Voysey. I also attended that school, and in the course of the first few years had designed a Cistercian monastery in corbelled stonework, a rustic Palladian town hall, an eighteenth-century town house with garages instead of stables, a Baroque garden pavilion, a Corbusian suburb, and a Mendelssohnian chemistry building. I have heard that Alison and Peter Smithson, following a similar course at Newcastle University, were renowned for their mastery of pastiche. It was a question of surviving the system. The schools had not yet adopted the modern movement in architecture as a teaching resource, and many teachers still thought of it as an unfortunate interlude, soon to be forgotten. It was not until the middle fifties that student excitement about new possibilities began to change the rules. In this atmosphere, Stirling would have learned as much about historical antecedents as about structural steelwork.

In addition, he came under a special influence during the session 1949–50, while he was preparing his thesis design, from the fact that his tutor for thesis was Colin Rowe, as he had been for me a year earlier. Colin Rowe had the erudition of a scholar, but the taste of an aristocratic amateur. He enjoyed architecture as a form of theatre, and he sent his students to the library not to study, but to crib ideas for their designs. Rowe's influence as a teacher was circumscribed in Britain by a puritanical refusal to express feelings in public, and architecture as a public art suffered under this constraint more than did poetry, which was generally proclaimed in private. In the United States, however, Rowe had an enormous influence on a whole generation, through being also adviser to Peter Eisenman at Cambridge University, and then through his relatively short period of teaching at Austin, Texas, before settling down to a long and fruitful career at Cornell. Rowe was not only a historian, he enjoyed modernism because it provided direct access to the perennial game of architecture, and as his seminal article on "The Mathematics of the Ideal Villa" makes clear, he enjoyed the continuity between modern architecture and its past. Le Corbusier virtually invented modern architecture, but at least in his earlier work, he was imbued with a classical spirit. Rowe's interest was in formal structures, and his writing gave a more intellectual status to cribbing than did the writing of Robert Venturi a few years later, Venturi being mainly interested in "effects".

During his student years Stirling developed a crush on Mackintosh and Hoffmann, as well as Baillie Scott and Voysey. And Asplund. He was also intrigued by the English baroque architects Archer, Vanbrugh and Hawksmoor, a taste no doubt prompted by Rowe (for I was subject to the same persuasion) and these were the first architects he went to look at as soon as he arrived in London.

As he left school he was already under the spell of Saxl and Wittkower's *British Art and the Mediterranean*, a book too large to put in the shelves, so left lying about on the floor to be consulted frequently, following the Rowe method. The influence of Le Corbusier, later characterised by him as "Europe's greatest architect", did not begin until his thesis year, so that was also undoubtedly initiated by Rowe.

In his speech "Architectural Aims and Influences", his response to the award of the RIBA Royal Gold Medal, Stirling acknowledges his interest while still a student in the "just arrived" modern movement — "the foreign version, as taught by Colin Rowe". He admits to having been somewhat eclectic in his tastes. By 1980 his interests have greatly expanded to take in the stripy brickwork of Butterfield, Street and Scott; the shingle style houses of New England; the concrete block houses of Frank Lloyd Wright; the art deco palaces of New York; and as preferred architects, the neo-classicists such as Soane, Gandy, Playfair and Goodridge; and their German counterparts Gilly, Weinbrenner, von Klenze and Schinkel. He expresses a preference for the period at the beginning of the nineteenth century when Neo-classicism was evolving into the Romantic. His personal library contained expensive volumes on English castles and French chateaux, rococo gardens in Bavaria and Italy, Venetian palazzi and English country houses: a truly eclectic range.

The Rowe influence must also have bolstered Stirling's natural curiosity about architecture as something for ever under our eyes, always accessible. Rowe's midnight perambulations with Henry Russell Hitchcock through the streets of London were legendary. At a personal level the interest started with the vernacular industrial buildings of the eighteenth century, seen particularly as precursors of the modern movement. This view of them as suitable models for "The New Empiricism" had been promoted by *The Architectural Review* during the early fifties.[1] Stirling was familiar with these buildings from observing the industrial landscape in the north of England. Train journeys were particularly enjoyed because they took the traveller across the exposed

[1] Stirling refers to a special issue of *The Architectural Review*, July 1957, on "The Functionalist Tradition".

backs of towns and through the industrial detritus, from which he later claimed to draw many ideas. These sources seem to have contributed to Stirling's appreciation of power and presence in a building, whatever its style, and may even have affected his feeling for proportions. More generally, he learned very early to take pleasure in *looking*.

This background perhaps goes some way to explain not only Stirling's tastes, but also his stances. Writing had a use for him in giving a certain substance to feelings that operated at the level of intuition. In public, he felt the need to state a position, to justify to a wider audience the results of his primary activity, which was and remained building.

At the outset of his career he was a straight modernist, and justified his work by reference to a functionalist creed that latched on to social needs and cost exigency, not so far removed from Hannes Meyer's creed of the true *sachlichkeit* architecture — function times economy. His method was to subject the brief to logical analysis, after which the solution would emerge automatically. In his contribution to the exhibition *This is Tomorrow*, he proclaims with iconoclastic zeal: "Architecture, one of the practical arts [...] has deflated the position of [...] the fine arts. The painting is as obsolete as the picture rail." A little later, in "Seven Keys to Good Architecture", when he was one of several architects interviewed by a newspaper, he says: "For architects to create monuments to their own aesthetic feelings is a worthless occupation, always [...] I believe that modern architecture has nothing to do with the past [...] While I enjoy past architecture in itself I do not accept that you can carry it over into our time as a lesson to assist you. It lacks relevance."

These are the opinions of a young architect determined to make good through the sheer efficiency and economy of his designs. In all the early work it was essential to meet strict cost limits if the job was to proceed. Of course, the claim to efficiency was *both* a matter of the functionalist creed, *and* propaganda for an effective professional service. Functionalism as a doctrine has been particularly welcomed by the British architect because it removes any suggestion that he is pursuing a secret agenda, or doing anything other than giving whole-hearted attendance to his client's needs. It provides a kind of alibi to prove that he is professionally responsible, not trying to use the client's state of want in order to advance his own career, or to express his own feelings, as the artist is allowed, even expected, to do. Those needs are embodied in the programme, and Sir John Summerson argued in a speech at the RIBA, given in June 1957, that the theory of modernism required that the programme itself could be considered as sufficient support for its legitimacy.

In the classical era, action was postulated as the result of applying principles, and only principles could guarantee consistency and unity in the result. With the modern movement, principles were apparently abandoned in favour of empirical necessity, the exigencies of the programme, which were subject to evolution in changing circumstances. In taking the programme as the origin of design, modern architecture accepted the accidental, and abjured personal expression. Architecture became contingent on matters outside its own domain. But then, according to Summerson, any purely programmatic unity lacks the element of expression altogether. If you accept the principle that the programme is the source of unity, the crucible of the architect's creative endeavour, you cannot postulate another principle, another crucible, at the other end of the designer's process, to satisfy the architect's craving for conspicuous self expression. You cannot have it both ways. You certainly cannot have two sources of unity! If architecture is contingent on the programme, it has no other source of unity.

This is the sort of logic that isolates the object of examination in order to eliminate any inconsistency within it. It ignores the distinction between doctrine and practice. Stirling adopted functionalism as a doctrine, but while addressing the priorities that his adopted programme required, he worked by intuition, following his own inner convictions. It could be said that he observed a British convention, parallel to the way that English law follows precedent rather than principle. This combination of external doctrine and inner motivation is precisely what sets up the field of decision, and the resulting action is as subject to impulse as to logic. Indeed, the combination of belief and logic is the defining characteristic of an ideological field, which today we have little difficulty in seeing as the all-pervasive framework of action.

The demand for unity arises from the desire to establish principles and secure legitimacy, and here again, it is possible today to recognize that the achievements of the Renaissance owe little to principle and a great deal to shared beliefs. These are not the same thing. What passed for theory during the Renaissance was just as much a matter of personal conviction as of applying principles. It is hardly any different from the theory embodied in Le Corbusier's *Vers une architecture,* which we would classify as a polemic.

Summerson's own masterly account of *The Classical Language of Architecture*[2] makes it clear that it was essentially a system of decoration, based on a corpus of structural symbols, and animated by an injunction to follow the rules — as in a game. Perrault, after all, had justified classical architecture as the result of convention rather than revealed truth,

[2] John Summerson: *The Classical Language of Architecture,* Thames & Hudson, London 1980, ©1963 Summerson and the BBC.

13

thereby enabling it to survive into the era of applied science. After Perrault it was a matter of observing the proprieties. In a sense, the strange history of Mannerism, dominant during more than a hundred years after the relatively brief period of the High Renaissance, demonstrates that the principles of architecture adopted at the outset of the cinquecento were a matter of belief, and already contained the seeds of doubt, later realized during the expansive period of the Baroque. In today's jargon, it provided a grand narrative, convincing to all who shared the beliefs of the times, no longer so convincing to us.

In an interesting passage, Summerson went on to suggest that any hankering after the unity of expression which programmatic architecture is denied, is due to a sense of loss, as if the architect were suffering from a species of amputation, longing for a source of unity that has been cut away, a unity that would restore the meaning to expression: "You must consider whether [...] the position of an architect who is concerned about the question of expression or style is not that of a man feeling his way back to classicism, or neo-classicism, or, to put the finest possible point on it, to crypto-classicism."

Was Stirling, then, a crypto-classicist, given the stance he took in his later work? There, he takes an evident pleasure in elaborating a game in which representational elements are inter-mingled with abstract elements in a synthesis that bears a highly personal imprint. In discussing the controversial Sackler Gallery at the Fogg with Michael Dennis, he stated: "Nowadays one can draw equally, without guilt, from the abstract style of modern design and the multiple layers of historical precedent."[3]

There is some irony here, insofar as Summerson was unexpectedly appreciative of Stirling's own vision of a post-

[3] Interview with Michael Dennis, Official Brochure for the Inauguration of the Sackler Gallery, Harvard, October 1985.

14

modern architecture. Reviewing the Clore Gallery, in which Stirling indulges in somewhat formalistic games in the sequence of entrance hall and staircase, Summerson approved the result as producing the kind of strange space that Soane would have enjoyed, and capped his article with the title "Vitruvius Ludens", the architect at play.[4] The idea of treating architecture as a game, with rules, was after all close to his own interpretation of *The Classical Language of Architecture*. Summerson returned to this theme in a later article "Vitruvius Ridens, or Laughter at the Tate", where he comments about a lack of support to a panel above the corner window: "leaving the brick panel in an apparent state of imminent collapse. One thinks of Giulio Romano's slipping voussoirs at Mantua." The risky game which Stirling plays is clearly close to the game of Mannerism, though Summerson hesitates to spell it out.

On the other hand, during the late seventies, Summerson was a guest critic of students' work at the Bartlett School for a project that asked the students to design an extension to the Dulwich Art Gallery, by Soane. It was clear from his comments that he detested all forms of pastiche, and hated the jejune efforts of some students to encompass post-modernism from a position of abysmal ignorance about the principles of classical architecture. As a teaching vehicle, he preferred modern architecture, bent to the needs of the programme and open to a common sense discussion. It is possible that Summerson himself felt the pain of amputation, and responded to Stirling's will to restore a game of architecture with all the concealed energy of a crypto-classicist.

However, if there was in Stirling a tendency to see architecture as embodying values different from its simple correspondence to the programme, this tendency is in evidence from the beginning. He enjoyed the play of abstraction, but

[4] Article titled "Vitruvius Ludens", in *The Architectural Review*, March 1983; also, by the same author: "Vitruvius Ridens, or Laughter at the Tate", in *The Architectural Review*, June 1987.

at the same time he always saw within that a parallel process of representation, and so an endless potential for expression. At the beginning expression was more or less limited to functional elements that would reveal an elementary meaning; later it was expected to encompass a wider array of cultural resonances. It could be said to approximate to a repertoire of coded meanings, that evolved in time from the conditions of a denotative to those of a connotative semiotic.

In his essay "The Functional Tradition and Expression", Stirling makes it clear that he saw in the functional tradition an alternative architectural expression to that of style or structure. This is by the direct expression of the actual accommodation volumes in relation to each element determining the plastic composition of the building. He goes on: "It is not assumed that every element should be expressive, but it is important that a hierarchy of the most significant volumes is recognizable in the ultimate composition [...] a design will start to emerge in the imagination when the relationship of spaces appears to have coherent organizational patterns."

It is interesting to note that, although the architect starts by identifying the most significant volumes according to an analysis of the functions, this is not the sole source of the design. The design, he says, will emerge *in the imagination*, and so results from a judgement about what appears to have coherent organizational pattern. With Stirling therefore we see that the hard facts of function are absorbed into a mental process which draws them together into a composition. The very use of the word *composition* implies judgement, as we expect whenever it is a matter of art and not of science. For Hannes Meyer, to speak of composition was to abandon the *sachlichkeit* imperative, to let go of objective reality and re-enter the world of personal and arbitrary decisions. It is important to note also that Stirling did not think of the functional as lying outside of culture, but saw it already embodied in a tradition.

In the same article, Stirling explains the use of earthworks as a containing perimeter in his competition project for Churchill College, not only as a response to the conditions of a sloping site, a matter of expediency, but as a form *associated with the symbolism of security and protection*. As such, he deemed them appropriate to form the boundary to a residential college. Such instances go a long way towards justifying his claim that abstract and representative factors have always been considered together in his designs.

Indeed, the bold buildings that first made Stirling's reputation, particularly the Engineering Building at Leicester University, in which James Gowan was his partner, already reveal concerns that go beyond the purely functional. He is at pains to point out that it was site constraints that induced them to build the research and administrative accommodation in the form of towers, forced to the very limits of the site, in order to leave maximum space for the engineering laboratories, which needed to be flexible and varied in layout to meet possible changes in their programme; again, it was the desire to minimise vertical circulation that led them to keep lecture and seminar rooms at the lower levels, leaving the upper levels, the personal rooms and the elevator to members of faculty. (The same argument is brought in to explain the vertical circulation in the History Building at Cambridge University.)

So functional matters are essential in defining the initial parameters. Then we go on to a series of decisions that are not functional alone, but that lead towards the appearance of a coherent organizational pattern. It may have been just such a concern that led the architects to contain the lecture hall at Leicester in a massive cantilever, but Summerson himself points out that this could be considered as following a precedent of Melnikov.[5] Again Stirling justifies the diagonal layout of the rooflights over the engineering laboratories by referring to orientation, but we may be forgiven for thinking that the architects enjoyed solving the resulting problem of the margins, where the termination of the angled roof structure provides a richly decorative effect. Indeed, the language adopted by Stirling and Gowan in this building goes so far beyond ordinary functional responses that Peter Eisenman could elaborate a highly mannerist reading of the building as following a series of formalist rules.[6] The rules are derived from the play of constructional elements treated, not as absolutes, but as purely formal values in a game of ambiguity and reversal, analogous to the "game" of Mannerism.

If there is some Melnikov in Leicester, there are certainly aspects of a distinctly constructivist origin in all the red-brick buildings. The project for residential accommodation at Selwyn, also designed with James Gowan, with glazing that staggers outward as the building rises, would appear expressionistically apposite today. The Florey Building at Oxford, which leans outward on tapering supports, has aspects of Melnikov and also of Breuer, in the model for an ideal town which he did just before leaving Britain for the United States. While not denying a certain stylistic aspect in these buildings, Stirling prefers to suggest "humbler" origins: at Leicester, a reference to the typical pre-war industrial estate where the office block is in front and the workshops behind; at Cambridge a reference to nineteenth-century public reading rooms with glass lantern roofs; at Oxford a reference to the traditional college courtyard.[7] He may not want to reveal

[5] Summerson, cit. He refers to the Rusakov Workers' Club in Moscow, of 1928.
[6] Peter Eisenman: "Real and English", in *Oppositions*, No. 4, October 1974.
[7] Speech in acceptance of the Royal Gold Medal, in *Architectural Design*, No. 7-8, 1980.

all his sources, architects rarely do, but the way he was taught at Liverpool would have encouraged him to treat the modern movement not only as an ideology but also as a tradition, no less engrossing than the functional tradition, and therefore itself a source of ideas.

In his article on "Methods of Expression"[8] Stirling again reiterates his attitude to expression. He wants to express the functional elements, as before, but now with a new interest in the cultural complexity that such an aim could encompass. He believes that the shapes of a building should indicate, and perhaps display, the usage and way of life of its occupants. Insofar as these are rich and varied, the expression is unlikely to be simple: "The collection [...] of forms and shapes which the everyday public can *associate* and be *familiar* with — and *identify* with, seems to me to be essential. These forms may derive from staircases, windows, corridors, rooms, entrances, etc. and the total building could be thought of as an assemblage of everyday elements recognizable to a normal man and not only an architect. For instance, in a building we did at Oxford University some years ago, it was intended that you could recognize the historical elements of [...] courtyard, entrance gate towers, cloisters; also a central object replacing the traditional fountain or statue of the college founder. In this way we hoped that students and public would not be dis-associated from their cultural past."

This restatement of his belief in the functional basis of expression is now undergoing a modification. It is no longer only a question of revealing the important volumes as a basis for a hierarchical composition, of a more or less abstract kind. The representative element now extends to include usage, familiarity, association, the need to identify. So the narrative is enriched, and the dimension of history which he had earlier rejected is now admitted.

[8] See *The Architectural Review,* May 1975, where it is published under the title "Stirling Connexions". The text was given as a lecture in September 1974 at the second Iran International Congress of Architecture held at Persepolis. An English text was also published in *A + U,* No. 2, 1975. In the same issue see also Kenneth Frampton on "Transformations in Style — the Work of James Stirling".

In opening this door Stirling needs to slam another. He is disenchanted with routine modernism. It may be stylistically correct, but it is lacking in imagination. He considers ninety-nine per cent of modern architecture to be boring, banal and barren, and usually disruptive and unharmonious when placed in older cities.

The year 1975 when Stirling wrote this article was also the year when he began to work on the designs for German museums, at Düsseldorf, Cologne and Stuttgart. The times are changing. Modernism is now turning into post-modernism. The comparative abruptness of this transition, we would do well to note, is peculiar to architecture. From the beginning of the century, in the other branches of modern art, from Joyce's *Ulysses* to Picasso's *Demoiselles*, from Eliot's *Waste Land* to Duchamp's *Grand Glass,* abstraction was henceforth mingled with representation. Allusions are essential to the fragmented form of *Ulysses* and *The Waste Land*, and Cubism, Conceptual Art, not to speak of Surrealism, would be incomprehensible without the web of allusions that they unfold. The two modes appear together in one work, abstraction allowing the free collaging together of the elements. Even with Constructive art, typical of artists like Naum Gabo, the proclaimed object-in-itself is still not entirely free from associations, indeed, it is the associations, however vague, that give it character. And even Mondrian, that purest of the pure, allowed one of his canvases to be titled *Boogie-Woogie.* Only within the myth of function, with its moral imperative substituting for the authority of natural science, could it be believed that buildings should be shorn of all allusions and kept in a sort of cultural refrigerator in a state of germ-free purity. Stirling is adjusting, and not with reluctance, to a change of fashion which for him was liberating, for it is after this moment that his art attains its plenitude, and that he achieves a masterpiece at the Staatsgalerie at Stuttgart.

In reacting to changes in society, Stirling has laid himself open to charges of being inconsistent, superficial, perhaps irresponsible. Especially in Britain, an aura of scandal always seemed to attach itself to his subsequent work. Stirling commented, in his conversation with Arata Isozaki, that in England architecture was a guilty profession, as though making a building was sinful or spending so much money somehow evil. The client should not be expected to subsidize the personal preferences of the architect. We may note that it is only now, at the *fin de siècle*, that architecture in Britain is beginning to be treated as capable of rising to the status of an art, and an architect like Zaha Hadid, who presents her work as art, is still treated with suspicion.

After problems arose in the public housing he designed at Runcorn, he received no new commissions in Britain between 1973 and 1980, when he was asked to undertake the extensions to the Tate Gallery — the Clore. In response to this somewhat hostile atmosphere, he was concerned to demonstrate that his work had not changed fundamentally, and that at the theoretical level, he had from the beginning paid attention both to abstraction and to representation. It evidently seemed more important for Stirling to be theoretically consistent than to achieve new commissions by whatever practical means. He points to his early interest in volumes expressive of function and his studies in village vernacular as showing a concern with meaning. The group of three houses which Stirling and Gowan designed in 1957 for Basil Mavrolean are clearly contextual, and in his project for the Arts Centre at St. Andrews University (1971) he combines new additions in the forthright style of the Olivetti Training Centre at Haslemere with an existing neo-classical house in a supremely contextual way. Concerned as he was to show his consistency, he never changed his thinking out of pure expediency, and when the Clore Gallery was opened, in 1986, it was not an act of conciliation, but boasted some fairly odd features, and got a mixed reception.

The personal style that emerges after the engagement with the German museums in 1975 is very different from the style of the red-brick buildings — Selwyn residential (which was not built), Leicester Engineering, Cambridge History, Oxford Florey — the first two of which brought Stirling and Gowan to fame. All of these employ brick as a facing material carried on a concrete frame, and employ cheap greenhouse glazing in large areas, and the result was felt as iconoclastic and technically innovative. Although there was no doubt that they were received as "modern", at a time when there was no post-modern, they were far from being in the idiom of modern then current, still less a continuation of the international style, which by then had become synonymous with business architecture. They appeared as original and even shocking. The use of brick facings and matching tiles was justified as a response to the British climate, where white walls would soon discolour. But it seemed to have had more to do with a refusal of the conventions of building new in the university, conventions which favoured the use of stone. Together they constituted a series, and Stirling has himself commented on this: "Looking back, it is a fact that our designs have sometimes come in series, which has led me, recently, to think that formal expression is maybe stronger than I would have liked to believe [...] Having always insisted that our designs emerge, as it were inevitably, from a logical analysis of the site, plus a functional interpretation of the building's requirements [...] there is nevertheless the matter of *presence* and *personality*, of *formalisms* and *style* in their appearance."[9]

[9] From "Three Loggias", in this collection of writings.

So Stirling has been brought to admit that style is an element in his approach. Yet it is not altogether a matter of superficial appearances, for the next series of buildings he undertook have in common not appearance, but method. The new theme derived from an interest in building theory, and the pre-fabricated concrete panels used in the Runcorn housing and the residential blocks at St. Andrew's University correspond to this interest, and even more the plastic panels used at the Olivetti Training School at Haslemere. This series could be thought of as an attempt to rationalize constructional method and achieve a more systematically high-tech image for his work. Although these buildings don't constitute such a clear stylistic progression, they do show a consistent interest in the constructional method. Yet certain elements are clearly due to personal preference, such as the bright colours used at Haslemere. The exhibition space there, with its variable configuration, is highly stylised in the direction of industrial design, the *raison d'être* of Olivetti the client, illustrating perhaps another kind of contextuality, at the level of making the appropriate response to the brief.

But the change of style that emerged with the three museum designs in Germany is more fundamental, and leads us into Stirling's mature period, when it was possible for him to compose in such a way as to combine the abstract and the representational in all the elements of the composition and so to achieve a richer synthesis. In his own words, it was now possible to draw equally, *without guilt*, from the abstract style of modern design and the multiple layers of historical precedent. At the same time, the writings take on a new note of assurance, as his theory comes closer to his own imaginative method, and allows his intuition a fuller rein.

In explaining the Staatsgalerie to a British audience in his

Gold Medal Acceptance speech, Stirling remarked: "The new building may be a collage of old and new elements, Egyptian cornices and Romanesque windows, but also Constructivist canopies, ramps and flowing forms — a union of elements from the past and present. We are trying to evoke an association with Museum, and I find examples from the nineteenth century more convincing than examples from the twentieth."

The following year, in his acceptance speech for the Pritzker Prize in Architecture (in which he was the third to be so honoured, after Philip Johnson and Luis Barragan) Stirling was able to "come out" publically as having always considered architecture as an art: "For me, right from the beginning, the 'art' of architecture has always been the priority."

However, as his subsequent remarks make clear, this did not mean an abandonment of modernity as such, but the continued search for a radical Modern Architecture, richer in associations, and free from the burden of utopia.

In subsequent writings describing his work, Stirling employs increasingly another concept, which has the virtue of freeing him also from the burden of chronological sequence, and this is the idea of a fluctuation between extremes. He starts to use the word *oscillation*, as in the following passage from his Gold Medal speech, which takes the idea of extremes in character: "Both extremes have always existed in our vocabulary; so, if we have a future, I see us going forward *oscillating*, as I did as a student — between the formal and the informal, between the restrained and the exuberant."

In 1990 this fluctuation had become more explicit: "Our work has oscillated between the most 'abstract' modern (even high tech), such as the Olivetti Training School, and the obviously 'representational', even traditional, for instance Rice University School of Architecture. These extremes have characterized our work since we began, but significantly, in recent designs (particularly the Staatsgalerie) the extremes are being counterbalanced and expressed in the same building [...] We hope that the Staatsgalerie is monumental, because that is the tradition for public buildings, particularly museums. We also hope that it is informal and populist — hence the anti-monumentalism of the meandering footpath, the voided centre, the colouring, and much else."

The idea of balancing opposing tendencies suggests something like a game. In tennis, restraint keeps the ball in court, exuberance risks hitting it out of court or into the net. It seems that Stirling has taken to heart certain effects in mannerist architecture, where rules are followed in one part only to be broken in another. If Stirling's writing comes second to his building, it still reveals the power of certain ideas, and it is very likely that these were ideas which he imbibed at university when Rowe drew his attention — and the attention of all of us who were his students — to the fascinating ambiguities in mannerism.

If Stirling writes after the event in order to justify the event, he still works within a certain body of theoretical ideas.

By comparison with Robert Venturi, whose theory of complexity and contradiction was highly explicit, and more influential probably than his built work, Stirling's built work was not conceived as the result of applying a theory. It is not simple enough to be rendered into a manual, and it is too personal to allow easy imitation. There have been few imitators, and there is no school that follows his method. But there is still an intellectual approach that none-the-less provides a theoretical under-pinning to his built work, and reveals the play of a powerful intelligence. And when it came to a game of associations, Stirling's knowledge of past architectures was extensive, and his attitude towards the past was, if not scholarly, certainly erudite.

Reviewing the writings as a whole, it is obvious that they have little life outside of the crucible of his design. Stirling can only be glimpsed through these writings; writing was not his medium of expression. There were many occasions when the need to produce text led him to cobble together excerpts from his client's brief, portions of the firm's official report, dead-pan descriptions of the layout, and finally quotations from the critic's reviews. Add a couple of jokes and a few self-deprecatory remarks, and someone not fluent in words could get by.

A special place must be given to the first two essays, which attained some prominence by being published in *The Architectural Review*. In writing these, early in his career, it is highly likely that Stirling took for his model the two seminal essays published in *The Architectural Review* by Colin Rowe, which we were all reading at this time, namely "The Mathematics of the Ideal Villa" (1947) and "Mannerism and Modern Architecture" (1950). Was he emulating his master? At any rate, "From Garches to Jaoul" (1955) and "Ronchamp. Le Corbusier's Chapel and the Crisis of Rationalism" (1956) have a weight as writing that the other pieces lack. They are proper essays, and they project critical insights that are valid independently from the built work.

Evelyn Newby, a friend of Stirling at the time, confirms that Rowe was frequently invoked in the conversations. At his request, she edited those two essays, in her words "turned them into proper English", and as a result the thought they contain is clarified and their impact is intensified.

The writing is at last adequate to the thought. In the last sentence of "From Garches to Jaoul", we reach a level of writing proper to an authoritative judgement. It's a pity that the other essays did not receive the same treatment.

Maison Jaoul,
section of the vault

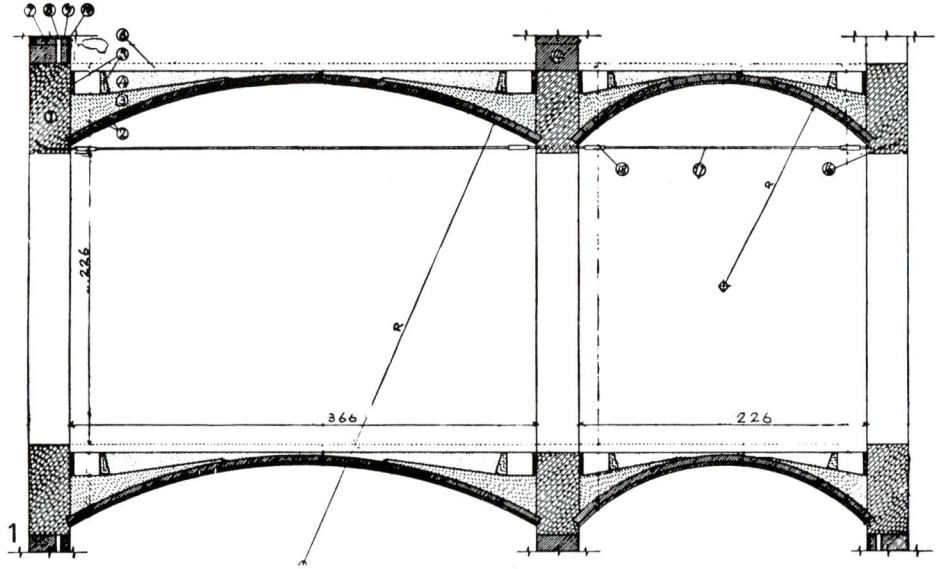

Garches to Jaoul. Le Corbusier as Domestic Architect in 1927 and 1953

Villa Garches, recently reoccupied, and the two houses for Mr. Jaoul and his son, now nearing completion, are possibly the most significant buildings by Le Corbusier to be seen in Paris to-day, for they represent the extremes of his vocabulary: the former, rational, urbane, programmatic, the latter, personal and anti-mechanistic. If style is the crystallization of an attitude, then these buildings, so different even at the most superficial level of comparison, may, on examination, reveal something of a philosophical change of attitude on the part of their author.

Garches, built at the culmination of Cubism and canonizing the theories in *Towards a New Architecture*, has since its inception been a standard by which Le Corbusier's genius is measured against that of the other great architects of this century. Inhabited, again by Americans, after fifteen years' splendid isolation, it has been painted in a manner more "de Stijl" than the original: walls white inside and out, all structural members black and single planes of primary colour on areas of lesser consequence. It is never possible to see more than one coloured plane from any single viewpoint. On the principal façade, the underside of the entrance canopy is painted sky-blue as the underside of the slab over the terrace. Inside, one wall of the living area is painted yellow, etc.

1955.
Published in
The Architectural Review, September 1956.

As with the still deserted Poissy, the deterioration at Garches was only skin-deep; paint decay, broken glass and slight cracks in the rendering; there has been no deterioration to the structure nor any waterproofing failures. Though the landscape has thickened considerably to the rear of the house, trees have not yet grown close against the main façades; where this has happened, at La Roche, Cook and Pleinex, the balanced asymmetry of the elevations, as total compositions, has been grossly disfigured. The one instance among the Paris buildings where trees are sympathetic is the Pavillon Suisse where they have grown the full height of the south elevation, significantly one of the most repetitive façades that Le Corbusier has produced. In more extreme examples of additive elevations, as in many American buildings, the presence of trees, naturalistic incidents, might almost be considered essential. The disembowelled machine parts of the Armée du Salut outbuildings have a similar juxtaposition to the neutral backdrop of the slab.

If Garches appears urban, sophisticated and essentially in keeping with *l'esprit parisien*, then the Jaoul houses seem primitive in character, recalling the Provençal farmhouse community; they seem out of tune with their Parisian environment. Their pyramidal massing is reminiscent of traditional Indian architecture and they were in fact designed after Le Corbusier's first visits to that country. Frequently accused of being "internationalist", Le Corbusier is actually the most regional of architects. The difference between the cities of Paris and Marseilles is precisely the difference between the Pavillon Suisse and the Unité, and at Chandigarh the centre buildings are indebted to the history and traditions of a native Indian culture; even a project for the Palace of the Soviets makes considerable reference to Russian Constructivism. Therefore, it is perhaps disturbing to encounter the Jaoul houses within half a mile of the Champs Elysées.

Assuming that the observer has become familiar with the architecture of Le Corbusier through the medium of the glossy books, then the first impression registered on arriving at the Jaoul houses is unique for they are of the scale and size expected, possibly because of the expressed floor beams. Usually, the scale is either greater or smaller than anticipated, that of Garches being unexpectedly heroic.

Differing from the point structure and therefore free plan of Garches, the structure of Jaoul is of load-bearing, brick cross-walls, cellular in planning by implication. It would, however, be a mistake to think of these buildings as models for cross-wall architecture as this aspect is visually subordinated to the massive, concrete, Catalan vaults occurring at each floor level. These vaults are to be covered with soil and grass to resist thermal expansion and the timber shutter-boards have been set to leave a carefully contrived pattern. Internally one-inch solid steel tiles are positioned at approximately fifteen-foot centres to resist diagonal thrust into the brick walls. At the external centre point of these vaults, bird-nesting boxes are formed, and occasionally concrete rainwater heads are projected from the side-beams, though the pipes drop internally. Rising from the underground garage through to the top of each house are dog-leg stairs, cast *in situ*; they are a development from the Marseilles fire-escape stair, with the treads cantilevered either side of the vertical concrete slab. By English standards, the brickwork is poor, but then the wall is considered as a surface and not a pattern. Masonry, rubble, or, perhaps more rationally in view of the vault construction, mass concrete walls could be substituted without difference to the principle of design.

Perhaps the only factor that Garches and Jaoul have in common is the considerable influence of the site on both. All Le Corbusier's buildings tend to fall into one of two categories: those in which the peculiarities of the site are a paramount factor in conception — most notably the Armée du Salut — and those where the site is of little consequence, being subordinated to a preconception or archetype, e.g. the Unité. To some extent this may account for the lack of inevitability, sometimes felt with buildings of this latter category, most particularly the Pavillon Suisse where, except as an archetype per se, there seems little justification for raising the building above ground, there being no circulation or view through. If the entrance hall, approachable from any direction, had been under and not to the rear of the slab, the raising of the block would not appear so arbitrary. None the less, the town-planning ideas which generated this form retain their urgent validity.

The exact relationship and planning of the two Jaoul houses have been motivated by the nature of the site. The circulation is on two levels and of two kinds. Cars drive straight off the road into the garage, a large underground cavern from which separate stairs rise through to each house. Walking circulation is above this garage on what appears to be natural ground level but which is actually a made-up terrace on which the houses stand. This level is linked to the road by a ramp. The differentiation of circulation on superimposed levels and the free movement around the houses are reminiscent in another medium of the suspended routes into the Armée du Salut.

At Maison Jaoul the only entire elevation that can be seen from a single viewpoint is to the rear and has to be observed over the garden wall of the adjoining private property. Owing to the narrowness of the plot, all other

Villa Garches,
axonometric view
of basic structure

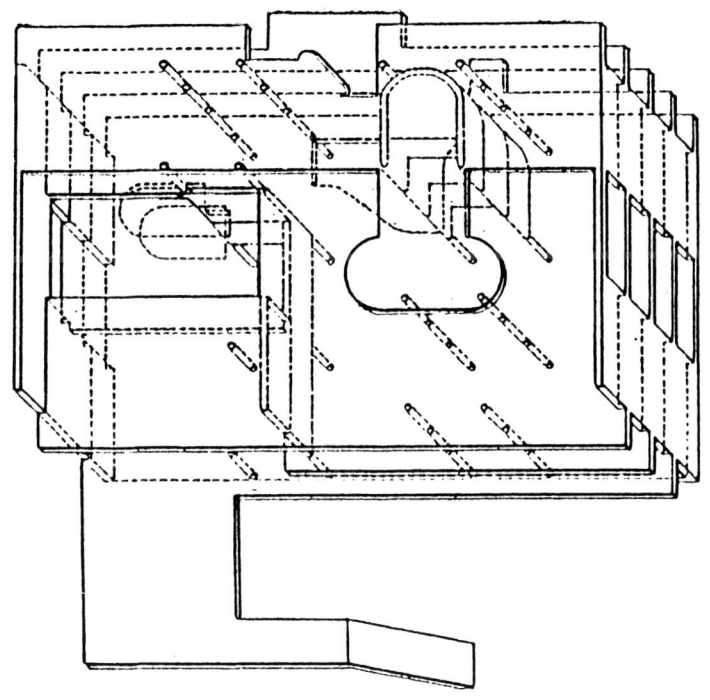

façades have to be viewed either episodically through the trees or close up at an oblique angle. The solid-void relationship of the exterior does not appear to follow any easily apparent scheme. This is a development from Le Corbusier's earlier work where at La Roche the drawing board elevation also cannot be seen at right angles and the studied balance of window to wall is destroyed. This is due not only to the trees which have grown since but especially to the necessity of viewing the elevation at a sharp angle.

The hierarchic presentation of external elements occurs also in the work of Frank Lloyd Wright, where the most important feature is the corner, and this may account for much of the undergrowth against the façades proper. It may be argued that the only exterior which can maintain interest, as the eye moves at an equal distance around the corner, is the cage or box. The most notable example of this is the Lake Shore Apartments where it would be inappropriate to suggest a "principal façade". Poissy almost comes into the category of the box but only on three sides; the fourth, receiving no undercut, becomes a vertical plane differing from the dynamic horizontality of the others. At Garches there is no point in moving around the corner for there is a very definite axis and the side elevations are of little consequence, their window openings positioned functionally make no attempt to arrive at a formal composition. The site boundary lines, defined by tall, closely planted trees are about six feet from each of these side elevations, making it almost impossible to see them. The long façades, on the contrary, may be seen head on from a considerable distance by the approaching visitor and their balanced asymmetry is masterfully exploited.

Internally, space departs radically from the structure; an explosion in terms of Cubist space is contained within the four peripheral walls which externally give little evidence of this phenomenon, contained except where it escapes and rushes out along the direction of the terrace, to be finally dissipated in the heavy landscape. However, space is not contrived for the sake of effect only, it invariably has a psychological as well as a functional context. For instance, on passing through the front door, the immediate double height and the presence of a stair indicate that the main floor is above. Similarly, the diagonal spatial stress across the first floor suggests the route through the house.

The main living areas are flooded with an even intensity of light, but, where accommodation and circulation are of lesser consequence, natural lighting becomes more restricted and as one moves through the house a continuous contrast in definition is attained. "The elements of architecture are light and shade, walls and space." The natural light which penetrates to the interior of the Jaoul houses is consistently subdued and not dissimilar to that found inside many Frank Lloyd Wright buildings.

Eventually somebody will have to consider the numerous similarities between Le Corbusier and Wright, and their common differences from the work of Mies van der Rohe. For instance, the pattern of circulation, repetitive on all floors as in the Pavillon Suisse and many of Le Corbusier's larger buildings, becomes in some of his and Wright's domestic works a route so complex and involved, as at Pleinex, that it is with the greatest difficulty that the stranger finds his way out. To a lesser extent, this applies at Jaoul and again, similar to Wright, the spatial effects, though exciting, are unexpected, encountered suddenly on turning a corner or glimpsed on passing a slit in the wall. Where double height does occur in one of the living rooms it appears as a dead area, having no secondary use such as the vertical height of the Unité flats which lights and ventilates the bedroom. If the space inside Garches can be considered dynamic, then here it is static; there is certainly no question of being able to stand inside and comprehend at a glance the limits of the house, as at Garches.

Implicit in the structural system, rooms tend to be small boxes with the living areas more generous. The internal finishes have a greater variety and richness of surface than at Garches, where, with the exception of the floor, the materials, though not the form, of the walls and ceilings are neutralized. Inside Jaoul, concrete is left shutter-marked, walls are plastered or brick fair-faced, floors are tiled and there is a considerable variety and quantity of timber and, most significantly, the ceiling or underside of the vaults is frequently finished in a dark clay tile which cannot be expected to amplify "the magnificent play of light on form". The "fourth wall" — the incorporation of shelving and opaque materials into the window opening — is symptomatic of Le Corbusier's recent attitude to surface depth. Windows are no longer to be looked through but looked at. The eye finding interest in every part of the surface impasto, does not, as at Garches, seek relief from the had textureless finish by examining the contours and form of the plane.

Maison Jaoul is no doubt dimensioned according to *Le Modulor*, a development from the application of the golden section by regulating lines as at Garches, where it is possible to read off the inter-relations of squares and sections as the eye traverses the façade and where, internally, every element is positioned according to an exact geometrical hierarchy. In fact, Garches must be considered the masterpiece of Neo-Palladianism in modern architecture, conceived in plan, section, elevation from two proportions which, owing to their particular inter-relationship, achieve an organic or

Maison Jaoul, site plan

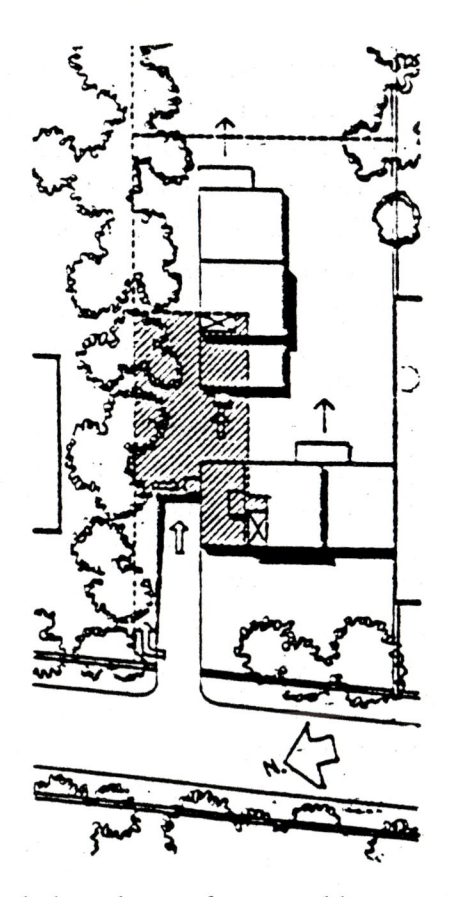

harmonic whole as distinct from an additive total. The variety of dimensions available from *Le Modulor* are considerable and as Bodiansky (the structural engineer for the Marseilles Unité) has said "there is always a figure near at hand to adjust to". This considerable flexibility may create a visually non-apparent geometry, as at Jaoul, but here the restrictions of the site already mentioned must be remembered when considering whether this is a valid criticism.

Garches is an excellent example of Le Corbusier's particular interpretation of the machine aesthetic. The body of the house, built by quite conventional methods for its time, has skin-walls of concrete block rendered to a monolithic, poured or sprayed effect; an aesthetic for a structural system not yet in being. Yet while Garches is not the product of any high-powered mechanization, the whole spirit of the building expresses the essence of machine power. To be on the first floor is to witness the Mumfordian end product of twentieth-century technology, "the silent, staffless powerhouse". The incorporation of rail-road and steamship fabrication is decidedly technocrat and the integration of architecture to specialist requirements extremely considered as the boiler-house disposed like an industrial engine-room or the timber-strip flooring obviously laid by ship's carpenters. The type of detailing in synthetic materials here and at the Armée du Salut is almost the last of the steam-age period; crude maybe, it is nevertheless powerful. After this date, the number of synthetic materials per building increases, and, as at the Pavillon Suisse, the detailing becomes more refined but somehow less memorable. There is no reference to any aspect of the machine at Jaoul either in construction or aesthetic. These houses, total cost £ 30,000, are being built by Algerian labourers equipped with ladders, hammers and nails, and with the exception of glass no synthetic materials are being used; technologically, they make no advance on medieval building. The timber window-wall units may be prefabricated but as with technology one suspects that prefabrication must begin with the structure.

To imply that these houses will be anything less than magnificent art would be incorrect. Their sheer plastic virtuosity is beyond emulation. Nevertheless, on analysis, it is disturbing to find little reference to the rational principles which are the basis of the modern movement, and it is difficult to avoid assessing these buildings except in terms of "art for art's sake". More so than any other architect of this century, Le Corbusier's buildings present a continuous architectural development which, however, has not recently been supplemented by programmatic theory.

As homes the Jaoul houses are almost cosy and could be inhabited by any civilized family, urban or rural. They are built by and intended for the status quo. Conversely, it is difficult to imagine Garches being lived in spontaneously except by such as the Sitwells, with never less than half a dozen brilliant, and permanent, guests. Utopian, it anticipates, and participates in, the progress of twentieth-century emancipation. A monument, not to an age which is dead, but to a way of life which has not generally arrived, and a continuous reminder of the quality to which all architects must aspire if modern architecture is to retain its vitality.

*Ronchamp chapel,
axonometric view*

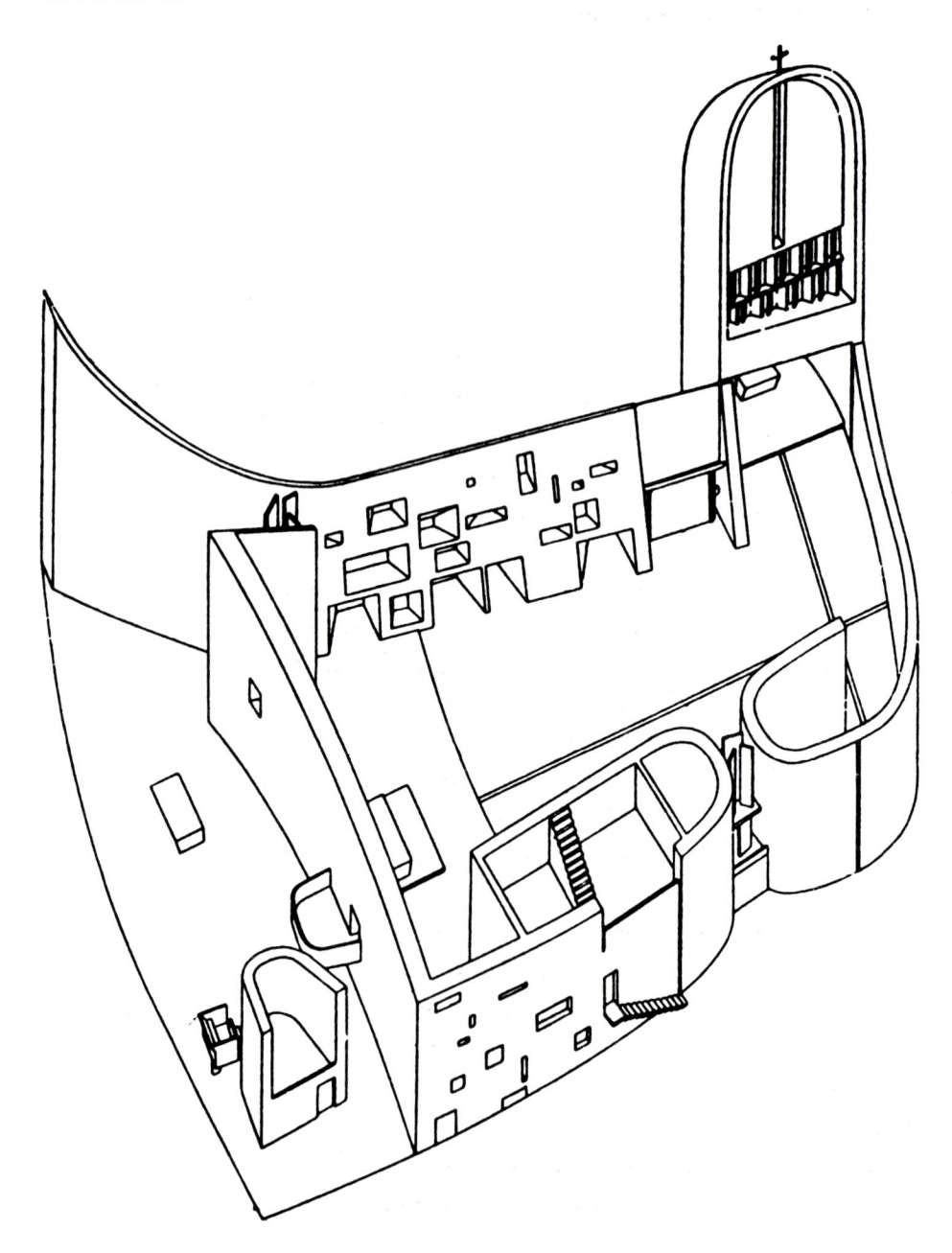

Ronchamp. Le Corbusier's Chapel and the Crisis of Rationalism

With the simultaneous appearance of Lever House in New York and the Unité in Marseilles, it had become obvious that the stylistic schism between Europe and the New World had entered on a decisive phase. The issue of art or technology had divided the ideological basis of the modern movement, and the diverging styles apparent since Constructivism probably have their origin in the attempt to fuse Art Nouveau and late-19th-century engineering. In the USA, functionalism now means the adaptation to building of industrial processes and products, but in Europe it remains the essentially humanist method of designing to a specific use. The post-war architecture of America may appear brittle to Europeans and, by obviating the hierarchical disposition of elements, anonymous; however, this academic method of criticism may no longer be adequate in considering technological products of the 20th century. Yet this method would still appear valid in criticizing recent European architecture where the elaboration of space and form has continued without abatement; and the chapel by Le Corbusier may possibly be the most plastic building ever erected in the name of modern architecture.

The south tower of the chapel, emerging as a white thumb above the landscape, can be seen for many miles as one ap-

1956.
Published in The Architectural Review, *March 1956.*

proaches the Swiss border. The rolling hills and green woodlands of the Haute-Saône are reminiscent of many parts of England and Wales, and the village of Ronchamp spreads along either side of the Dijon-Basle road. After climbing a steep and winding dirt-track, leading from the village through dense woodland, one reaches the bald crown of the hill on which the chapel is situated. The sweep of the roof, inverting the curve of the ground, and a single dynamic gesture give the composition an expression of dramatic inevitability. The immediate impression is of a sudden encounter with an unnatural configuration of natural elements such as the granite rings at Stonehenge or the dolmens in Brittany.

Far from being monumental, the building has a considerable ethereal quality, principally as a result of the equivocal nature of the walls. The rendering, which is whitewashed over, has been hand thrown and has an impasto of about two inches. This veneer suggests a quality of weightlessness and gives the walls something of the appearance of *papier-mâché*.

Notwithstanding that both roof and walls curve and splay in several directions, the material difference of rendered walls and natural concrete roof maintains the conventional distinction between them. They are further distinguished on the south and east sides by a continuous nine-inch glazed strip, and though the roof is not visible on the north and west sides its contours are suggested by the outline of the parapet. There is a similarity between the chapel and the Einstein tower which is even less conventional, but only inasmuch as the walls and roof are fused into one expression.

The whitewashed rendering is applied to the interior as well as to the exterior and the openings scattered apparently at random over the south and north walls splay either inwards or outwards, similar to the reveals of gun-openings in coastal fortifications. On the inside of the west wall these openings splay inwards to such a degree that from the interior the surface takes on the appearance of a grille. It is through this grille that most of the daylight percolates to the interior, yet the overall effect is one of diffuse light so that, from a place in the congregation, no particular feature is spotlighted as in the manner of a Baroque church.

Where the roof dips to its lowest point, a doublebarrelled gargoyle projects outwards to shoot rainwater into a shutter-patterned concrete tub. This element is surprisingly reminiscent of South Bank festivalia and something of the same spirit is conveyed by Le Corbusier in his stove-enamelled murals covering both sides of the processional entrance door. The same applies to the inscriptions on the coloured glass insets to the window openings. These linear applications suggest a final flourish and appear superfluous and even amateur in comparison with the overpowering virtuosity in moulding the contours of the solid masses.

The usual procedure in examining buildings — an inspection of the exterior followed by a tour of the interior — is reversed, and sightseers emerging on to the crown of the hill proceed to walk around the building clockwise, completing $1\frac{1}{2}$ circles before entering the chapel where they tend to become static, turning on their own axis to examine the interior.

Echoing the sag of the roof, the concrete floor dips down to the altar-rail which appears to be a length of folded land. The various altars are of polished pre-cast concrete (probably with a marble aggregate) which are cast to a marvellous precision. The roof, together with the concrete alms-boxes and swivel-door, represents an incredible French ingenuity in using this material.

The wall adjacent to the choir gallery stairs is painted a liturgical purple and the whitewash on the splayed reveals of the openings returns on to the purple wall to a width of three inches, thus resembling the painted window surrounds on houses around the Mediterranean coast. Small areas of green and yellow are painted over the rendering on either side of the main entrance and also on the reveals to the opening which contains the pivoting statue of the Madonna. The only large area of colour is confined to the north-east chapel and tower; this has been painted red for its entire height so that light pouring down from the top gives this surface the luminosity of "Dayglow". The three towers which catch the sun at different times of the day and pour light down on to the altars are in fact vertical extensions of each of the side chapels.

Even with a small congregation, the superb acoustics give a resonance suggesting a cathedral space and the people using the chapel do so naturally and without any sign of embarrassment. As a religiuos building, it functions extremely well and appears to be completely accepted. It is a fact that Le Corbusier's post-war architecture has considerable popular appeal. The local population, both at Marseilles and at Ronchamp, appear to be intensely proud of their buildings. Remembering the pre-war conflicts, it is difficult to ascertain whether the change is a social one, or whether it lies in the public or Le Corbusier. Garches is still regarded with suspicion by the public, either on account of its style or the manner of living of its inhabitants.

It may be considered that the Ronchamp chapel being a "pure expression of poetry" and the symbol of an ancient ritual, should not therefore be criticised by the rationale of the modern movement. Remembering, however, that this is a product of Europe's greatest architect, it is important to consider whether this building should influence the course

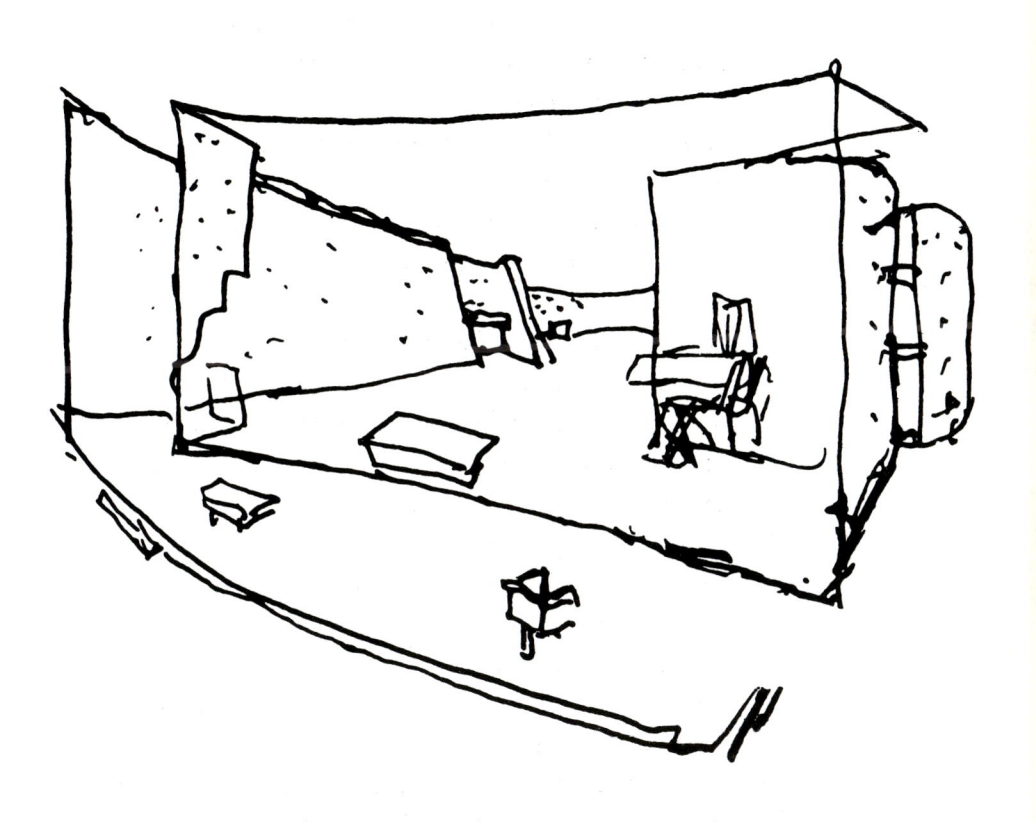

*Ronchamp chapel,
sketch of the interior*

of modern architecture. The sensational impact of the chapel on the visitor is significantly not sustained for any great length of time and when the emotions subside there is little to appeal to the intellect, and nothing to analyse or stimulate curiosity. This entirely visual appeal and the lack of intellectual participation demanded from the public may partly account for its easy acceptance by the local population.

Basically it is not a concrete building, although it has all the appearance of a solidifying object; the walls, however, are constructed in weight-bearing masonry. The initial structural idea of outlining the form by a tubular metal frame wrapped over with wire-meshing on to which concrete was to be sprayed, for some reason was not carried out. With no change in the conception, this outline was filled in with masonry, rendered over and whitewashed to the appearance of the initial idea. The interior of the west wall became so interrupted with openings that it was found necessary to imbed in the masonry a concrete frame to form around the window openings. This freedom from the precept of the correct use and expression of materials, apparent in other post-war European architecture, has little parallel in the New World where the exploitation of materials and the development of new techniques continues to expand the architectural vocabulary.

With the loss of direction in modern painting, European architects have been looking to popular art and folk architecture, mainly of an indigenous character, from which to extend their vocabulary. An appreciation of regional building, particularly of the Mediterranean, has frequently appeared in Le Corbusier's books, principally as examples of integrated social units expressing themselves through form, but only recently has regional building become a primary source of

Le Corbusier,
No Title, *1955*

plastic incident. There seems to be no doubt that Le Corbusier's incredible powers of observation are lessening the necessity for invention, and his travels round the world have stockpiled his vocabulary with plastic elements and *objets trouvés* of considerable picturesqueness. If folk architecture is to re-vitalise the movement, it will first be necessary to determine what it is that is modern in modern architecture. The scattered openings on the chapel walls may recall de Stijl but a similar expression is also commonplace in the farm buildings of Provence. The influence of popular art is also apparent in the priest's house and the hostel buildings. The external wood-work is painted sky blue and areas of smooth rendering painted over in patterns are decoratively applied to the outside walls; their situation and appearance do not express any formal, structural or aesthetic principle. All the walls of these outbuildings are in concrete, and large stones have been placed in the mix close against the shuttering, so that when the boarding is removed the surface of these stones in exposed.

Since the Bauhaus, the fusion of art and technology has been the lifelong mission of Gropius, and yet it is this aspect which denotes his least achievement. The Dessau building itself presents a series of elevations each of which is biased towards either art or technology. The suggestion that architecture has become so complex that it needs to be conceived by a team representing the composite mind may partly account for the ambiguity which is felt with buildings generated in this manner. On the other hand, Maillart, who evolved his aesthetic as the result of inventing theories of reinforcing to exploit the concrete ribbon, achieved in his bridges an integration of technique and expression which has rarely been surpassed. The exaggerated supremacy of "Art" in European Architecture probably denotes a hesitant attitude towards technology, which itself has possibly been retarded by our derisive attitude towards the myth of progress, the recent belief that true progress lies in charity, welfare, and personal happiness, having replaced the Victorian idea of progress as the invention and perfection of man's tools and equipment.

If the application of technology is of little consequence, nevertheless the appearance of industrial products still has some importance for Le Corbusier, as shown by the handrails to the stairs on the chapel. These handrails, which appear to be cut-offs from an extruded section of rolled steel joist, are in fact specially cast and the top flange is set at an acute angle to the web. The movable louvre is a logical development in resisting intense sunlight and it is surprising to find them above two of the entrances to the chapel; however, a closer inspection reveals that they are four-inch static concrete fins set at arbitrary angles, suggesting movability.

The desire to deride the schematic basis of modern architecture and the ability to turn a design upside down and make it architecture are symptomatic of a state when the vocabulary is not being extended, and a parallel can be drawn with the Mannerist period of the Renaissance. Certainly, the forms which have developed from the rationale and the initial ideology of the modern movement are being mannerized and changed into a conscious imperfectionism.

Le Corbusier, proceeding from the general to the particular, has produced a masterpiece of a unique but most personal order.

*House at Woolton,
1954, study sketch*

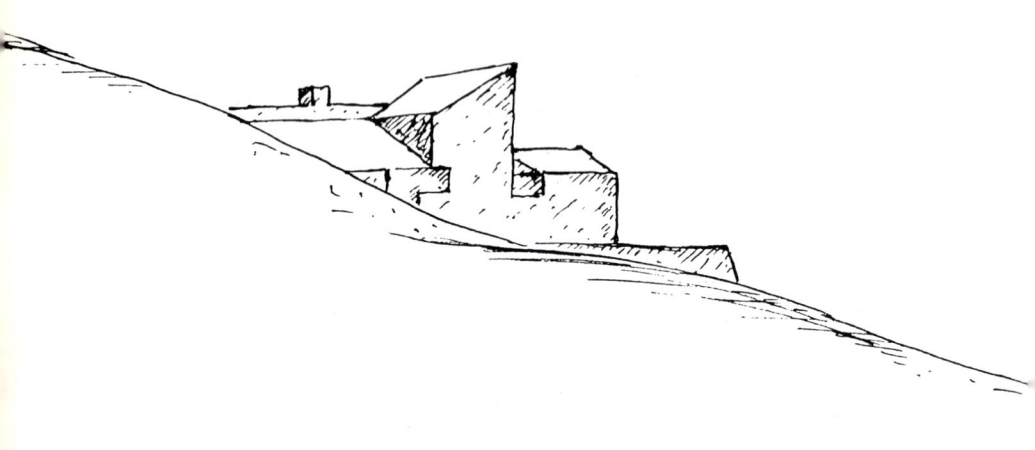

Regionalism and Modern Architecture

In post-war Britain, two styles or minor movements have emerged from the Schools of Architecture in addition to the eclecticism that is normal to them. The first style, which probably reached its peak about 1950–54, has been termed "neo-Palladian" in deference to Professor Wittkower's *Architectural principles in the age of Humanism*, published in 1949. The usual asymmetry of Modern Architecture was reconsidered and axially conceived schemes became more common. Various proportional systems were applied, in part due to the influence of Le Corbusier's publication, *Le Modulor*. The expression of this style is closely related to the "use of materials", and designs in steel or brick are frequently derivative of Mies van der Rohe, those in concrete or stone of Le Corbusier. It would appear that this style is in decline in some of the Schools, although it is to be expected that the students of these post-war years may eventually build in this manner. This trend finds a parallel in the USA where the interval between qualifying and building is apparently shorter. The work of Johnson, Rudolph and others might loosely be considered neo-Palladian.

The more recent trend in many ways is a reaction from the former and could be considered approximately a re-assessment of indigenous and usually anonymous building and a

Published in Architects' Year Book, *No. 8, 1957*

revaluation of the experience embodied in the use of traditional methods and materials.[1] Le Corbusier's assimilation of Mediterranean domestic and native Indian architecture into his most recent buildings is symptomatic of this new manner. The most visually stimulating chapters of Kidder Smith's recent book *Italy builds* were not those on Italian Modern and Italian Renaissance but that on the anonymous architecture of Italy.

Today, Stonehenge is more significant than the architecture of Sir Christopher Wren.

Whereas the former movement was primarily an aesthetic one, the latter can advance considerable arguments with respect to economy, practicability and policy, not least of which is the assumption that Authorities will be more inclined to grant aesthetic approval to such design rather than to "modern". The MARS Group's contribution to CIAM X[2] was a most consistent example of this indigenous trend, but it is significant that this group was entirely concerned with low cost housing.

Immediately after the war, much of the thinking about and some of the attempts at solving the problems of housing were in terms of prefabrication and mass production. This rational approach no longer appears acceptable either at an aesthetic or at a practical level, and creative thinking is now mainly directed towards the utilisation of existing building methods and labour forces. This exploitation of local materials and methods is perhaps the only alternative to the conventional or the "contemporary" which is left open to the European Architect when he is confronted with a minimum budget. The building industry of this country cannot subscribe to "modernism" in the design of a "one-off" house. It is significant that the new traditionalism is mainly confined to Europe, except Germany, and finds little response in

[1] See "The Functional Tradition", in *The Architectural Review*, July 1957.
[2] See *Architects' Year Book*, No. 7.

*House at Woolton,
1954, plan and section*

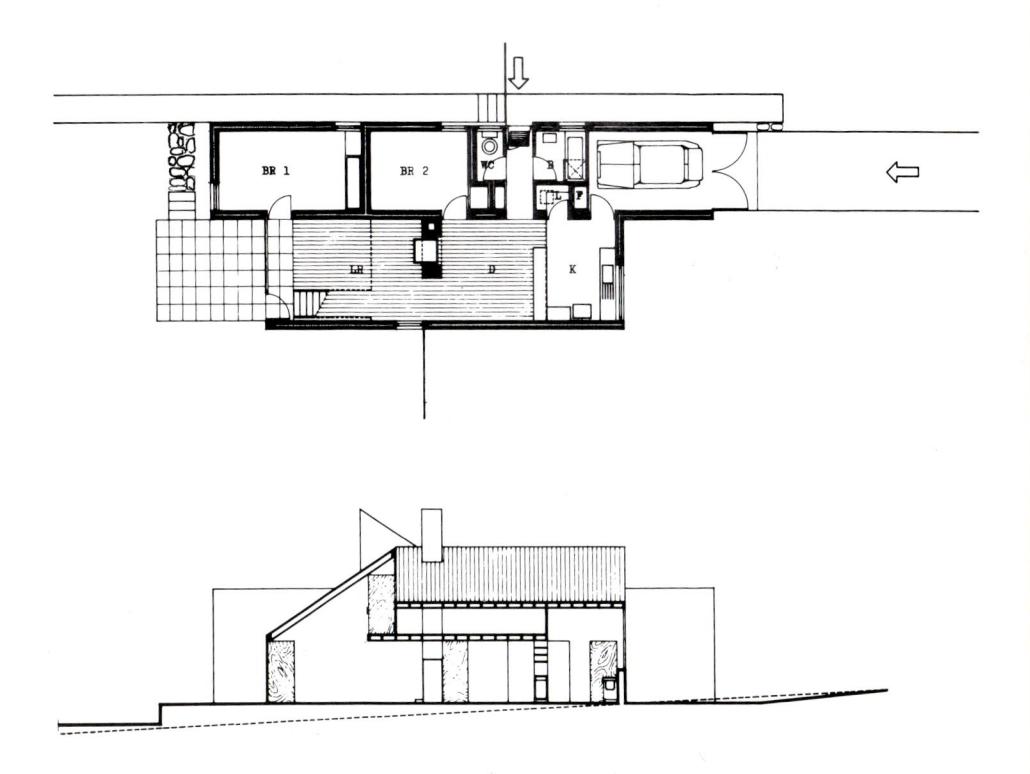

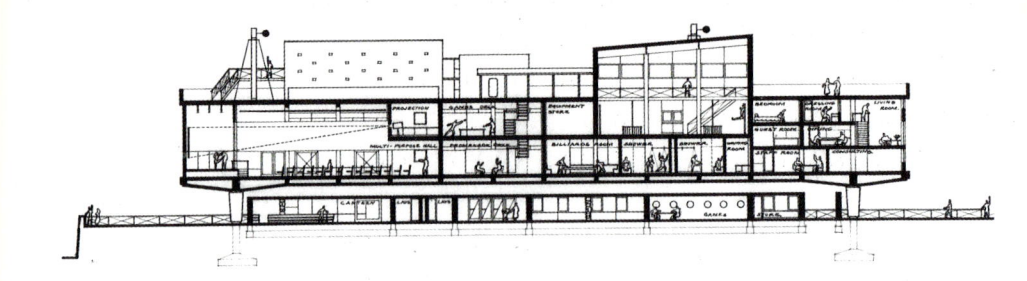

Community Centre, longitudinal section (from James Stirling's thesis, 1950)

America where technology and aesthetics have kept more evenly apace, and the schism between designer and constructor is less apparent. An American middle-income family can afford a house built by new methods and materials, the vital aspect of progressive Architecture. In this country, the decline of technology, particularly in Building and Civil Engineering, is forcing Architects away from the radical or science fiction outlook. One only has to compare the Crystal Palace to the Festival of Britain, or the Victorian railway stations to recent airport terminals to appreciate the desperate situation of our technical inventiveness in comparison to the supreme position which we held in the last century. Whereas the Hertfordshire schools might be considered our best post-war effort, they do not set a standard either in conception or style, though at least they were initially motivated by a will to modernity.

The appearance of regionalism amongst our younger architects is but a reflection of the spread of this style in post-war Europe where, significantly, the only major architects who are not now resident in the USA — Le Corbusier and Alvar Aalto — are, of course, the innovators. Swedish architecture has surprisingly little influence on this new movement whose prime manifestations in this country appear to be:

a. The plastique of folk and anonymous architecture. Initially stimulated by Mediterranean building, recently this interest has moved nearer home, with the examination of such anonymous buildings as Martello towers, oast-houses, brick-kilns, etc., and also including aspects of the nineteenth century, warehouses, office buildings, etc.; in fact, anything of any period which is unselfconscious and usually anonymous. It should be noted that the outside appearance of these buildings is an efficient expression of their specific function whereas today they may be appreciated picturesquely and possibly utilised arbitrarily.

"The method of design to a modern mind can only be understood in the scientific, or in the engineer's sense, as a definite analysis of possibilities — not as a vague poetic dealing with poetic matters, with derivative ideas of what looks domestic, or looks farmlike, or looks ecclesiastical — the dealing with a multitude of flavours — that is what architects have been doing in the last hundred years. They have been trying to deal with a set of flavours — things that look like things but that were not the things themselves. Old farmhouses and cottages are things themselves — cottages and farmhouses."[3]

b. The application of orthogonal proportion and the obvious use of basic geometrical elements appear to be diminishing, and instead something of the variability found in nature is attempted. "Dynamic cellularism" is an Architecture comprising several elements, repetitive or varied. The assemblage of units is more in terms of growth and change than of mere addition, more akin to patterns of crystal formations or biological divisions than to the static rigidity of a structural grid. This form of assemblage is in contrast to the definitive architecture and the containing periphery of for example, a

[3] W.R. Lethaby: *Form in Civilization*, 1922.

building such as Unité. It is significant that in large single-cell and usually symmetrical structures, e.g. a stadium and auditorium, an aspect of neo-Palladianism is most relevant, particularly in the work of Catalano, Candela and the North Carolina school.

c. A return to the last significant period of English Architecture: a revaluation of Voysey, Mackintosh and the turn of the century when we last held the initiative in Europe. It is obvious that the Architecture of this period is still the most modern that we possess but in returning to the point of departure we may be implying that the Continental innovations of the twenties and early thirties are incapable of development, presumably because they were foreign to our own experience and today they are academic and no longer valid in our present situation.

"The New Movement is anti-intellectual, anti-posh, and anti-official minded..."[4], so commences a description of "The Movement" in post-war English Literature to which the new architectural trends have some obvious affinities. At both the Third Programme and the Elvis Presley levels there is a revival of interest in folk art. The metropolitanism of Sartre and Moravia is being replaced on one hand by "Lucky Jim" provincialism and, on the other, by the "mythissmus" of Dylan Thomas and Bert Brecht. It appears that the recent trends are nationalistic and more the reflection of a "cottage" culture than the expression of supposedly undesirable ad-mass society.

The number of book references in this article is considerable, and indeed one of our vices is an overliterary approach to Architecture. It would appear that theories of building are more important than realisation. The influence of the camera must also have affected our observation. The range of the

[4] George Melly: *Intimate Review*, 1956.

camera lens is a small angle, focusing attention on the particular and distorting the overall. These media of communication have been useful in the last fifty years when programmatic Architecture has almost entirely been built outside this country, but their effectiveness is limited, and the transference from picture to reality — picturesque. A good aspect of the recent trend is the ability to be stimulated by actual contact with a local object even though its author may be unknown, and theories appertaining to its appearance unwritten.

By the end of the twenties, the strength of modern architecture lay in the closeness of its extremes. At about the time of the Bauhaus, a common synthesis of the recent past and a definite attitude towards the future was, in fact, if not international, at least universal in Europe. The works of Gropius and Aalto at this period for instance had a more or less common appearance. From the public's viewpoint this was an asset, and the new architecture convinced by its logic and style a small but influential part of that public. By the late thirties, modern architecture had percolated into remote corners of the world, encountering the infinite idiosyncrasies of locality, and, at the same time, Architects, feeling the limitations

Community Centre, general perspective (from James Stirling's thesis, 1950)

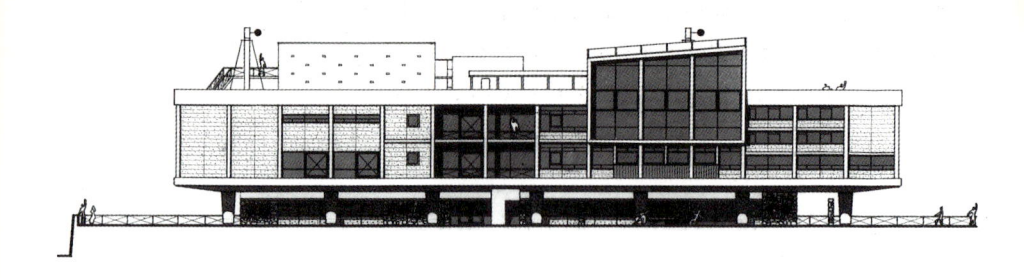

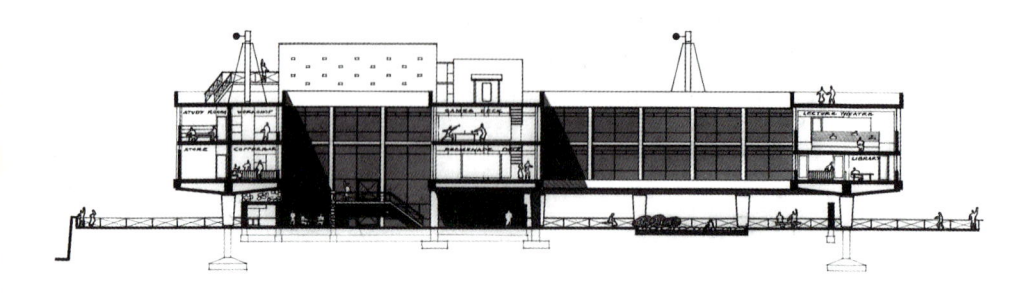

Community Centre, main front and longitudinal section (from James Stirling's thesis, 1950)

of their style and becoming intent upon extending their vocabulary, embarked upon a process of diffusion, assimilation and personalisation. This process is still going on with the result that today it can in no way be said that there is any similarity in the recent work of Gropius and Aalto. If this period of dispersal is coming to an end, attempts may again be made to achieve a synthesis, with the possible revelation that modern architecture has divided into two, approximately one for either side of the Atlantic. The Old World exploiting, and contorting, traditional ways and means, and the New World inventing techniques and developing the appropriate expression of the modern attitude.

As a nation, we will probably get the architecture we deserve and, at this stage, we might reconsider these new trends which may ultimately be recognised as standing apart from the mainstream of modern architecture.

"Thirty years ago there was something called 'modern' poetry. Go back to the *Waste Land*, and, if it is any length of time since you read it, I guarantee that one of the things you will notice is how much more *modern* it is than anything being written now; I mean 'modern' in the sense that Bauhaus architecture, Cubist painting, etc., are modern. This quality, this modernity, which was supposed to represent the twentieth century and set it apart from the nineteenth had many absurd features, and the reaction away from it was quite justifiable; but it is becoming obvious by this time that the baby has been emptied away with the bathwater."[5]

[5] John Wain: *The London Magazine*, 1956.

*House in North
London, 1953,
axonometric*

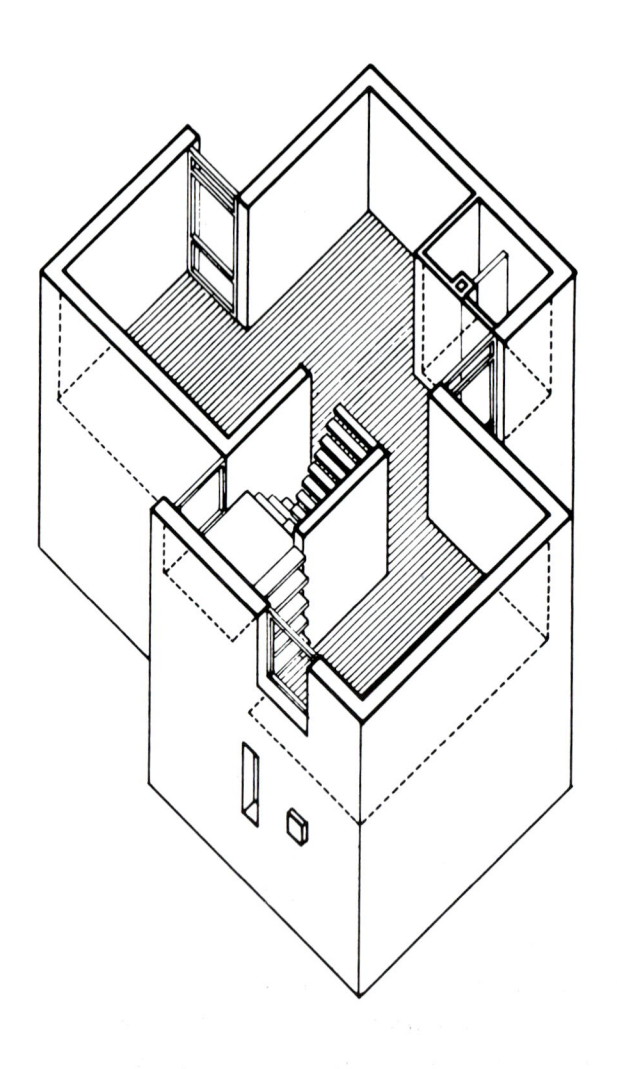

A Personal View of the Present Situation

Almost from the time when architects became "top people" the route from obscurity to respectability has been initiated by the private house.

To-day this traditional procedure has become meaningless and it is extremely doubtful if a house, a fraction the architectural equivalent of Indigo Jones' Queens House or Lutyens Deanery Garden, Sonning, would get by the "aesthetic controllers", "restrictive convenantors", "preservationists" or "fine arters".

In microcosm the house is the genesis of multi-cellular space organization, and the research expended on the house has been influential on many architectural problems; unfortunately, however, no revolutionary house has appeared, or been allowed to appear in this country since the war; certainly nothing comparable to the white architecture of the thirties.

Perhaps this appears as the perennial dissatisfaction of the young, seeking after the re-adjustment of values normal to every generation, but there is now a profound difference; the opposition is not only entrenched, it is legalized.

In the USA, where the personalization of the house may soon be taken over completely by its gadgets, we have nevertheless watched Rudolph, Kahn and many others develop in

Published in Architectural Design, June 1958.

the space of twelve years, by the traditional route from small private houses to involvement in city planning.

This traditional and normal way of establishing and extending a practice, has, with few exceptions, been cut from under the feet of the younger generation of architects here (those who have qualified since the 1947 Town and Country Planning Act). Recently the more usual way of setting up has been through winning a competition and/or by sheer luck. From the viewpoint of society as well as the individual, neither of these is very satisfactory in principle, as the lucky breaks go most frequently to the "best connected", regardless of ability, and the quality of competition wins is closely related to the choice of the assessor. A count of the "good wins" against the bad over the last ten years will show the former to be greatly in the minority.

The competition winner may either be straight from school or have spent years employed in a non-responsible capacity with regard to total design. Suddenly he is confronted with the reality of a large building without an interim period of direct experience. Formal lessons of mass, proportion, junctions, etc., can be taught; but a sensitivity for the juxtaposition of materials, and an understanding of the effects of light, etc., can only be acquired through personal contact. In the past an architect, by the time he had acquired a major building, would be capable of avoiding eclecticism and have had sufficient experience to acquire some degree of personal design convictions. It is the absence of an indication of a personal idiom which is most disappointing in the works of the younger generation, notwithstanding (or perhaps because of) the fact that we live in a period of stylistic *laissez faire*.

In the field of private building, quantitatively speaking, the state of architecture (and the status of the architect) has never been worse. Suburbia continues to spawn over the country unchecked and accepted by the establishment. All the regulations invoked ineffectually to control this blight, work against good architecture, originality is suppressed, and, with a few notable exceptions, the standard of speculative development lags far behind the public taste exhibited in popular monthlies, and women's magazines. Even in the worst period of Victorian expansion there was more social and constructional innovation in low density housing, even accepting the ugliness of the stylistic merry-go-round.

It is an indication of the cynicism of "welfare state" goodwill that the very same authorities who give approval to the chaos of speculative building and restrict the private architect, may ironically be producing some of our best schools and mass housing (but from another room in another department), mainly as a result of the take over by the younger generation, many of whom find that the only outlet for their ideas is from within the local authority.

It is a fact that much of the best architecture produced in this country since the war is for the unknown client, and doubtful assumptions have to be made regarding the users of schools, flats, etc. In this situation the architect is handicapped, for the idiosyncrasies and personal requirements of the client are frequently the sparking point of a solution, and it is not surprising that buildings designed *in vacuo* often have the appearance of "no personality". Without hard thinking on this problem, an easy acceptance of pre-solutions becomes the norm: thus schools have all glass façades, high density housing is slab-blocks, and maisonettes are "cross wall". The influence of the client is replaced by that of a "system", frequently structural, and post-war we have seen the birth of many patent methods of building, including precast concrete and curtain walling, which are likely to be considerably developed because of their particular aptness to the linear qualities of English architecture. However, without the intervention of the architects' personality, that which is originated rationally may soon become characterless.

This is an age of multi-aesthetic styles, and each problem appears to have its appropriate aesthetic, in contrast with the twenties, when much of the strength of the movement lay in the naïve conviction that all buildings could be designed in "international style".

The greatest advances technologically are being made from the top downwards, primarily in single problem buildings, such as domes, auditorias and large span structures where cost is probably of lesser importance. Possibly in trying to conceive the lowest costing of "non-specialized" buildings — the individual house in "house of to-morrow" terms — is reverse about face in regard to this trend. In multi-problem buildings where planning, psychology, construction and humanism may be of varied importance, coupled with the necessity for building at a minimum cost, it would appear that from the bottom upwards a new interpretation of vernacular seems to be evolving in England.

Packaged Deal and Prefabrication

In spite of its widespread use, the term "packaged deal" in housing has very little meaning. It belongs to the jargon of the selling agent along with terms such as split-level, supermarket, Hi-Fi and do-it-yourself; all derived from the better-living vocabulary of American advertising. As such, it is frequently used to sell the all too familiar houses of the speculative builder to willing suburbanites.

Published in Design Magazine, *March 1959.*

On examination packaged deal housing seems to cover three different systems, namely: a packaged superstructure; packaged internal services; and the totally prefabricated assembly of superstructure and interior.

The first of the three is produced by a number of manufacturers both here and abroad, and usually consists of timber-framed superstructures which are planned and designed for the unknown individual buyer, rather than for redevelopment schemes or mass housing programmes. These superstructures are sold and despatched (with the cost of haulage sometimes included) to the site, previously acquired by the purchaser, where a local builder is waiting to transform the package of components into the wall, floors and roof of the new house. Subsequently he installs the equipment, servicing and fittings, and completes the finish and trim, all to the owner's personal taste. The image of speed and efficiency which in theory is evoked by this process — indeed its *raison d'être* — may probably become a little blurred as the builder and his local know-how take over; and the cost of the initial package is likely to become more than doubled before the house is finished.

Nevertheless there are many variations of plan and accommodation offered on one or two floors, and there is a range of accessories by which the house buyer can express his individuality (i.e., hipped oriel window, coronation porch, etc). However, the final price is not likely to be much less than the architect-designed and supervised house which, of course, can be personalised to the minutest requirements of client and site.

A less direct version of this system is the American range of Techbuilt houses designed by Carl Koch, but these include a pre-determined interior as well as an exterior shell. This is also the system of Wates's Dormy houses. Both are licensed by the marketer to selected local contractors who construct them from a standard set of working drawings. Unlike the Dormy house, however, Techbuilt achieves considerable variety by dividing the house into two basic units, i.e. bedroom/bathroom unit and living/kitchen unit, each in four sizes, making a total of sixteen plan combinations of different sized living and sleeping areas.

The "package" can also mean the prefabricating of the mechanical utilities, i.e. service stack, heating unit, or on a larger scale, a combined kitchen/bathroom assembly. Several of these packages could constitute the guts (and almost half the cost) of a house, and they could be arranged in an infinite variety of plans. These packages can be mass produced in an advanced technology, and if the system were rationalised on a national scale it could undoubtedly improve efficiency, lower cost, and be adaptable to almost any size and

Living unity Stiff Domino, 1951, general structure with fixed and openable windows

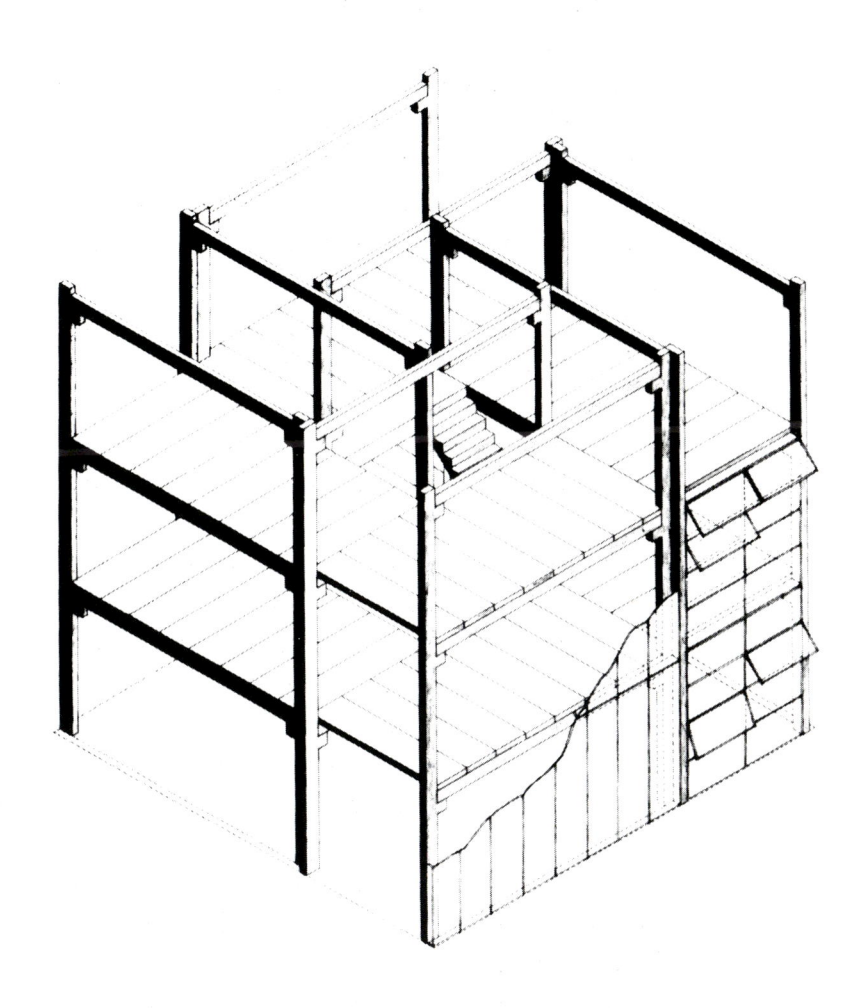

type of plan and superstructure — traditional, "contemporary" or modern. With the detached house on a suburban plot, this limited system of prefabrication would appear to have all the advantages, particularly in regard to orientation, variations in site, and the personal requirements of the house buyer.

An interesting aside on prefabrication has been made by Charles Eames, who has constructed his own house in California entirely of components selected from the trade catalogues of industries not usually interested in housing, such as marine and aircraft fittings and factory building units. To design a series of variations according to this system would require a very considerable organisation, sifting through catalogues, price tagging and collecting information. It would also require an artist to select the parts and compose the building; in the hands of a sub-standard designer the result might be at best whimsical or at worst chaotic. Nevertheless, in any country with an industrial backlog, there is an enormous range of available objects, ranging from agricultural sheds to cast iron staircases, which could be utilized in such a way.

The combination of a packaged superstructure and packaged internal elements results in the totally prefabricated house. However, unlike packaged deal, the term "prefabrication" is a nasty word, with overtones of the war, standardisation, working class and temporary building. Immediately after the war there was a tremendous programme of mass produced housing — prefabs to accommodate families from the blitzed areas. The Arcon Mark V, which was shown at the Tate Gallery in 1944, was a highly efficient and technically intricate construction. It was also rigid and unadaptable, as it had been designed in an emergency to cope with one situation. Inevitably the prefabricated house must include a built-

Living unity Stiff Domino, 1951, agglomerate of three unities

in idea of flexibility so that it can accommodate itself to any site levels, be adaptable to any orientation, and capable of expansion.

The experimental house built by Buckminster Fuller in 1946 comes nearest to this specification. It arrived in a package, was quickly and easily erected, and was suspended from a central core, around which the house could revolve, following the sun.

Unfortunately the considerable achievement in mass production methods attained during the post-war housing drive has been largely dissipated, leaving only the technically diluted packaged bungalows which several manufacturers have available for export overseas. The prefab estates are gradually being replaced by traditional (and cheaper) houses erected by the speculative builder for the expanding middle class.

The presumed advantages of prefabrication are, briefly, speed of erection, low cost, and the increased functional efficiency of the house as a whole. However, it must be realised that the house is the embodiment of its owner's individuality. Even though the public accepts the mass produced car, school, refrigerator and so on, the average householder sees his home as the ultimate stronghold of his personal tastes, indeed as an extension of himself, and never as a production line job. Whether this attitude is logical, particularly if the house is expensive and inefficient, is beside the point.

It would seem that beyond a certain number any standardised and fashion-motivated house will be resisted, except perhaps a product of very high efficiency and very low cost, and this could only be feasible by using conventional fabrication techniques if millions were mass produced. The concept of prefabrication as a modular and complex assembly of pressings and skeletals may already be obsolescent in comparison with the simplicity of balloon-spraying, pre-casting and form reinforcing techniques, and ultimately conditioned environments.

At a point always short of perfection, the technology of a product reaches the condition whereby it can be slightly improved only by a disproportionate increase of complexity. At that stage greatly increased performance can only be attained when the development of the product is taken over by an entirely different, simpler and usually more recent medium. This applies from astro-engineering to road constructing and indeed in all fields of technology; it is certainly the case with building prefabrication.

Any designer or manufacturer involved in prefabricated housing in this country must be prepared to take into account and resolve a conflicting set of requirements, ranging from the style implications of production methods to the uncertain and sometimes irrational preferences of the consumer and the class he represents. In the media of existing technology and prevailing social patterns the packaging of internal elements, utilities, storage units, walls, furniture, etc., seems the most realistic approach. This system suggests a great freedom in the planning and modulation of spaces, at the same time allowing the owner either to conceal his way of living or exhibit his personality in the final appearance of the home.

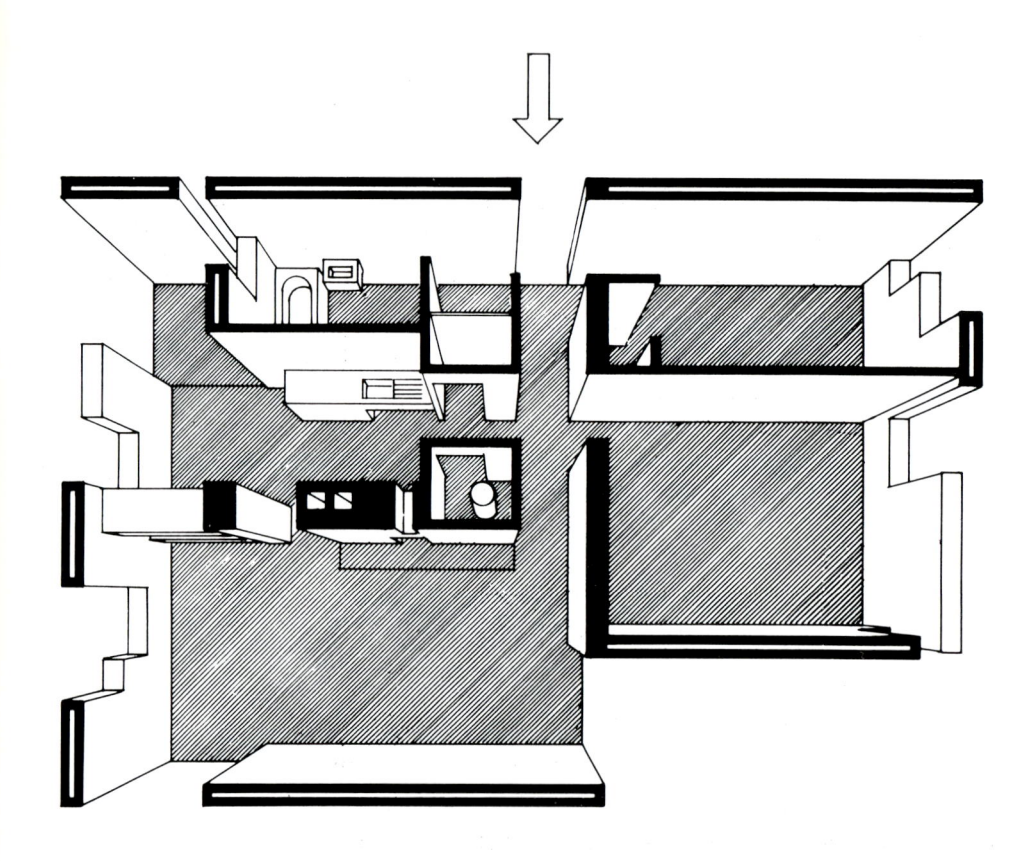

*Flats at Ham Common
(with James Gowan),
1955–58, vertical section*

72

Afterthoughts on the Flats at Ham Common

Normally in the past the architect has attempted to achieve an integration of exterior and interior, and this has been a special obsession in the development of modern architecture. But in designing houses for the open market and the unknown occupier, the architect finds himself in an ambiguous situation where discrepancies eventually become apparent between his intention and the actual use of the dwelling; a situation which is due to the lack of an accepted form of taste and the divergence of visual outlook between specialist and layman.

These flats were designed for middle class purchasers, and the developer in asking us to produce a modern solution was no doubt bearing in mind the recent sales success of contemporary styled housing estates and the mounting propaganda of the "better living" magazines, as well as his own preferences. Nevertheless, of these thirty flats, only three or four of the purchasers have furnished and fitted their flats in a contemporary manner, and it would be interesting to know how this proportion compares with that found in the SPAN [a Development Company that produced, in the late fifties, standard housing] estates, although one could expect the brisk fashion-forming publicity attending sales of these to yield higher results.

Published in Architecture and Building, May 1959 (with James Gowan).

On talking with the owners after they have moved in, it would seem that "modern" is approved for the outside of the building, but that inside the flat will be personalised by the occupier regardless of the design of the existing exterior or even of the interior. As this is the majority opinion, it might be more realistic for the architect to accept this situation and provide a completely negative interior (as Mies is supposed to have done at the Lake Shore Apartments) or to provide only the outer shell and an open floor space to which the occupier at his leisure could add partitions, fittings, and furnishings which would be alterable at will. Perhaps the architect should recognise the fact that the design of interiors has become the province of interior decorators, both amateur and professional?

With these flats we tried a middle course, and certain elements such as the fireplace, servery and kitchen fittings which were designed in accord with the external expression, were provided in the hope that they would influence and indeed assist the occupier in completing the furnishing of his flat. However, even with the few contemporary-styled interiors one feels that the owners have been less influenced by what they found than by pre-formed ideas of house decorating. No one has taken the left interior as a point of departure for a personal but sympathetic interpretation, either by contrast as the Italians do so well, or in direct harmony as the Americans seem to do almost automatically. The lack of understanding between the intentions of the designer and the tastes of the occupant shows itself most clearly in those elements of furniture and fittings which are visible from the outside.

In speculative development it is quite usual for the building owner to make lease conditions regarding the colour and materials of curtaining, so that the variety of individual taste

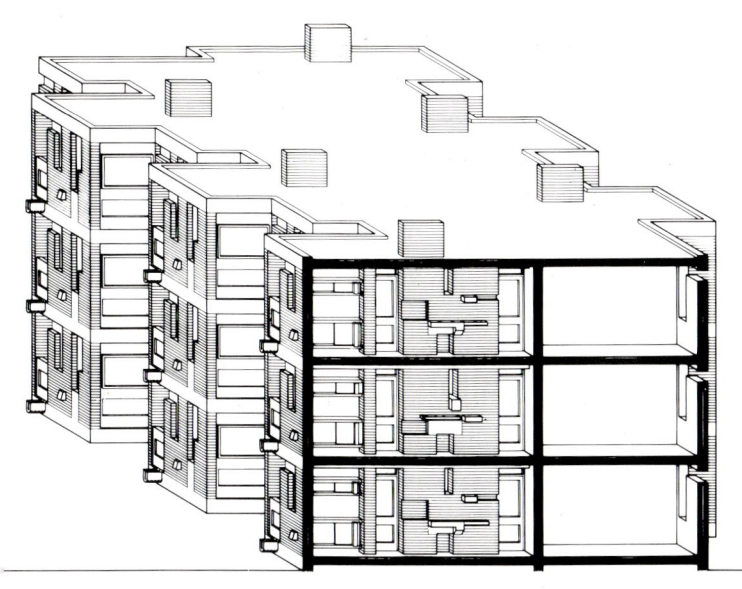

Flats at Ham Common (with James Gowan), 1955–58, axonometric section of the three-storey block

does not obtrude on the exterior, destroying the balance of a repetitive window pattern; and the dull but neutral white laced curtained windows of many pre-war flat blocks can be seen in an area such as St. Johns Wood (also the Lake Shore Apartments). Here we have tried to suppress the disruptive aspect of unrelated curtaining by imposing a very bold arrangement of window members, but this does, of course, pre-determine a very thick proportioned architecture. Where the treatment of window bars is more delicate as with some of the best LCC [London County Council] terraces, the curtaining chaos becomes more assertive than the actual buildings, and the finer aspects of the architecture are lost. Windows continue to get larger and from the viewpoint of the man in the street, the building front has changed from being a relationship of walls and openings to a complicated façade of curtaining.

The chances of the exteriors of these flats surviving as a design entity are slight if the multi-variety of the occupiers'

Flats at Ham Common (with James Gowan), 1955–58, plan of the first and second floors

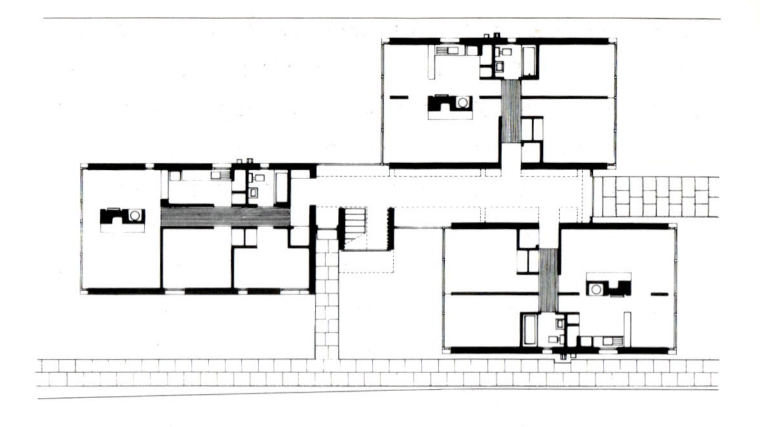

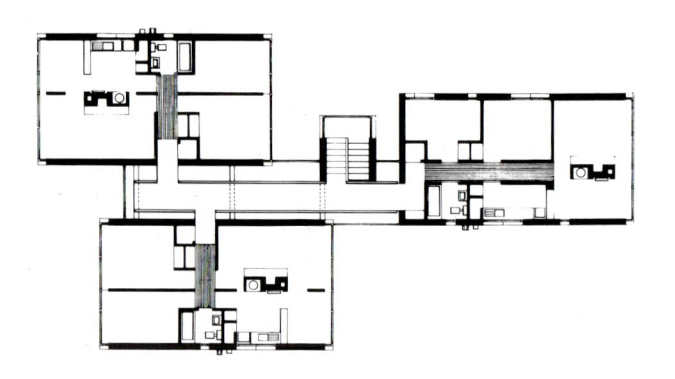

taste obtrudes on the outside of the buildings and in the grounds. Unless this is prevented from happening by close co-operation between the occupiers and the building owner, and by the conditions of the lease, any housing of modern design may rapidly become a visual shambles, as has already happened with some post-war local authority developments. At a period when there is anarchy of taste, only a strictly maintained lease can ensure survival, whether it be a Georgian Square, the Nash Terraces or the SPAN estates.

It has been suggested that these flats are brutalist in design, whatever that may mean. The client's brief was that he required the maximum accommodation for a low cost (approximately £ 1,900 per dwelling), and this factor alone predetermined the use of simple and everyday materials. The walls are of load-bearing brickwork, and were calculated structurally to get the maximum of window openings and clerestories in certain places. The brick pointing was recessed and appears in oblique shadow as the site is orientated north/south. The concrete floor beams were patterned by the formwork, as rendering or aggregate exposing would have been more expensive. The softwood EJMA [English Joinery Manufacturers Association] window sections were painted white to contrast with the yellow bricks (London Stocks).

We do not know if this specification is in accord with the "new brutalism", a term which we used to regard on the one hand as a narrow interpretation of one aspect of architecture, specifically the use of materials and components "as found" — an already established attitude; and on the other hand, as a well-intentioned but over-patriotic attempt to elevate English architecture to an international status. But whatever the term might initially have meant it is clear from recent and repeated derisive journalistic asides, that it must by now have created in the public eye an image of pretentiousness, artiness, and irresponsibility, and as such the continuation of its use can only be detrimental to modern architecture in this country.

*House at Woolton,
perspective
of the interior*

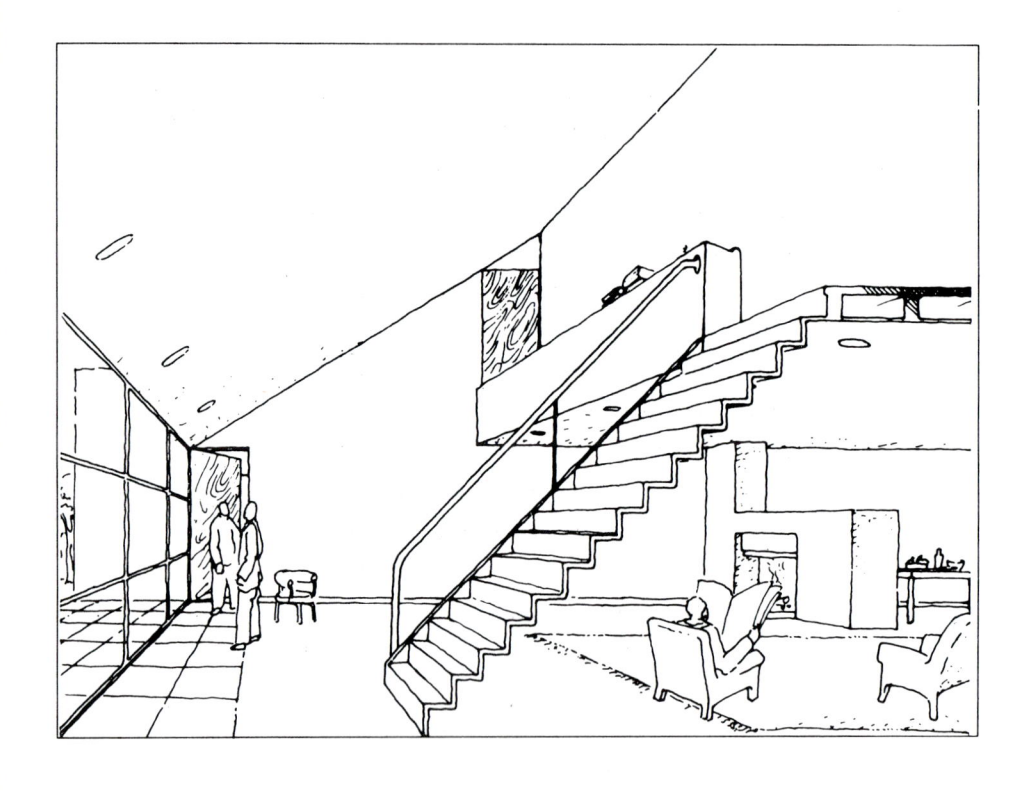

The Functional Tradition and Expression

The Architectural Review published in July 1957 a special number called "The Functional Tradition"; this illustrated many anonymously designed buildings in England of a regional type, such as farmhouses, barns, warehouses, mills, etc. This selection was perhaps a little narrow, faintly Georgian, and too nearly confined to early industrialism. It could have included fortifications, village housing, and early office building. Sibyl Moholy-Nagy has also published a book illustrating similar buildings in America.

The merit of this type of building as seen by an architect today is that they are usually composed of direct and undecorated volumes evolved from building usage and particularly from the functions of their major elements. They adapt to a wide variety of materials and locality and their structural support is sensibly derived from the organization of the building. Though dating back to medieval times, they are peculiarly modern, suggestive of the early ideas of Functionalism, but probably less of the machine aesthetic, which was primarily a style concern. Le Corbusier has always been aware of the uncompromising appearance of this type of building, and as the theoretical impetus of the modern movement has diminished, their influence upon him has become apparent, particularly in his later work.

Published in Perspecta, *No. 6, 1959.*

The flats of Ham Common were probably influenced by de Stijl and the Jaoul houses, but at the same time we were fascinated by the quality of vernacular brick buildings such as the Liverpool warehouses, and in general by the great virtuosity of English nineteenth-century brick technology. The design of a small house in the country was probably affected by the roof complexes of traditional farm buildings, and the pyramidal massing results from giving the living-room a double height space with a sloping ceiling, and by placing a studio/bedroom on the upper level. The roofs are simple lean-to's spanning between walls.

On both sides of the Atlantic the current dilemma of modern architecture seems to be that top architects are absorbed in becoming either stylists or structural exhibitionists and as the "functional tradition" indicates, there is an alternative architectural expression to that of style or structure. This is by the direct expression of the actual accommodation volumes in relation to each element determining the plastic composition of the building. ("The section is the elevation" — Le Corbusier.) The architectural quality of a solution will of course depend upon the particular organization of the accommodation, circulation, services, etc., and vernacular buildings usually have an unsophisticated but successful integration of large and small elements achieved with a degree of inevitability. In modern architecture, an over-formal solution may avoid the realities of the accommodation and this is the case with Louis Kahn's project for the Trenton Community Centre where the silhouette of the gymnasium, which is the biggest single volume, is determined by a roof-bay system which is mainly appropriate to the corridors and small rooms.

In America, "styling" appears as the application of frills and grilles, the introduction of historical fragments, and the indiscriminate use of glass curtain walls. Structural exhibitionism appears as the over-articulation of columns and floors. Both are obsessed with the outer building skin and both are equally effective in masking the volumetric dimensions of the spaces behind the façade. Recent "after-Mies" architecture can be seen in fact as a more decorative elaboration of the Miesian peripheral structure solution. Arising from axial plan arrangements of classical origin, the structure is often unrelated to the shape of the internal space, and it tends to stand evermore in its own right accounting for the principal appearance of the building. The ideology of the "free plan" included the independence of spaces and walls, where necessary pushing through the constrictions of the structural cage; and on the exterior of Le Corbusier's early Paris houses, the shape and purpose of the internal spaces is suggested, bringing the scale of the human being and the room back into the city.

Modern architecture has recently gained its real foothold in England through the necessity for low-cost building, whereas more fortunately its acceptance in America appears to be synonymous with prestige. We have therefore only recently taken up with the application of curtain walling, but as our buildings have neither the scale or the expense of their American equivalents they appear cheap and undistinguished. ("Money equals quality" seems to be a factor in this style of architecture.) We also have a complete alphabet of "contemporary style", fashion-promoted by the public press as avant-garde, and this will soon create more harassing problems for modern architects than the dying protests of the academic conservatives.

In the Georgian squares, each house has an elaborated entrance and the location of the principal room, usually on the first floor, was indicated by wrought-iron work, canopies, etc.; thus the extent of the dwelling and the location of its main accommodation was indicated on the terraces of the eighteenth-century city. This identification of the house in its environment is repeated by Le Corbusier in the Unité, with the expression of the dwelling cell, several of which comprise the total building, whereas in the Lake Shore Apartments the location of the dwelling is of little consequence. "Styling" encourages ambiguity and in most of our Victorian terraces the identity of the individual house has also disappeared. The styled uniformity of these street façades was achieved with rendered walls, repeating windows, and horizontal cornice, but the true organization remains visible on the backs where it can be seen that building is made of bricks; it has a pitched roof, rooms are at different levels and of unequal size, and outhouses define the property walls.

With the design for a house in the Chilterns, the organization of stacked room volumes resulted from using each half-landing of a central staircase as access to, in principle, one room at each level. This formation adapted well to the site which was sloping in two directions.

A few years ago, Luigi Moretti illustrated in *Spazio* the plaster castings taken from inside accurate models of certain historical buildings. By treating the external surface and the inner constructions of a building as a three-dimensional negative or mould, he was able to obtain solidified space. If space can be imagined as a solid mass determined in shape and size by the proportion of a room or the function of a corridor, then an architectural solution could be perceived by the consideration of alternative ways in which the various elements of the programme could be plastically assembled. It is not assumed that every element should be expressive, but it is important that a hierarchy of the most significant

Chilterns House (with James Gowan), 1956, general view

volumes is recognizable in the ultimate composition. Within practical limits, room shapes are variable and the different ways of assembling accommodation, circulation, etc., may be almost infinite; nevertheless a design will start to emerge in the imagination when the relationship of spaces appears to have coherent organizational pattern. At this moment of coagulation, however, the cerebral exercise loses its abstract value as it is necessary for it to materialize as substance; and a successful transition from organizational pattern into structure and materials is dependent upon the author's structural vocabulary. Through its selection the method of support should assist the ideogram of the space organization.

Le Corbusier's monastery at La Tourette grammatically explains a pattern of cellular repetitive spaces (the monks' cells) related above the varied proportions of the halls and refectories and set alongside the dense single mass of the chapel. The structural grille of the Unité defines the space and describes the dwelling, and where the shape of the accommodation radically changes so does the structural system, setting free the drama of the roof.

With a complex building of different shapes and sizes of accommodation, it appears essential that several appropriate methods of support should be used, each specific to a particular organization; and this was the case with our design for the new main building at Sheffield University. The Architecture, Arts and Administration Building was in principle a long terrace of varied accommodation planned either side of a centre axle of horizontal circulation. From left to right are located the Architecture studios, the Arts classrooms, the Arts lecture theatres, tutorial rooms, and finally the University Administration offices. Each of these groupings is joined by a shaft of vertical circulation. The classrooms and tutorial groups are of mass concrete walling, and the remainder is supported by columns and beams. At roof level there is a terrace, and underneath there is a covered access walk, and situated off each are nonrepetitive elements also in mass wall construction. Before reaching the point of considering an architectural solution, there has presumably been a considerable and perhaps lengthy buildup, amassing and analysing information, and factors of site, access, and orientation may account for principal decisions. At Sheffield the long terrace of the new building was intended to direct the flow of space and people within the precinct in addition to being a visual retaining wall counteracting the slope of the ground which was tending to spill the University out into the adjoining area.

In New Haven, Louis Kahn makes reference to the realities of an urban situation, and the Yale Art Gallery is not conceived as a pavilion; instead it exploits the asymmetry of a site on the boundary of the campus, presenting on one side an open glass window to the University and on the other a closed brick façade to the city. The science building for Pennsylvania University, also designed by Louis Kahn, can be seen as a juxtaposition of towers (vertical circulation, services) and horizontally stressed laboratories, and the over-all appearance is therefore of an organized pattern of accommodation, not of a structural system or applied styling.

A disquieting aspect of "functional tradition" buildings is that when the usage of an element is not obsolete then its form retains a validity (i.e. pitched roof) and it is perhaps not surprising that the light and ventilation towers over the side chapels at Ronchamp are similar to those over peasant houses on Ischia; the function they are serving has not changed.

In England a number of architects were recently asked to prepare designs for an entirely new college at Cambridge, intended as a monument to its founder, Sir Winston Churchill, whose ancestral home is Blenheim Palace, exemplar of the English Baroque.

The programme issued to the architects required on the one hand that it should be a modern design and at the same time impressed on the competitors the validity of the traditional courtyard solution, and it has to be conceded that the working of a residential college has changed only slightly in the last few centuries.

The site is an open windswept field north of the town, somewhat overlooked by suburban houses, and we considered it necessary to create an internal environment, private, enclosed, and protected.

It was also required that the college should be built in

four separate stages and yet remain an entity at each stage.

This was attempted in the first instance by building an outer ring of accommodation with the following stages as additions of inner court and slab buildings. The size of this main court was almost three times that of Trinity Great Court and was not dissimilar in outline to medieval castles and walled cities. Earth-works which are often associated with the symbolism of security and protection resulted from the placing of the new buildings on a turfed podium of banked and cut earth, a necessary adaptation to the sloping site; also the programme implied that the new college should maintain a traditional attitude to access and security.

The two basic types of accommodation were the residential quarters which comprised the bulk of the college, and the non-repetitive elements of the Library, Dining Hall, and Common Rooms; the latter were spanned by precast concrete roof trusses indicating the scale of the volumes and at the same time allowing clerestory light into their interiors.

A college is a sort of camp and the location of the students' quarters is of less consequence than the expression of the home, and in the over-all context the main distinction was of studios with floor-to-ceiling windows and sleeping areas with sill-height windows.

These rooms and sets were treated as a series of related and interlocking blocks of space evolved as additions to a basic cell; and like building blocks they could be lapped, butted, and interlocked in various combinations, and their over-all arrangement was conditioned by the site, staging and other factors. In the outer wall or stockade, these accommodation blocks were laid horizontally with access off a cloister and a roof walk, but with the inner court and slab buildings the vertical stacking of the accommodation resulted, from staircase access with entry off the half-landings.

The upper floors of these inner buildings had double height studios and it is their broken silhouette which appears above the outer wall of the college.

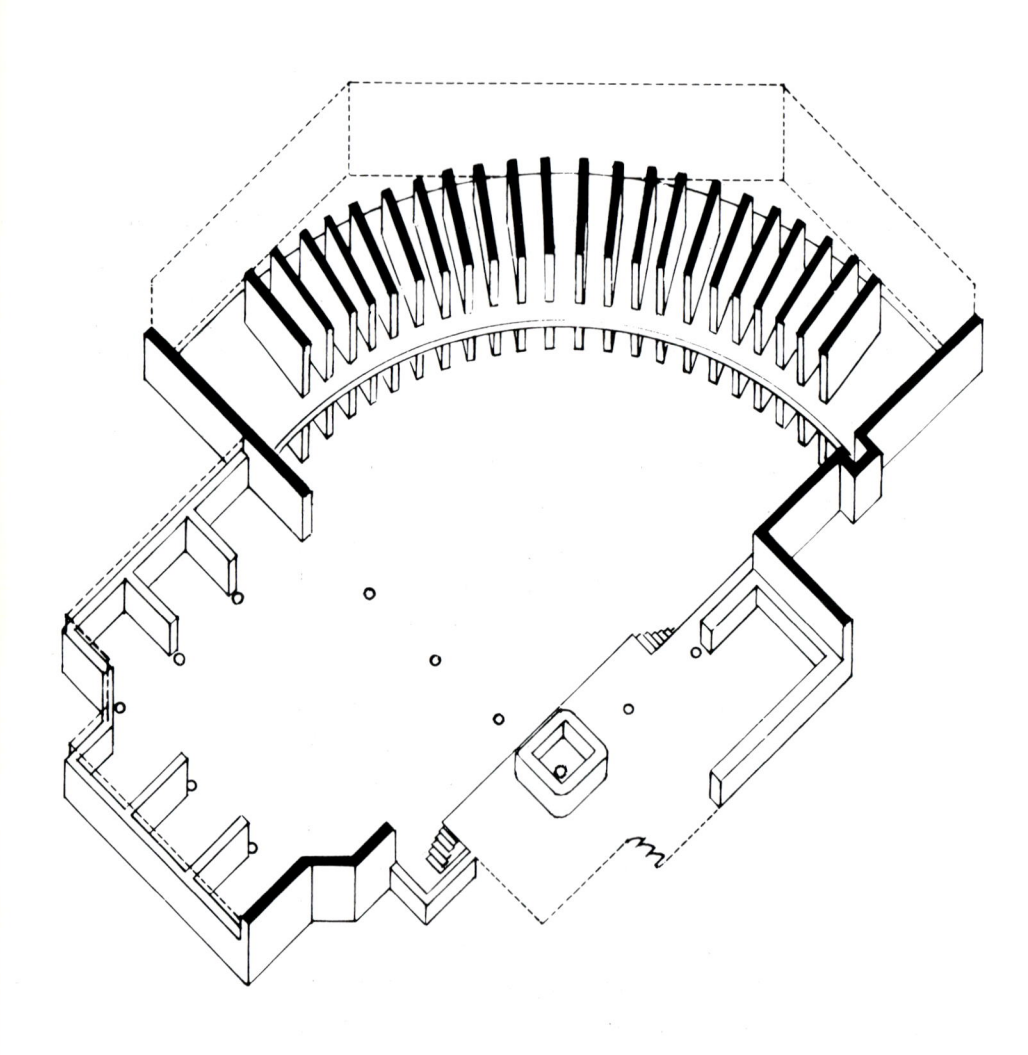

*Cambridge, Faculty
of History, 1964–67,
axonometric view
of the reading room*

An Architect's Approach to Architecture

I might as well come clean and reveal the awful truth by showing my thesis (1950). We all had this event at the end of our school training; though I'm told there are now some schools where you can get through five years without designing a building.

I grew up in Liverpool — a fashionable thing to do these days — but I left school without a school certificate let alone "A" levels. Under the present system of admittance I would not get into a school of architecture or even night school. However, I was lucky and got a service grant to Liverpool University — a wartime system which does not, of course, operate today.

The School of Architecture was in tremendous ferment as the revolution of modern architecture had just hit it [1945] secondhand and rather late. There was furious debate as to the validity of the modern movement, tempers were heated and discussion was intense. Some staff resigned and a few students went off to other schools; at any rate I was left with a deep conviction of the moral rightness of the New Architecture. Probably this issue is not really felt as being significant, or even discussed by students any more. At that time the School was under Professor Budden, a liberal without opinion in regard to the great argument. He believed that

Published in RIBA Journal, *May 1965. This article is based on a paper given at the RIBA on 23 February by James Stirling, who has summarized both the paper and his answers to questions.*

quality, whether neo-Georgian, modern, etc., was all that mattered — an attitude that was maybe an asset to the school at that time.

My thesis was a Community Centre in a New Town and it was influenced by the principles of the "free plan". Rooms and circulation were intermixed and no doubt compromised each other functionally, which is always the case with a *plan libre*. Circulation is excessive and varied types of accommodation are fitted into a rectangle; "compressed" is a more operative word, describing the forcing of volumes as different as restaurants, assembly hall, libraries, offices, into a constricting box.

In 1951 I came to London, coinciding with the South Bank Exhibition, which, after the puritanism of my academic conversion, I found a nasty experience, finickity, decorative and inconsequential compared with Asplund in 1936, or Paxton in 1851, which the exhibition was commemorating.

I took a course in town planning at APRR where, unfortunately, they rarely got down to urban planning, being more concerned with national and regional problems, which I thought unrealistic as decisions at that level are more likely to be political. Believing that the quality of an environment is almost entirely the result of making the correct three-dimensional physical proposals and getting little instruction in this, I didn't stay to complete the course. Instead I did a series of competitions.

The first was for Poole Technical College. I was beginning to re-act to my thesis and schooling in the principles of "Towards a New Architecture", although I still felt the last significant architecture was the white masterpieces of the twenties and thirties. The problem now, however, was to move to the next stage, which I saw as extending the range and the clientele of modern architecture; beyond luxury villas and apartments to public buildings of low cost (particularly relevant here as, unlike other European countries, our rich seemed notoriously ill-disposed towards modernism).

In this situation of expediency a principle of the new architecture which had to be changed was the excessive circulation and compromised room usage that is inherent in the free plan. Materials also had to change; the white rendering of Villa Garches or Tugendhat was never structurally relevant, or even appropriate, as an external finish in this country. Brick is our traditional low cost material and, in the design for Poole, it was used as the external veneer to the high block; window openings being located according to the type of room and their size and shape determined by the room usage. However, the reinforced concrete frame showed through indicating that the external surface was not structural. The high block accommodated staff rooms and offices over a canteen and social rooms, and the lower block was an assembly hall over three gymnasiums. The external walls of the assembly hall were Herts School concrete panels, used out of context (perhaps there is hope for CLASP [Consortium of Local Authorities System Production] if used out of context!). More important however, was the necessity to re-think the role of circulation (corridors, lifts, staircases, etc.) and to re-state it as the dynamic and motivating element of the building. It was essential to create not merely corridors in the institutional sense but to construct something of fundamental organizational significance, like an armature or skeleton on to which rooms fastened, allowing them to become again private spaces, separate from circulation and movement.

After this competition I had to find a job and I went to work for a firm of private architects, and also did the Sheffield University competition (1953). At ground level the main building was a covered way linking buildings at either end of the site and, as the site sloped down into the town, it also had to act as a retaining wall to the campus. From left to right it included a School of Architecture, then a battery of classrooms; in the centre a cluster of lecture theatres, entered from two levels, then a group of staff rooms, and finally the University administration. Each of these groupings was separated by a shaft of vertical circulation — a recessive element which visually articulates the different types of accommodation. The horizontal circulation was regarded as a spine or driving axle on to which rooms were connected, like a mechanized assembly. The planning of spaces and rooms was secondary to the creation of a circulatory system. This design I regret not building, though if I'd gone into practice at this time it would have been without experience, which would have been inhibiting in building subsequent projects.

After this, I settled down to three years with Lyons, Israel and Ellis, and learnt a great deal about detailing, running a job, how to make a building stand up, keep out the rain, etc. I think it essential to gain this degree of experience and confidence before pushing off into practice.

While working in offices I did a project for Team 10 (1955) that was a reaction to driving through country villages and finding at the other end perhaps half a dozen houses tacked on by the local authority, usually semi-d's, unsympathetic to the scale and materials of the village. One had to propose a system appropriate to the size and formation of the English village and, therefore, it had to continue the linear street pattern. In principle it was a strip of three structural walls making two internal bays of different width. The rooms of the house can easily be accommodated in two bays, the larger for living-room and main bedroom, the smaller for other bedrooms, kitchens, etc. From the outer walls spanned a lean-to roof, and walls and roof were to be made of any material, according to locality. I think the resulting aesthetic has now become rather common-place. This particular scheme was never intended as a solution for new settlements or in New Towns, only for extending existing villages.

We used the forms of this village extension on individual houses in an attempt to get aesthetic approval. At this time I was trying to start a practice with six private houses, four of which were rejected as being aesthetically sub-standard. This was rather a heavy loss. However, in the case of a house at Woolton this approach came off. The site on a hillside overlooked the Lancashire plain and the contractor started the foundations, got down about 2 feet and found 6 feet solid of compressed tin cans. So much for rural England! The building had to be abandoned. At this stage we suffered badly from the aesthetic opinion of architects who had the authority to reject and throw out schemes. The likelihood of starting a practice designing individual houses of some architectural merit is now very remote, though it used to be the traditional way and this is a tragic situation for young people starting up. On the other hand practically every commission we have received since this time has come directly or indirectly from other architects. It's difficult not to see the profession in terms of good and bad guys. The large and very public buildings we are putting up nowadays don't get rejected on aesthetic grounds; it appears that only the small isolated house, often in a wood where the public will never see it, gets turned down.

Indirectly, the Sheffield competition took me into private practice. The Architectural Association students had an exhibition of the four schemes which they thought best (others were by Colin St. John Wilson, Peter Smithson, and John Voelcker) and, as a result, I was asked to be a visiting tutor.

Later, the father of one of my students became my first client. He wanted to build flats at similar construction and selling price to the nearby SPAN housing. (I think his previous architects had been traditional, and he asked his son to recommend someone who could design in the contemporary idiom.) He was quite unlike the normal speculator and had great trust in launching an unestablished person into practice with quite a large commission.

I left Lyons, Israel and Ellis with James Gowan in 1956, and we built the flats at Ham Common. Materials, and therefore trades, were limited to the minimum — bricks, concrete, and timber windows (which were designed as permutations of opening light, clerestory, vertical slit) put together in different ways according to the type of light required inside.

The Old People's Home for the LCC [London County Council], also a structural brick building, is shown out of sequence as it was completed a year ago. The site was badly overlooked by terraced houses, three- and four-storeys high

Enlargement of Sheffield University, 1953, main front and transverse section

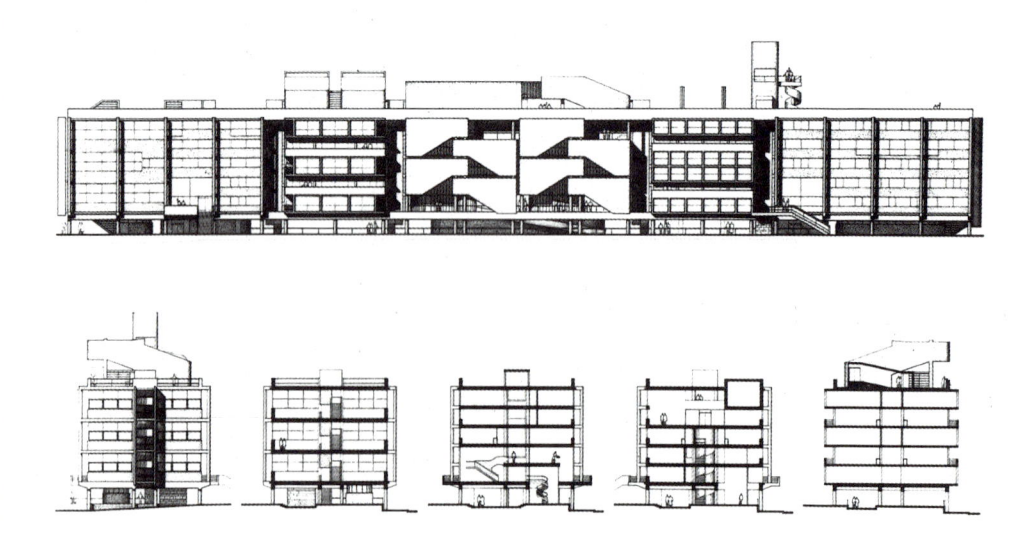

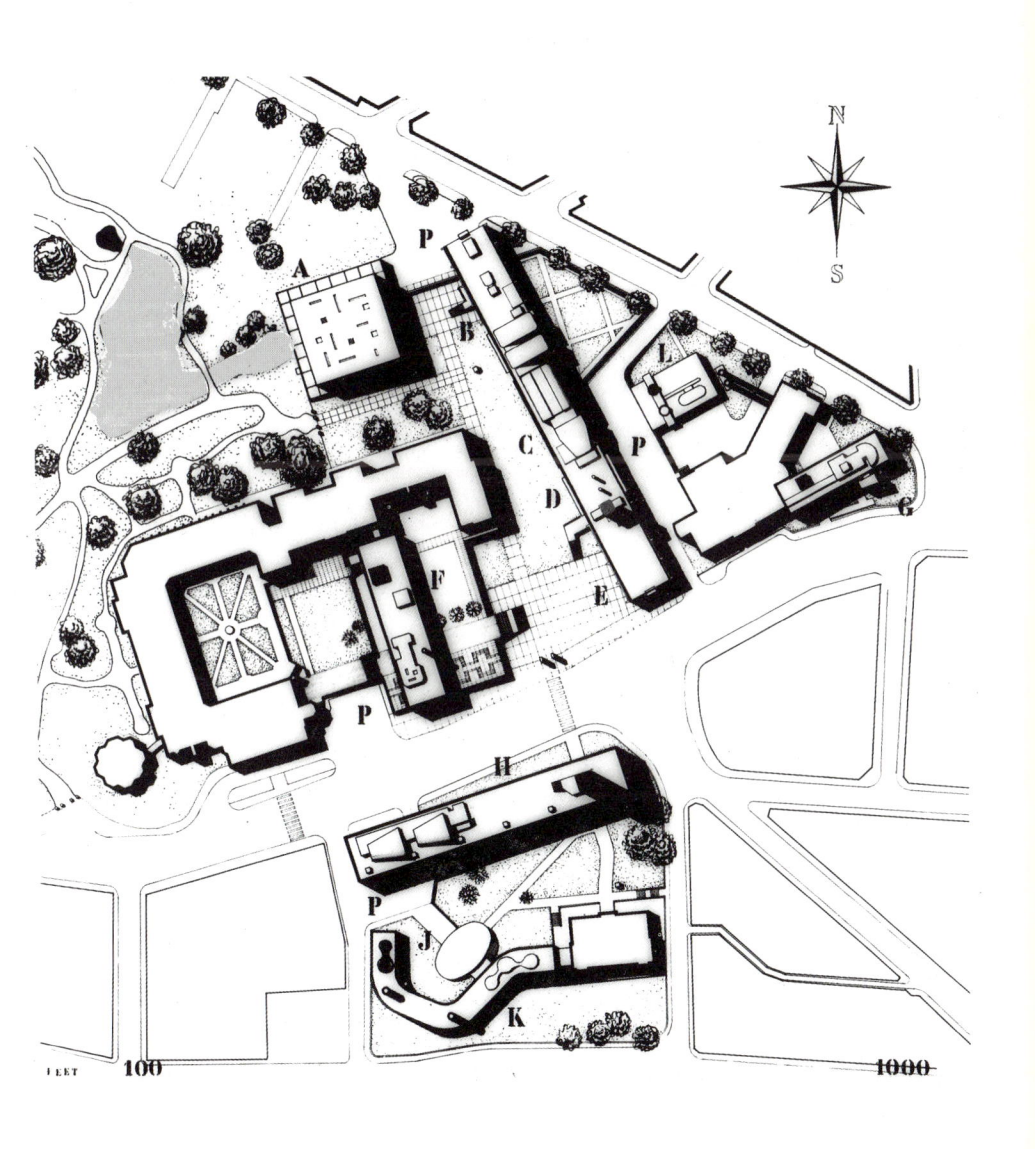

Enlargement of Sheffield University, 1953, general planimetry:
A Library;
B Architecture;
C Arts; D Staff;
E Administration;
F Physics; G Chemistry;
H Medical; J Hall;
K Union & Refectories;
L Boiler house;
P Car park

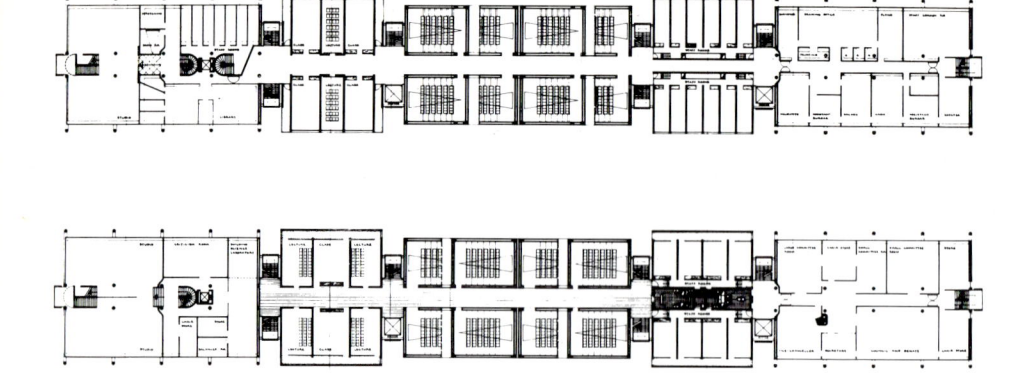

Englargement of Sheffield University, 1953, plan of the first and second floors

and we thought it essential to create a private garden where the residents could sit out in fine weather and not feel spied on by the neighbours. (They are very sensitive about this.) The building, therefore, was bent round a courtyard garden and kept lowest on the south and west sides allowing maximum penetration of sun and daylight into the courtyard. The corridor-route through the building is the organizing element of the plan. As it moves round the building it swells out or reduces according to location, widening where it is also the lift lobby and when it becomes the entrance hall, narrowing between bedrooms and service rooms. As it is always bending there are never long institutional views down it.

The interior has what might be called a "soft inside", negative without play of double height or architectural space and contrary to another principle of the modern movement that the inside of a building should be similar to the outside. This is not normally reasonable, as what happens inside is quite different from what happens externally. We had been a little disillusioned with the flats at Ham Common, where we tried to maintain the external appearance inside with the brick fireplaces and carpentry; with the exception of the architects who live there, we found that the occupiers frequently plastered the fireplaces and "fabloned" the servery units. We therefore came to the conclusion that when building for the anonymous public (particularly older people) it is better to make a neutral interior which can be altered. In fact the LCC descended upon the Home and managed to wallpaper every bedroom (62) in a different pattern.

It is inevitable that in building low cost small buildings one uses brick construction and, I dare say, this building looks a bit Victorian. In fact, the nineteenth century had great knowledge in detailing structural brickwork (very evident in railway and warehouse buildings) and there is no reason why we should not learn from these when, for cost reasons, we have to put up a brick structure.

The project for extending Selwyn College was an important move in the direction of our present designs. The proposed new building also acted as a wall, maintaining the privacy of a fine garden for members of the College, like the courts in other Cambridge Colleges. The planning of the first stage building was very directional and all rooms focussed with a view across the garden and the existing college. The glass screen was really an enormous window faceting in and

Old People's Home, LCC (with James Gowan), 1964, plan of the third and fourth levels

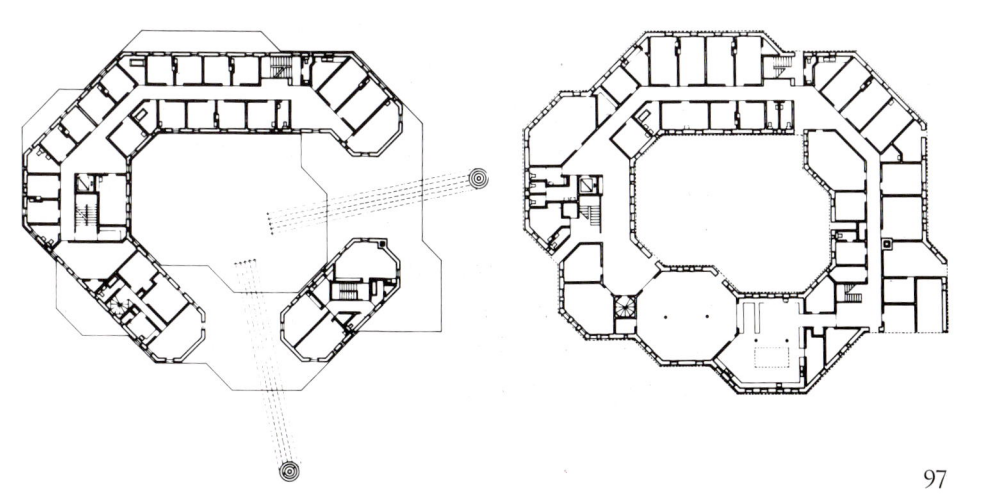

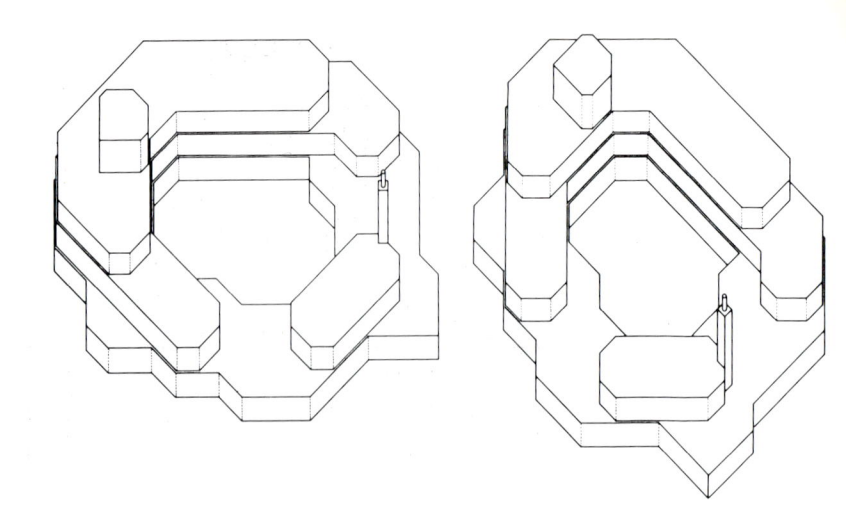

Old People's Home, LCC (with James Gowan), 1964, general axonometric

out approximately indicating on the exterior the scale of the students' rooms and sets; and college members walking in the grounds would have seen reflected in the glass a shattered cubist image of the trees in the garden. The circulation and service rooms were external to the building and these became a series of towers retaining the back wall and marking the entrances. Unfortunately, this project divided the college fifty fifty and, as C. P. Snow readers will know, it's necessary to have almost 100 per cent voting approval before getting action on a major decision.

The Leicester Engineering building has been overdone in the glossies and I shall not describe it in detail. The site was too small, and however we had planned the building, part would have been a tower — the first at the University — with a view over the adjoining park. The original "brief" by the Professor of Engineering was very good though brief — three pages of foolscap, and, on occasions, specialist staff, as they were appointed, would visit the half-finished building, and comment "we must have a noise cell", etc. — various requirements which had then to be incorporated. Architects

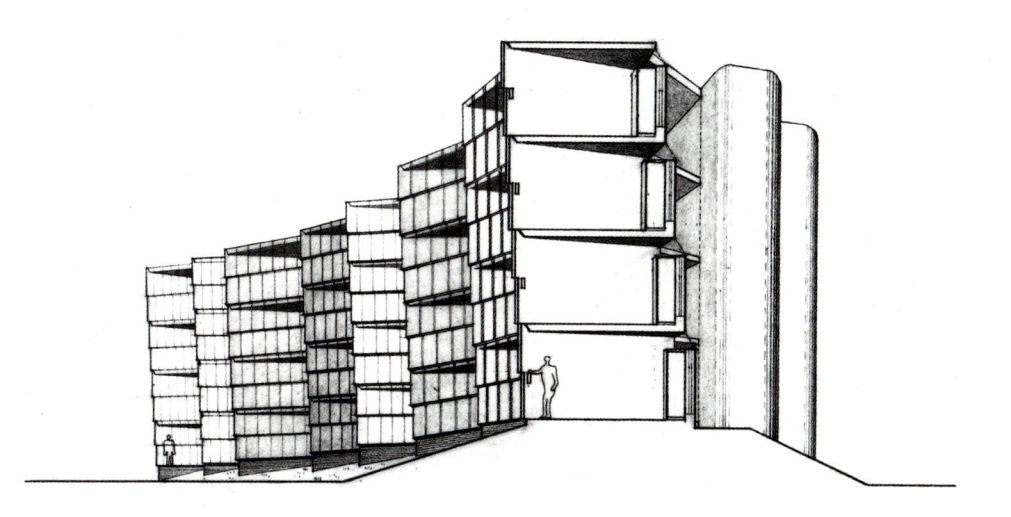

Cambridge, Selwyn College (with James Gowan), 1959, perspective section

are in a difficult position with buildings of a highly scientific nature as they don't have the specialist knowledge to query the "brief"; with this particular building you would have needed a degree in about four subjects to have been able to dissect it. In this situation it is essential to propose a generalized solution which can take change and has inherent flexibility. We regarded the workshop shed in this way, the only expressed units of accommodation are those we understood at the level of our own experience and felt reasonably confident would not change — lecture theatres, staircases, etc.

At ground level the circulation routes which are drawn in from the shed and entrances, come together and turn upwards into the tower as vertical shafts of circulation, stopping off individually at the higher levels, leaving one stair and lift to go to the top. The decreasing size of landings adjacent to these stairs accords with the diminishing number of people occupying the upper levels. The tapering section of the tower and building derives from the way circulation has organized the building form. There are about 300 students in the building and, by making it like an iceberg, the bulk of

Cambridge, Selwyn College (with James Gowan), 1959, standard plan

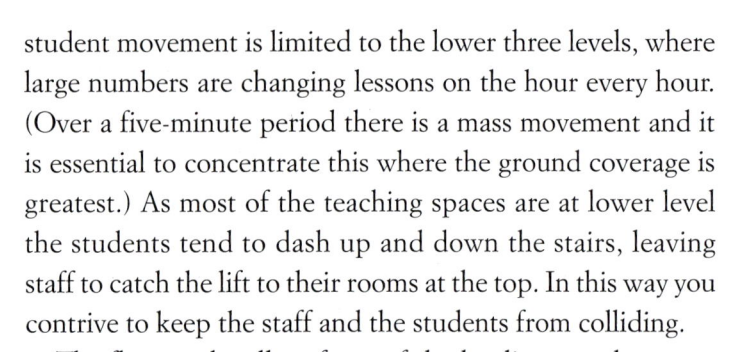

student movement is limited to the lower three levels, where large numbers are changing lessons on the hour every hour. (Over a five-minute period there is a mass movement and it is essential to concentrate this where the ground coverage is greatest.) As most of the teaching spaces are at lower level the students tend to dash up and down the stairs, leaving staff to catch the lift to their rooms at the top. In this way you contrive to keep the staff and the students from colliding.

The floor and wall surfaces of the landings up the tower are tile veneered like the external surfaces of the building and it is difficult to be sure, in certain places, whether you are inside or out. However, the lecture theatres have the ultimate "soft inside" as it would be unreasonable to have these acoustic studios (with structurally disconnected and absorbent walls and ceilings) resemble the exterior. The interior design of the research labs is also different from the rooms in the shed. There is no attempt visually to relate any of the rooms to each other when the activity which takes place in them is different.

The University magazine did an issue on the building — staff, students and visitors wrote articles. There was some criticism at the level of taste (colour, shape) but all the contributors ended by saying it was tremendously stimulating to be in the building, and they felt intensely alive working and studying there. This is the ultimate compliment for the architect, as it is his unique responsibility to raise the human spirit by the quality of the environment which he creates, whether in a room, a building, or a town.

As always (in my experience) the contractor was led protesting through the operation. As well as producing a great number of working drawings, we visited the site sometimes once or even twice a week and, in varying degrees, had to become surveyors, administrators, site agents, etc., all for five per cent.

The History Building at Cambridge originated as a limited competition and the judging committee co-opted two members of the History Faculty to examine the drawings and report from the users' point of view. They reported in favour of this scheme, primarily on two accounts:

1. The reading room (50 per cent of the total accommodation) can be supervised by one man from the control desk. The running cost of staff would be minimal.

2. The reading room is an integral part of the building (the other competitors had made two buildings out of it) and they felt that the History Faculty was an entity and should be housed in a single building.

Perhaps I was lucky as the competition coincided with an outbreak of thefts in the College Libraries which was widely publicized and, at the time, everyone was very supervision conscious.

The design was presented to Senate where every teaching member of the University is invited to debate its merits, and this was led off by the Professor of Classical Archaeology who, in fine Roman stance, stood at the lectern and began his speech — "This building is like no building I ever learnt to love", and finished with an impassioned plea for architects to return to the sanity of the orders. Along the way he slipped in a description of the building — "You come to the desk and you realize you are in an Edwardian hotel; either you go up to your room or you pass beyond into the tea lounge with light coming in from above and no doubt a palm court orchestra playing." An apt description in a strange sort of way!

This building also has a tapering section. The reading room (280 students) has the greatest density of occupation and, therefore, is at ground level. Staff and student common rooms are at first and second floor level and above are the seminar rooms; staff rooms are on the two top floors. Student movement around the lower levels is by stairs, with the lift relatively free for staff to get to the top.

The circulation is the primary organizing element and the corridors around the upper floors are designed as tiers of galleries. These appear under the roof lantern which lights the reading room: as you move along them you may be seeing out across the roof, and the next moment you are alongside it looking in, seeing the mechanics of the building. The roof lantern (at its deepest a floor thick) contains ventilators, heaters, cat-walks, lights, etc., and is really a controlled climate cushion, thermostatically adapting to the weather outside. Walking further along the gallery you see down into the reading room. As you move about the building you are, therefore, always visually referring to the *raison d'être* of the Faculty — the reading room (where students are waiting for seminars to change, the walls of the galleries bow into the roof space forming lay-bys to avoid restricting movement). Fresh air enters the reading room from the window beyond the book-stacks and is drawn across the heated floor, rising upwards to the top of the roof lantern, where it is sucked up by large extract fans and discharged out through the side of the roof. The walls of the galleries which appear in the reading room are veneered in fibrous plaster, perforated with acoustic slots for sound absorption, and the whole of the interior is considered a "soft inside" in contrast to the brittle, reflective, glass skin of the exterior.

Glass buildings are, I think, appropriate in the English climate. We are, perhaps, the only country where it is seldom too hot or too cold and, on a normal cloudy day, there is a high quality of diffused light in the sky. A glass covering keeps the rain out and lets light through. This is eminently sensible in comparison say, to Japan where they build massive concrete structures which, when they want to see out or let the light through, they have to puncture with a window. Glass can resolve all these functions as well as being low cost, light weight, and quick to install. I think of glass rather like polythene, to be pushed in and out enveloping the shape of the rooms, which are considered as always having an ideal shape according to their use. It is necessary to maintain the shape of rooms at their most functional without compromise by forcing them into an overall constricting form and in designing a building one compiles these various room shapes to become the complete assembly. This can then be covered with a membrane of glass, not structurally a difficult thing to do. We asked the specialists to invent a gantry with telescop-

Cambridge, Faculty of History, 1964–67, longitudinal section

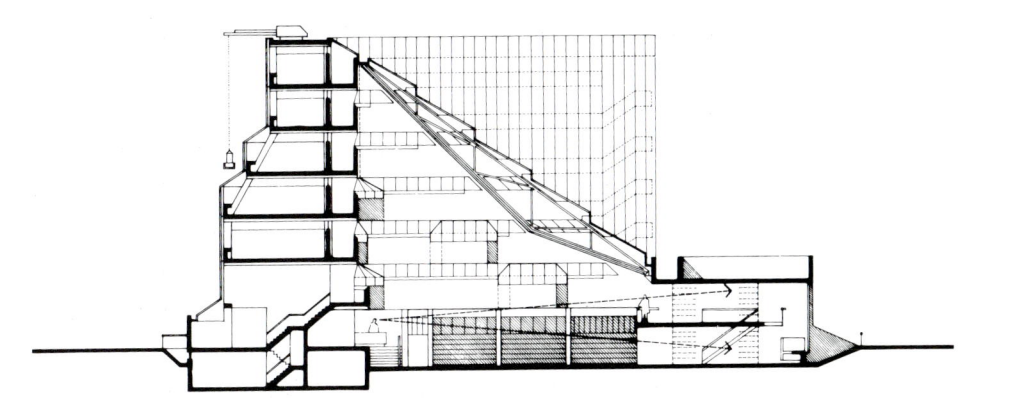

ic arms so that the men in the window-cleaning boat could travel up, down, horizontally, but also step out over the widening floors at the lower levels. It is always necessary to trace back to source the inhibiting factors (in this case window cleaning) and then change them in order to achieve a supra-rational solution.

In modifying and even rejecting principles on which the New Architecture was founded, it is necessary to replace them with working rules and methods which are realistic in a situation of low cost and expediency.

Debate

What buildings do you think have influenced you most in your attitude towards architecture, and what architects?

Different things at different times. Fifteen years ago it would have been Corb, Marseilles, etc., but I think one grows out of being influenced by other people's work, also I find I am less interested in specific buildings. Today it might be the support structures at Cape Canaveral and Jodrell Bank.

In the past an aesthetic was established by a duologue between the client and the architect. Today one is dealing with a committee, no member of which has any particular idea of any aesthetic. One would be interested in your comment on this problem.

I don't find dealing with committees particularly difficult. It seems there are always at least one or two members vitally interested in putting up a decent building — you spot them pretty quickly; often they are the most dynamic personalities on the committee. It then becomes like talking to one man, and you make sure he personally understands what you want, if necessary contacting him before meetings so he's had a chance to talk the committee in the right direction.

Do you think about the town planning and general development of an area, and how what you build fits in with what is there or what is going to be alongside?

My greatest concern is to produce a building with a high degree of environmental quality (one-off or not) which somehow improves the human condition and I wouldn't let neighbouring buildings be inhibiting in trying to achieve this. Nevertheless, if there was an adjoining building which had something, obviously one would be influenced by it. Unfortunately, universities have this habit of selecting a different architect for each job, ending up with a campus like an exhibition. I would prefer to have several adjoining buildings instead of odd ones dotted here and there.

In conceiving a new town I'm sure it's necessary to make a skeleton or structure from the elements of movement and gathering which is so intense that, whatever building is attached, it would always be secondary. I wouldn't mind attaching a building to a connector which I considered to be fundamentally relevant.

Lou Kahn has said that the idea of trying to do a skeleton for any group of buildings is hopeless, and that all any architect can do is to concentrate on his own building. All the environments you can think of are, in fact, groups of a whole lot of related buildings, but do you think that creating a skeleton would create difficulties for architects to come and work within it?

I think if the skeleton had great significance no architect would mind relating to it. Kahn is probably cynical about this, as actually the American situation is worse than the potential English situation. We do have this tradition of authoritarian planning and I think it's possible to achieve something, here, perhaps more easily than in America.

Cambridge, Faculty of History, 1964–67, axonometric view of the interior routes

You say that you think the kick has gone out of modern architecture. Do you think that we are going to continue to "freewheel" for some time on the remainder of that impulse or can you foresee some new impetus arising?

I would like to think of myself as in the mainstream, perhaps "free-wheeling", but I think architecture at the moment is rather static because I think architects are cynical about the society which they have got. It seems to me that in the twenties and thirties Corb, the constructivists, futurists, and others, had an intense vision of a society which was about to arrive, and now that it has come we are all somewhat disillusioned. In the West we have the affluent society, and in the East communism. In neither case is this at all the Utopian way of life envisaged by the pioneers of the modern movement. I think the vision which they had gave them a consistent plastic inventiveness, something which is lacking now. A new culture will, in time, become apparent, quite unlike what we know now, maybe an entirely interior one. It won't be anything to do with Bloomsbury Square or plazas or piazzas or anything like that.

Could you say something about the sort of investigation you do into the functions of the building and structure?

Structure is something which holds a building up and stops it falling down. An architecture over-concerned with structure or services expression is really superficial. We have a normal responsible attitude to research; we analyse the "brief"; we do user research; we visit similar buildings and we do general academic research. We examine the site and see what inevitable inhibiting factors there are. Then, after programming the hierarchies, we set about putting together a relevant organization. For this I have a staff (nowadays called a team) gathering together material, analysing, programming, drawing up and detailing; one is assisted all the time by others who are involved in all the factors and are also working on design options. However, an actual decision as to what is correct or not in a design has to be my responsibility. Even so, we don't find many design possibilities come up, as we tend to fasten on to appropriate functional solutions and then try to find other relevant factors, and so on gradually building up. I think every building must have at least two ideas in it.

If you find the present state of society so depressing, what makes it worthwhile going to the trouble of designing well-detailed, good buildings? Is it a love affair with the client and his "brief", or is it just sheer professional pride?

It is more like a love affair with the building. Undoubtedly one is emotionally involved with one's building. I know this is so because when they are finished and the clients are about to move in I have a sort of resistance. I think they are going to do all the wrong things when they get inside. I keep coming back and hanging around, and probably pester the daylights out of them. Eventually it fades on you, usually because you are getting involved with the next one, and after a period of time, maybe a year or so, I seldom go back. However, architecture is not a game. One is really trying to produce buildings which are the most apt for a site and function, it's not a question of style or appearance, it's how you organize spaces and movement for a place and activity, initially nothing to do with appearance.

With respect to your initial failures — five out of six — do you feel that this can be got over by the general public seeing more of stimulating architecture?

It could easily be got over by sacking planning officers and not having aesthetic control. I know the argument is that if we didn't have it much worse things would get built. But I don't think this is so. All over the country one sees hideous developments which don't appear to have been subjected to any aesthetic test. If there isn't a consistent cultural level you are really operating in terms of a gamble, and it depends whom your scheme goes in front of as to whether it gets turned down or not. In this situation it would be better not to have control.

You worked very much under the competition system. Do you see this as a good system?

Whether a competition is worth doing or not is related to whom the assessors are. If the assessor is no good it's not much use going in for it if you are trying to win. There are few assessors one really trusts and, therefore, the number of competitions that younger people enter with a realistic intention of winning and thereby starting a practice is limited. When I did competitions it was not because I was seriously trying to get into practice, I was working off a surplus of ideas which had accrued in the first years out of school.

The reason you said you liked glass was an emotional one, as I understood it, not because you could build more quickly or because it was cheaper or anything of that sort. This also, I feel,

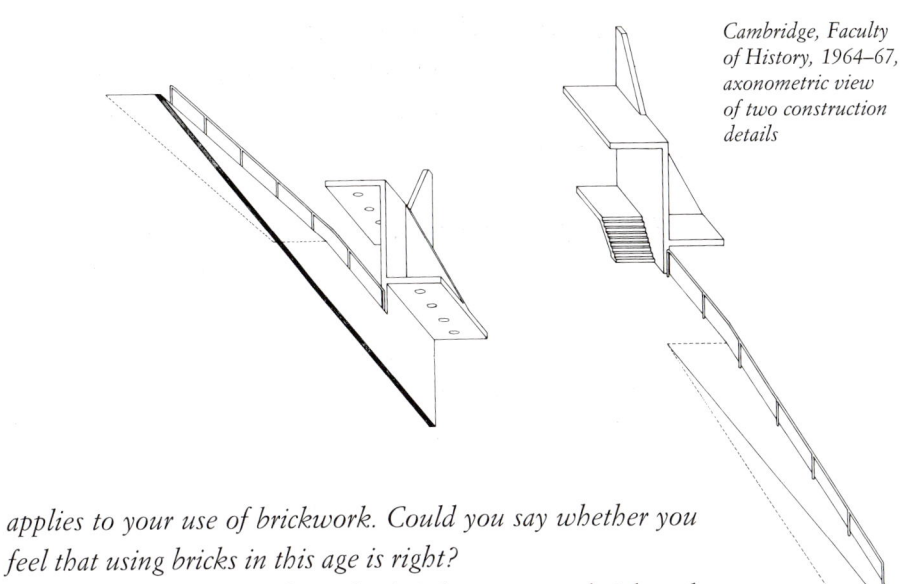

Cambridge, Faculty of History, 1964–67, axonometric view of two construction details

applies to your use of brickwork. Could you say whether you feel that using bricks in this age is right?

You are quite wrong if you think I choose to use brick and glass on an entirely emotional level. I use glass skins because they are light-weight, rapidly applied, low in cost, keep out the rain, self-cleaning, let the light in, let you see out. These seem to me to be very practical arguments for using glass. Likewise with brickwork, bricks are low in cost, need little maintenance, and can also be the structural support. These seem to me to be very good practical reasons for using brick. I never select materials emotionally; they are chosen entirely at a practical level, but then, of course, they must be transformed to cohere at a level of significance.

I'm all for system building, but it's just another method of construction. In itself it can't revitalize the environment. Bricks are a 9" × 4½" pre-cast system, likewise patent glazing is a sheet cladding system. Everything is a system though possibly not poured concrete; perhaps the distinction is whether you are using molecular pre-formed unity or something poured. It's not what you build of, but why and how you make it that determines the quality of our physical existence.

*Leicester, laboratories
of the Faculty
of Engineering
(with James Gowan),
1959–63, general
axonometric*

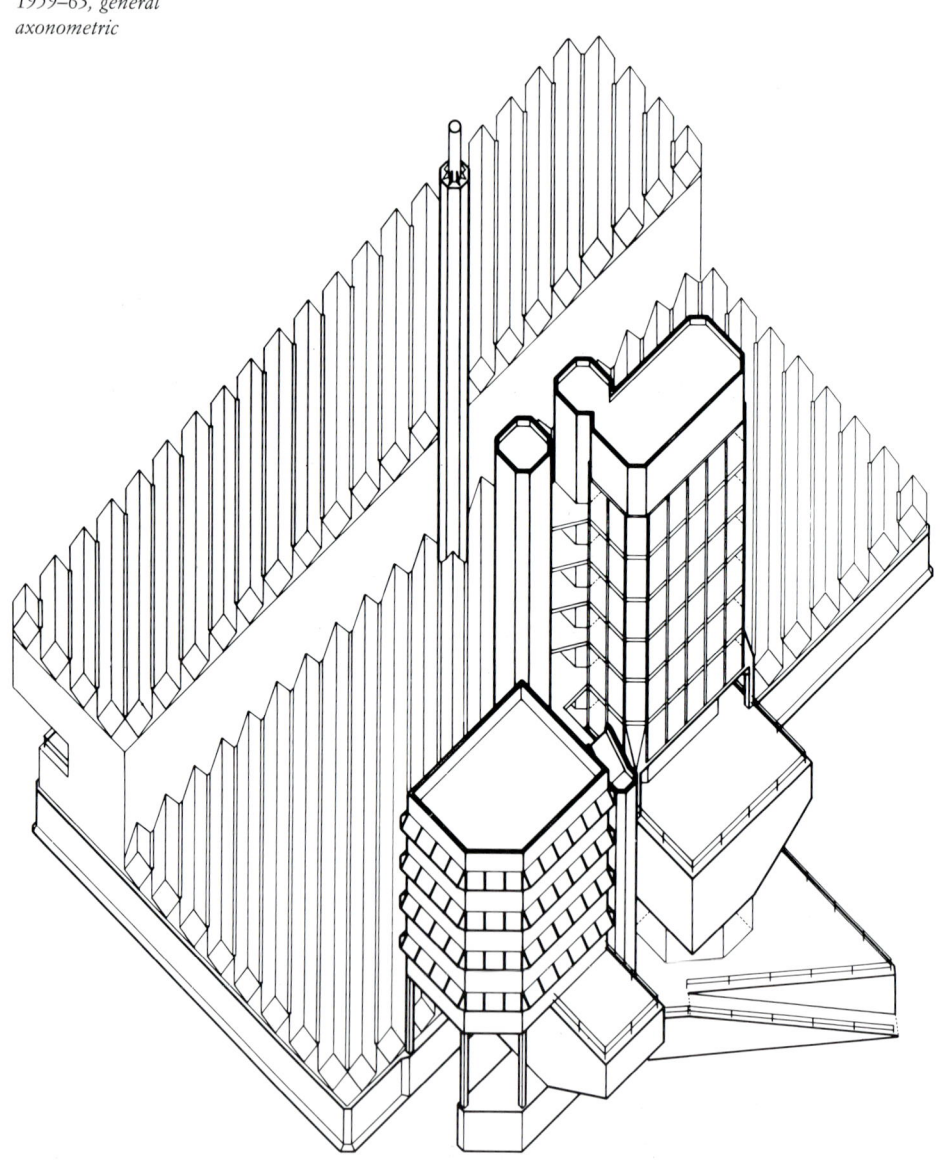

110

Anti-Structure

I understand the subject for discussion at this Symposium is the relevance of structure in architecture. This is not a very appropriate subject for me as I have a rather *ad hoc* and expedient attitude to structure particularly as a design element and I usually manage to prevent it from intruding in the architectural solution. I'm more concerned with sociological, environmental, and organisational problems which I regard as being more important in the evolution of a design.

I suspect I'm considered by many English architects (and some of the architectural press) as a somewhat irrational designer. (We have inherited the Bauhaus mentality just as America has inherited the Beaux Arts.) However, I would argue that our buildings usually evolve from a broad but complex understanding of logic. Logic is many-faceted and its properties are normally not the same for every building. Each project has its own importance hierarchy, sometimes indicated by the client's brief and always determined by the sensibility of the architect. I would like to comment on some factors which have influenced our work, and as you may be familiar with these projects, I will try to keep to aspects which have not been described previously.

In the design for a children's home in South London we thought social considerations should have priority. The chil-

Published in Zodiac, *No. 18, 1969.*
A slide talk given by James Stirling at Bologna University during a symposium (November 1966) to mark the retirement of Professor Michelucci from the School of Architecture.

dren who grow up in these homes are either orphans or have been taken from families where the parents cannot look after them. We wanted the new buildings to over-compensate for the lack of a real "home". Small in size, they are almost a caricature of the domestic house and they have the small scale of doll's houses and children's toys. The more costly decision to make two buildings instead of one was in order to reduce the size of the "family" to about fifteen children per house instead of thirty as it would have been in a single building. We thought it important not to make the scheme institutional. Each house is looked after by a married couple who really become foster parents and, like an ordinary house, the children's bedrooms are on the upper floor. Seen from outside, each room steps back, causing the façade to recede and articulate the bedrooms, indicating them as the important spaces within the building. Children playing in the gardens are able to identify with their own particular room.

The expression (articulation) of the important accommodation is something we have always been concerned with and in our first project — the flats at Ham Common — the entity of the dwellings was indicated by the forward and backward movement of the façade. These flats were built in the garden of a Georgian house and we made the new buildings of similar materials and kept to the same height. Modern buildings need not necessarily be visually disruptive to adjoining old buildings.

In the re-housing scheme at Preston, the front door of each dwelling is onto an elevated footpath and opposite this door is a storage outhouse. This outhouse identifies the position of the dwelling within the terrace and, although the density is twice the existing, the new buildings are of similar height and materials to the houses in the adjoining nineteenth-century streets. I have doubts about the accepted solution for re-building slum areas in the form of slabs or towers, which are physically disruptive to a neighbourhood and probably create an inferior social community. Lifts, in their present form, are a crude and anti-social way of approaching one's home.

Probably as a country we spend less per square foot on our buildings than most countries of Western Europe and all the projects I have worked on are of low cost. With the smaller buildings, we have resorted to our surviving craft tradition of bricklaying. This slow hand-made process does, of course, pose philosophical problems in the middle of the twentieth century. However, if it is still a viable economic/labour method for our building industry, then it is surely realistic for us to use it.

After six or seven years designing very articulated buildings, we decided, in the old peoples' home at Blackheath, to do the opposite. Here, none of the accommodation is expressed; all rooms are concealed behind a screen of structural brick walls which wrap around an internal garden. Perhaps this is our only perverse building, and maybe, it has some resemblance to style *à la liberté*, popular here some time back.

All these projects were domestic in function and concerned with maintaining the *status quo* in relation to their environs; and they are essentially conventional in their restatement of traditional internal use.

With the engineering building for Leicester University we had to build a new institution of a scientific/educational type. The tower at the front contains the fixed non-expanding accommodation and is intended to be a grouping of identifiable volumes of accommodation, i.e. vertical shafts which are for lifts and staircases, wedge-shaped volumes which are lecture theatres, etc. The back of the building is considered as a shed, within which there can be continuous re-equipping and adjustment of spaces.

The total building should read as a conjunction of fixed, specific activities and of a variable changing situation, both reflecting the educational curriculum. The organisational circumstance which was different from our previous experience is the fact that 200 to 300 students move rapidly through the circulation in a stop/go process several times a day, changing classes; this movement factor largely influenced the planning solution and the building section. The vertical circulation, which includes lay-bys adjacent to the lift and staircase shafts, is the skeleton onto which various rooms are hung and the circulation routes are the only consistent visual element running through the building, in comparison to the differing visual characteristics of specific rooms. We have not attempted to carry through an "interior design" idiom and the function of a room has been the sole determinate of its internal appearance. This is different from some contemporary buildings, for instance the Yale School of Architecture which contains a lecture theatre, staff rooms, library, guest suite, etc. as well as studios, and all are treated in a similar interior aesthetic-ribbed concrete (brought in from the exterior). The same materials and surfaces are used throughout, inside and out, which I would have thought incompatible and illogical for such divergent activities. In the engineering building each type of room has its own interior aesthetic and, in a similar way, the structural support changes for different parts of the building — the type of construction chosen being the most appropriate to the dimensions and activity of a particular space, i.e. industrial space-frame roof across the workshops; disconnected acoustic shell within a reinforced concrete *insitu* box for the lecture theatres; reinforced concrete diagrid spanning between periph-

Leicester, laboratories of the Faculty of Engineering (with James Gowan), 1959–63, view from the river

eral columns over the research labs. There are as many structural systems as there are major differences in function and the choice of the type of structure was a later decision in the design evolution.

There is however, a more important aspect to structure than the selection of constructional systems and this relates to the initial concept of the building mass.

All built form has weight and properties of stability or instability dependant on shape and it is necessary to make a grouping of masses which is inherently stable. In the engineering building, the weight of the towers above counterbalances the overhang of the lecture theatres under, or to say it another way, the extent of the cantilever of the lecture theatres is dictated by the amount of weight over; if you removed the top floor the building would overturn. No doubt there is a certain architectural quality inherent in the composition of stable masses particularly when they are a-symmetrical.

The small elements of a building should, wherever possi-

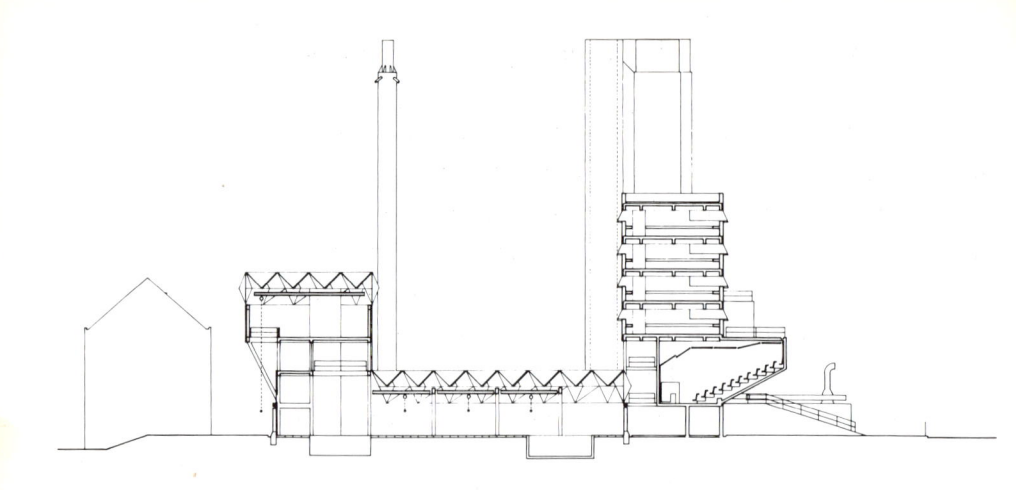

Leicester, laboratories of the Faculty of Engineering (with James Gowan), 1959–63, transverse section

ble, be multi-functioning, a more subtle requirement than the simplistic relationship of one to one elements; for instance, the sloping underside to the large lecture theatre is also the canopy over the entrance porch. At a smaller scale, the beams normally at the ceiling are on the floor of the offices and they are made as upstand beams which are simultaneously a window seat, a horizontal duct for services and a fire barrier between floors, as well as being structural beams. The shafts which contain the lifts and staircases are the vertical service ducts as well as being structural buttresses.

The diagonal displacement of the roof over the workshops was necessary to obtain north lighting but it also allowed a superimposition of two geometries, the normal (right angular) and the distorted (at 45°) like a Cubist image. There is liberation and a greater number of planning choices available when more than one geometry is integrated into the design. It has also been said that axonometric drawing technique has influenced the design of this building.

The History Faculty for Cambridge University is also intended to be read as a grouping of identifiable elements, i.e. lift and staircase shafts and most obviously the large tent-shaped roof indicating the library reading room below, the largest internal space.

A vast amount of modern architecture is banal, partly through the easy acceptance of compressing room accommodations into simple overall building forms. We usually try to retain the ideal shape of a room and avoid distorting it to fit a structural module or a preconceived building shape. In the History Faculty the room shapes are stacked to become the total building form and it is possible to see that the smaller rooms are on the top floors, increasing to larger and largest rooms at the lower levels.

The open steel truss roof which leans across the reading room allows daylight to filter into the library and, at the upper levels, it also allows light through into the circulation corridors. This roof is also a technical element, a controlled climate cushion containing heaters, ventilation louvres, fan extracts, lights, etc. automatically adjusting to the outside climate to maintain a constant atmosphere within. The thrust from this "lean-to-roof" is stabilised by the buttressing effect of the "L" shaped block and the total building mass is a resolution of various structural forces.

The exterior is of similar materials to the engineering building — glass, tiles, etc. — hard, brittle and reflective surfaces appropriate to the outside climate. These materials are not brought into the interior and the walls of the library, etc. are lined with acoustic finishes.

The visual aesthetic inside is, if anything, more like that of a television studio. The corridors are thought of as galleries running around the upper spaces of the reading room, they are glazed for sound and are the primary circulation system. The students moving about the building are visually in contact with the library, the most important working element of the Faculty. This interrelationship was developed from an implication in the Faculty's brief for the new building.

The next projects are significantly different as both have an external appearance of expressed structure. This is not however a rejection of our previous work; it is just that these buildings have extraordinary circumstances which made considerations of structure top of the importance hierarchy.

The new buildings for St. Andrews University are in the north of Scotland where there is no local building material (not even bricks) or workmen (who have all come south). The problem was how to erect a battery of student residences as a continuous building process over a period of six or seven years. The only method which seemed possible was to design a kit of precast concrete elements to be manufactured elsewhere. These are taken to the site where they are lifted directly off lorries by mobile cranes and placed onto the building without touching ground. The factory is in Edinburgh, about eighty miles south of St. Andrews. Each building is assembled from a range of precast wall and floor units and there are about thirty-two different moulds which will be re-used for the later buildings. The first building is expensive but the cost should be more economical with the later residences and the overall cost could be similar to that of traditional buildings.

There are 250 students in each residence (both sexes) and the students' bedrooms are positioned in the fingers, which are pointed towards a magnificent view of the North Sea and the Scottish mountains. The non-repetitive accommodation (i.e. dining hall, games rooms, etc.) is located in the web where the fingers join. There is a glazed promenade level about halfway up the building and, from this, internal staircases give access up or down to the students' rooms. This promenade is the main artery of circulation and is intended to be the major element of sociability. Off the promenade

St. Andrews University, students' residence, 1964–68, standard plan

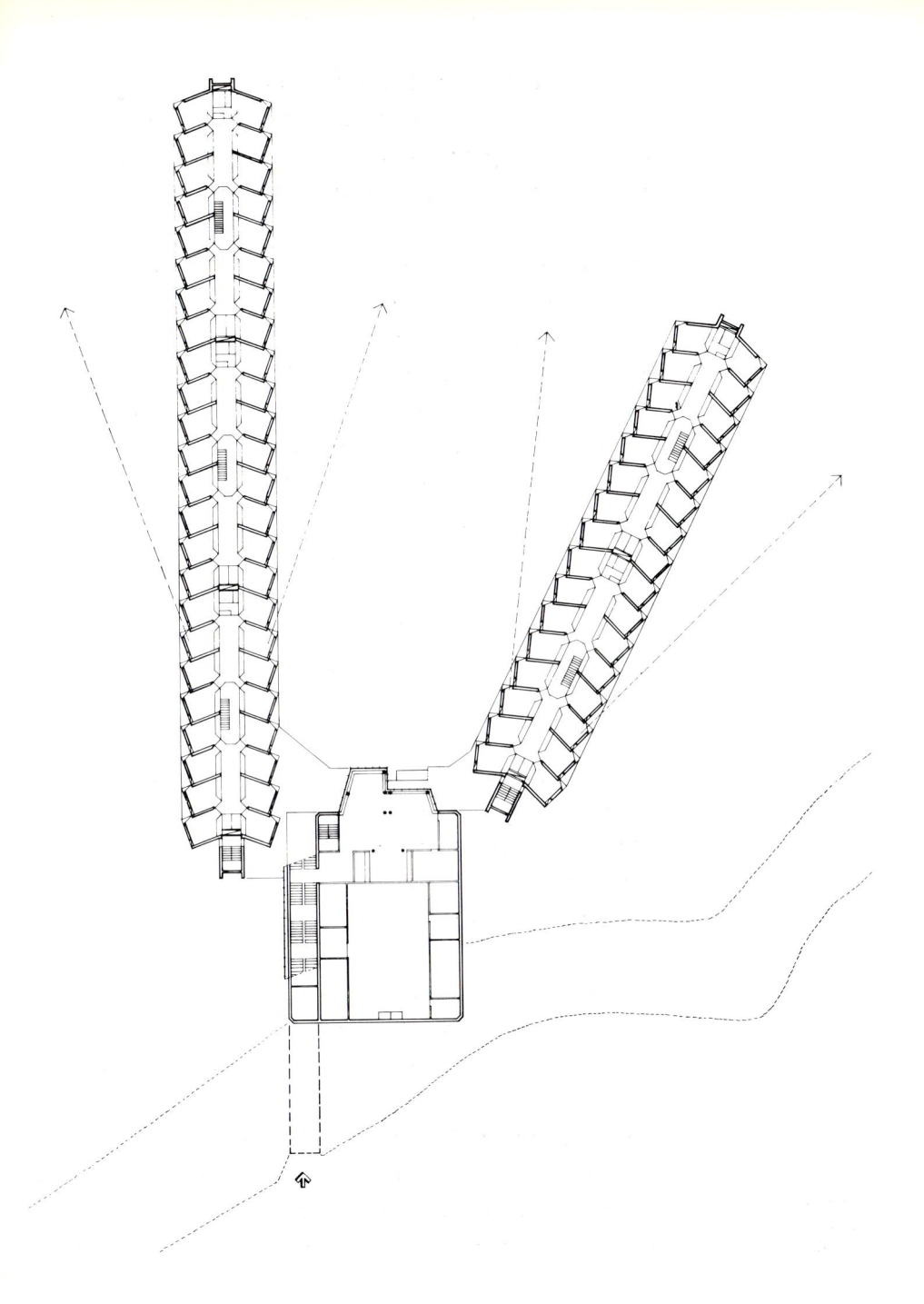

and adjacent to the staircases are lay-bys containing seats and vending machines. In these areas it is hoped that much of the social life in the residence will take place and, in using the promenade on route to their rooms, every student will inevitably come into contact with everyone else. On the floors above and below the promenade the staircases give onto short, unpleasant corridors (deliberately narrow and underlit) to the students' rooms. Sometimes it is necessary to design unpleasant spaces in order to increase the usage of areas where activity is intended. There was an elementary problem of identity inside the internal staircases — at what level does the promenade occur? — how to know when to get out. To help visually locate, large circular holes were cut into the walls of the staircases at promenade level; not an inside/outside window in the normal sense, it is therefore different from the rectangular windows used elsewhere. The sexes change with each staircase though I don't think the University realise that, as fire exits were required onto the roof, it should be possible for the students to cross over at night unseen. The student's private room is obviously the most important accommodation in the building and every room has a window angled like an eye towards the view. This angling which is a displacement of the room articulates its position on the façade and therefore, even with a very structurally motivated scheme, we have maintained as fundamental the expression of the most important accommodation.

If the site at St. Andrews is idyllic, then the site for the Dorman Long building must be considered satanic; positioned at the end of the steel mills and surrounded by the symbols of heavy industry — slag mountains, cooling towers, flaming chimneys, etc. Dorman Long are England's largest producers of rolled steel columns and beams and they have a long history of civil engineering from Sydney Harbour

St. Andrews University, students' residence, 1964–68, assembling of the pre-fabricated elements

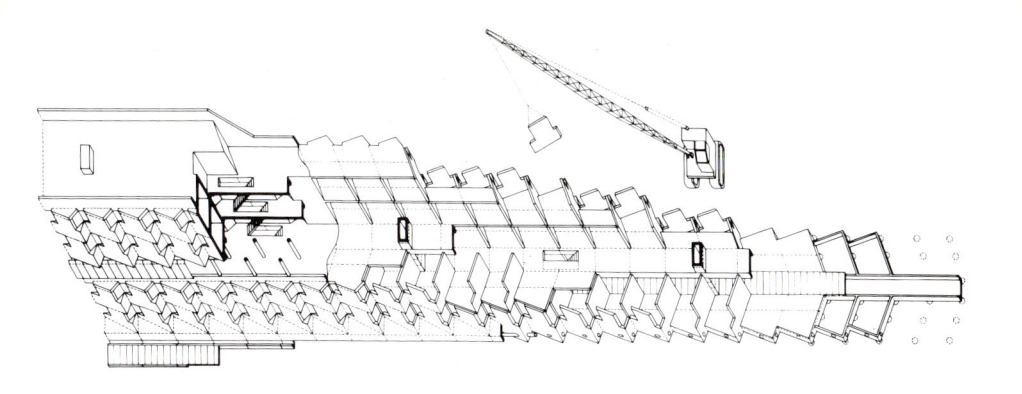

Bridge to radio telescopes. They asked for the building to be of steel construction and for it to be an exposition of their standard products. Not only had the building to be made of steel, it had to be seen to be made of steel. This was a commercial requirement and we accepted it, partly as we think the future will see a considerable development in the steel medium for building (as well as assemblage methods of erection — i.e. St. Andrews). Inevitably their request meant that the appearance of a structural system would dominate the architectural solution.

The headquarters office building is fourteen storeys high, and almost 1,000 feet long. The accommodation includes many small rooms — secretaries, managers, directors, etc. and areas of large spaces — drawing offices, open plan offices, canteen, library, computer centre, etc., amongst others. The larger spaces are on the lower floors and this accounts for the thickening of the building section towards the ground, indicated by the splayed front. The thrust created by this splay is counterbalanced by the shafts of vertical circulation pulled out behind which act as buttresses stabilising the total building form.

The English steel industry is about to be nationalised and there are doubts as to the future of this project, though as the

St. Andrews University, students' residence, 1964–68, perspective plan of a standard apartment, lighting study

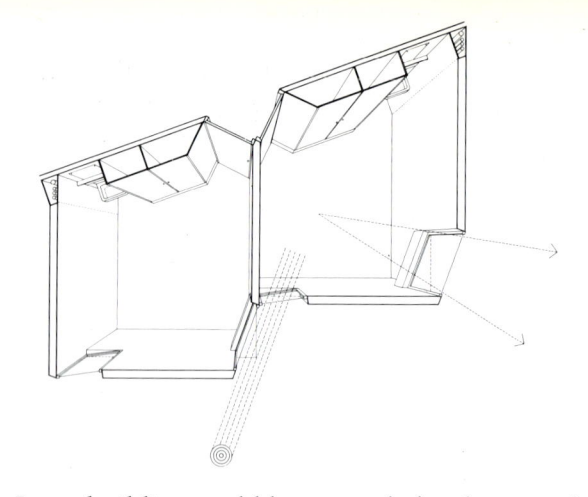

Dorman Long building could be expanded to become the headquarters of a north-east steel group, the building might grow to be three times longer. It would then be lying across the intended siting of a new motorway which the local authorities are reluctant to move. However, the road could go straight through the building, or dip down under (Orly Airport) and the building would then also be a bridge.

An interesting situation arose when a particular design of the external grid of columns and beams was being considered by the structural engineers. It transpired that there was a choice of about six alternatives for this structural mesh, all using approximately the same weight of steel and all of similar cost, i.e. it could be all diagonally braced, or it could have horizontal stiffener beams at every floor level, etc. The choice of a particular structural appearance was therefore arbitrary, reinforcing my opinion that a design, which is primarily dependant on expression of structure is likely to be superficial. To resolve this problem we made an architectural decision and kept the horizontal wind stiffener beams adjacent to each floor on the upper part of the building, but on the splayed front we omitted them at every other level, replacing them with diagonal struts to maintain the strength of structural mesh. The scale of the structural grid therefore relates to the building section and graphically indicates the smaller accommodation at the top and the larger accommodation below.

In England I find that, when making a presentation to the client, we must never talk about aesthetics and explanations should always be in terms of common sense, function and logic. If you mentioned the word "beauty" their hair might stand on end and you could lose the commission. Perhaps this philistine attitude is, in some ways, beneficial as it probably means that a design can never be too far removed from common sense and logic.

The structural content in architecture is likely to increase as traditional methods of construction decline and new buildings get larger and more complicated. However, I think it will be ever more necessary for architects not to rely merely on the expression of techniques for the architectural solution. Humanistic considerations must remain the primary logic from which a design evolves.

*Halsemere, Olivetti
Training School,
perspective of the
multifunctional space*

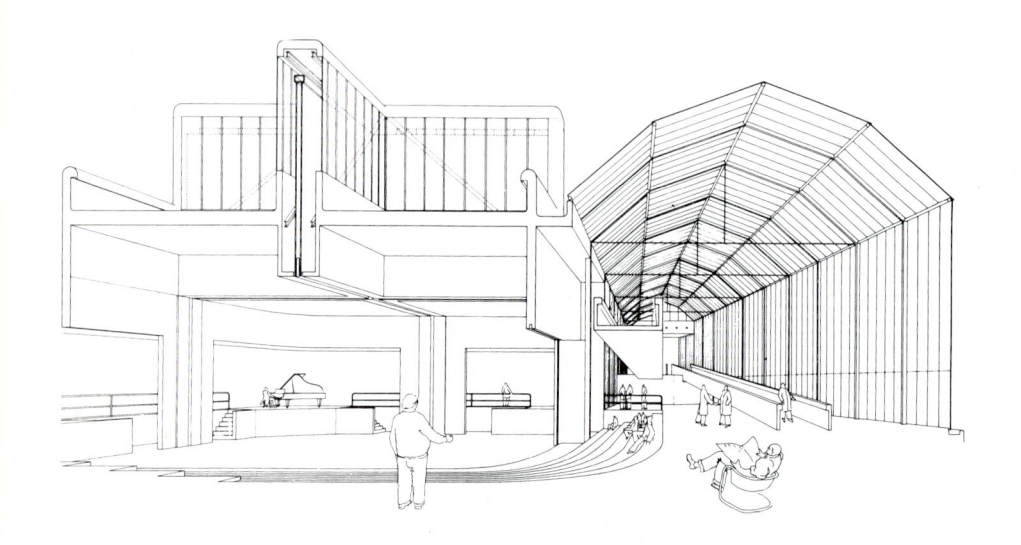

Methods of Expression and Materials

Like Professor Quaroni, I consider 99 percent of modern architecture to be boring, banal and barren and usually disruptive and unharmonious when placed in older cities.

In England the Government, either local authorities or central government, are politically concerned to build the greatest number for the common good — be it schools, houses, factories, etc. Private Enterprise Developers are concerned with building the greatest quantity of square footage (i.e. offices) at the least cost to maximize profits. Both see shoebox style modern architecture with its stripped down puritan aesthetic and repetitive expression as very suitable for building to the lowest costs. Government and Developers are eliminating the perhaps more costly element of "art" in architecture; and many would agree that this is right and proper in a social democratic society. In this situation an architect who is concerned to produce architecture has to revert to low-down cunning to make his buildings of any consequence.

Today's theme (at the Congress) is "Materials and Methods of Expression". I would prefer to re-phrase it "Methods of Expression and Materials". I ceased to believe in Frank Lloyd Wright's philosophy of "truth to materials" when I saw for the first time a building by Palladio — where the peeling columns showed that the columns were in fact made

Published in A+U, No. 2, 1975. The statement was made at the second Iran International Congress of Architecture, held in 1974 at Persepolis organised by the Iranian Government.

of bricks — and not of marble or stone which I had naively assumed from the books.

I believe that the shapes of a building should indicate — perhaps display the usage and way of life of its occupants, and it is therefore likely to be rich and varied in appearance, and its expression is unlikely to be simple. The collection (in a building) of forms and shapes which the everyday public can *associate* with and be *familiar* with — and *identify* with — seems to me essential. These forms may derive from staircases, windows, corridors, rooms, entrances, etc. and the total building could be thought of as an assemblage of everyday elements recognizable to a normal man and not only an architect. For instance, in a building we did at Oxford University some years ago, it was intended that you could recognize the historic elements of courtyard, entrance gate towers, cloisters: also a central object replacing the traditional fountain or statue of the college founder. In this way we hoped that students and public would not be *dis-associated* from their cultural past. The particular way in which functional-symbolic elements are put together may be the "art" in the architecture.

I am wary of what seems to me banal and arrogant solutions of tents, space frames, domes and bubbles covering everything — which technocratic solutions may be valid for single usage spectator activities, but if carried into normal everyday building can only *subvert* the richness and variety of life. If the expression of functional-symbolic forms and familiar elements is foremost, the expression of structure will be secondary, and if structure shows it is not in my opinion the engineering which counts but the way in which the building is put together that is important. It is desirable not to eliminate the traces of the human hand in carpentry or bricklaying and by the same token it is necessary to express the assemblage process of most prefabricated systems: similarly with the use of color pigmentation in plastics to delineate the separate parts.

We are not much concerned with the imagery of space flight or super-advanced technology as I think an architect usually has to make do with the technology which is normal and is cost-wise available to him. According to what is appropriate for a particular building problem, a building could — I think — be made of any materials — old or new — traditional or technological and the whole spectrum of the past, from earth works to plastics is usable according to the differing economic/climate conditions prevailing in different countries.

Hopefully there might be some humor in modern architecture, and in this context there is a rich vein in serious puritanical modern that can be satirized and commented upon. I realize that an interaction between the design for a new building with associations of the past is a dangerous tightrope to walk with compromise and sentimentality on either side.

I would like to end by showing a sequence of slides which indicate in pairs a relationship between the past and one of our projects. Not that the first slide of each pair has in any way influenced the design of the building which follows, but nevertheless there is, I hope, a connection, be it in material, constructional method, or association.

Non-Modular
A primary non-modular way of building is by pouring concrete into specially made formwork which is erected on site to contour the building shape. The making of this formwork is of paramount importance though it usually has a single life and is destroyed after the act of creation. These formworks — like the building they make — are unique and singular.

Modular

Almost all ways of building, ancient and modern, are modular at basis (traditionally in the UK for example, bricks and timber framing). Prefabricated methods of building depend on repetition and consequently have parts of recurring appearance and are therefore modular.

All modular building methods involve the process of assemblage, the units being made away from the site are then brought to the site and assembled to make the building. Therefore I think the expression of "assemblage" should be apparent in the finished building and with axonometric drawings of this type we try to show "how" the building is put together — not give an image of a complete building.

The type of "unit of prefabrication", whether traditional or modern, will be determined by labour and building costs prevailing at the time — this applied as much in the 17th century as it does now. Today bricklaying is expensive (more so in some countries than others) whereas sheet cladding is less expensive (also more so in some countries than others), fortunately suggesting that national differences will continue to exist in building technology — even prefabrication.

The following are some comments with slides related to our limited experience in trying to find an appropriate aesthetic expression for some normal (modular) building materials.

Bricks

The handlaying process is apparent through variations in joint widths and the irregular set of brick to brick. The surface of the wall should not look too mechanical or machine made.

Walls can be mathematically calculated relative to the maximum crushing strength of the bricks and thus influence the shape and size of window openings that can be cut out and leave supporting areas of brickwork — which appear as piers.

Windows can be aligned vertically so that the wall areas between become continuous vertical piers of brickwork. Alternatively smaller random openings not creating particular structural problems can be positioned to fit the brick module.

Cills, plinths, parapets, etc., can be made from "standard brick specials" as produced by brick manufacturers in the UK.

Precast Reinforced Concrete

It is appropriate to make a repetition of precast units when there is repetition of accommodation — usually rooms. Much less appropriate to make a repetition of structural elements in order to design a building system.

Buildings are seen as mass from the distance but are seen as assemblage close to.

"Expression of assemblage" is achieved through the visual articulation of each unit in the wall, optically assisted by adjoining units having contra-diagonal ribbing on their surface and also by the plain edge margins outlining the edge of units. These edge margins are also necessary to give protection to the ribbing, particularly when units are being moved in the factory and transported and handled on site.

The ribbed surface of the unit is achieved by placing corrugated sheets (aluminium or rubber) in the moulds prior to pouring concrete. The resulting texture of normal/cheap concrete is more appropriate as a finish to cast concrete than other methods such as exposing aggregate (a mosaic of stone chippings, marble, etc.) or chemically treated surfaces which have the aspect of being disguises.

Controlled weather staining — water is routed via the ribbing in diagonal runs across the building surface. Sunlight and rain falling on the panels create geometric patterns.

Factory in-fitting of windows/doors (into hole in the unit) or after fit on site of windows and doors into spaces left between units.

Glass

The modular spacing of mullion bars which flow over the contours of the building and graphically emphasise the building form. The closeness of the mullions makes the glass surface a web or mesh, not just a transparent void. Close spacing of mullions is also related to using cheap thin glass in small widths.

Glass is used as cladding (like sheet metal) to sheath the building and because of lack of weight and thickness it close fits the building profile like skin or polythene — fitting in and out to express the building section.

At complicated intersections sheet glass can be cut on site like cardboard and has the facility of carpentry. Glass can be used transparently, translucently or reflectively.

Steel

In the UK (as elsewhere) structural steelwork has to be encased for fire protection except when used in single-storey buildings or where structure is externalized. Therefore direct expression of steel fabrication is limited to single-storey parts of buildings, or when it can be placed externally clear of the building envelope.

Civil Engineering expression (i.e. bridges). At Dorman Long headquarters, we designed a grid of standard (from the catalogue) rolled steel joists and columns which were placed external to the building. An architectural decision was made to use a particular scale of grid to suggest the larger and smaller spaces inside the building.

Industrial Building expression (i.e. factories). The horizontal steel trusses at Leicester University are inclined to form a north-light roof with peaks and valleys running across the workshops.

Roof trusses (i.e. market halls or railway stations). At the Cambridge Library the trusses lean up six floors but as this is still a single-storey volume they do not need to be protected for fire and can be painted decoratively and are a major visual aspect within the building. The trusses also support upper and lower areas of roof glazing and carry the primary services in the building.

Plastics

A refined expression of plastics has been achieved in the much smaller scale field of industrial design — for example the objects shown in the *New Italian Landscape* exhibition at the Museum of Modern Art, New York.

We use two tone colouring on adjoining panels to articulate the unit in the mass of building, an expression of lightweight clip on assemblage, aided by emphasising the joints between units and also through having surface (citreon style) corrugations to make rigid the thin layer of GRP (Glass Reinforced Polyester) against distortion and warp, particularly necessary when the unit is being lifted out of the factory and again when lifted onto the building.

Water drainage channels on the external surface of the unit also produce corrugations strengthening the unit and at the same time keeping water away from the joints.

In-fitting of windows and doors into the unit before it leaves the factory.

The modular units for Olivetti (UK) were not produced by normal Building Contractors, but prefabricated in the works of the pleasure boat industry. Is this architecture or industrial design?

*Design School,
Rice University
(with Michael Wilford),
1979–81, axonometric
of internal spaces*

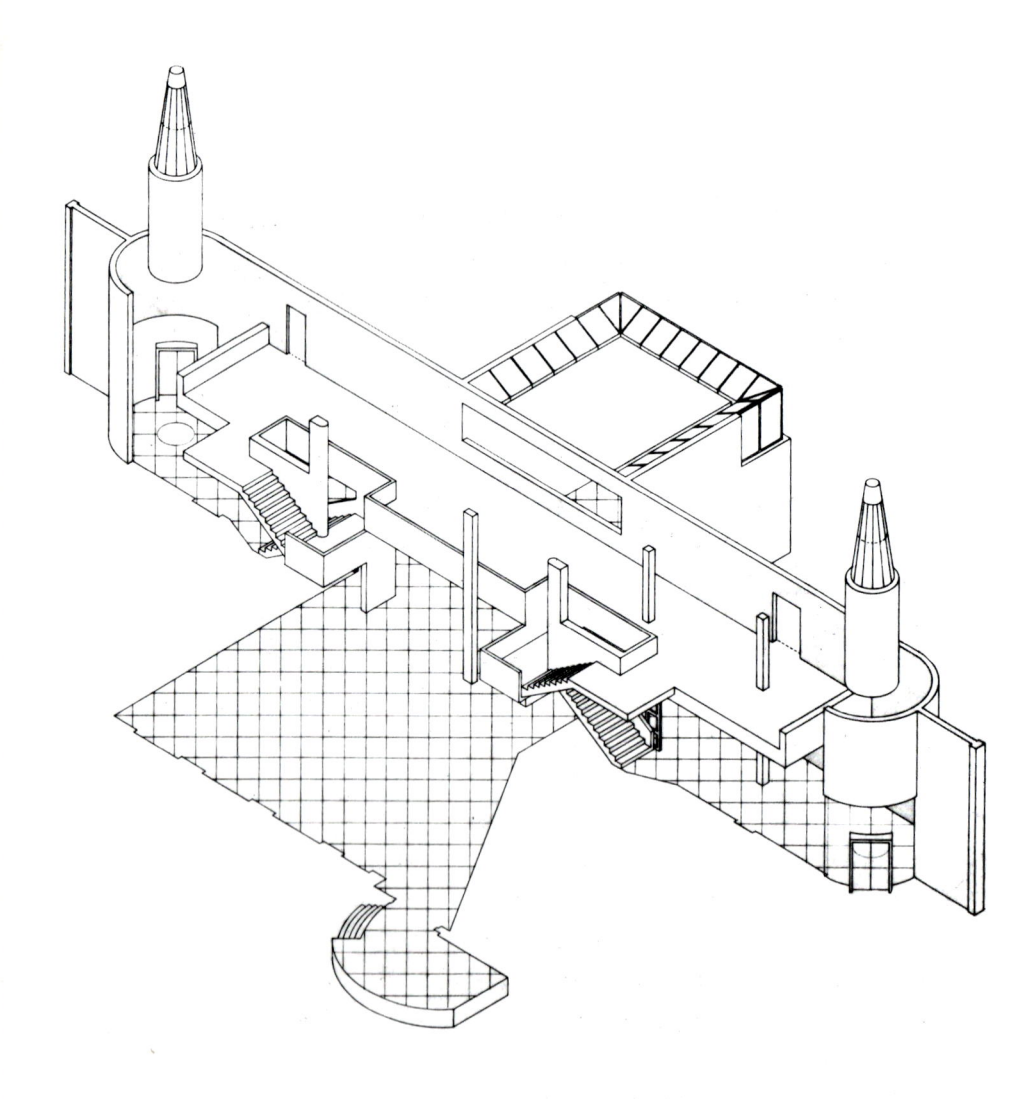

James Stirling: Architectural Aims and Influences

There are many who have helped me and I must start with some thanks. Firstly, going back to the beginning, to my mother who was a Scottish/Irish schoolteacher and who early on perceived that I had no heart for my father's wish that I should follow him in going to sea — my father was the archetypal Scottish chief engineer. Ironically it was my discovery of his "apprenticeship" drawings — beautiful blue and pink wash sectional drawings of machine parts, turbines, ships' engines — that first opened my eyes to the elegance of functional draughtsmanship.

Later at architectural school I would thank my good friend and teacher *then* as *now*, Colin Rowe. I must have been one of the first of the many hundreds, perhaps thousands, of students he has stimulated.

In London I would thank the architectural firm of Edward Lyons, Lawrence Israel and Tom Ellis (Lyons, Israel and Ellis) where I finally settled and learnt the conventions of job running, contracts, site visiting, etc.

Then I would thank my first client, in particular, Leonard Manousso, for whom we built the flats at Ham Common. He had great trust in encouraging me in 1956 to set up an office and start a practice.

I particularly wish to thank everyone who has worked

Published in RIBA Journal, September 1980. Address given at the ceremony for the presentation of the 1980 Royal Gold Medal.

with me — consultants, staff, associates, and partners — at the beginning James Gowan and in the last several years Michael Wilford.

Then there are the patrons — almost all our work has come directly or indirectly from fellow architects, both in the UK and abroad, and I would especially mention Sir Leslie Martin who recommended us for several university projects and who also greatly helped many of my contemporaries.

I've always been a designer with wide ranging interests and perhaps eclectic tendencies; as a young man I did not work in an office or through the English system of being an articled pupil — a practice which seemed to be dying out (about 1945) just as I went to architectural school — so my problem was not one of working for a master or of getting out from under the influence of one.

Rather, at Liverpool under Professor Budden, to succeed, one had to be good in many styles — in the first year we did renderings of classical orders followed by the design of an antique fountain, and at the end of that year we had to design a house in the manner of C. A. Voysey — quite a span of history.

In following years we oscillated backwards and forwards between the antique and the just arrived Modern Movement — which for me was the foreign version *only* — as taught by Colin Rowe. In addition to *Towards a New Architecture*, the book which influenced me most at this time was Saxl and Wittkower's huge atlas-like *British Art and the Mediterranean*, this much more so than Wittkower's later *Architectural Principles*. This large book was the one that none of us students could even get to fit onto our plate glass and wire Albini style bookshelves. It just lay around on the floor and got looked at.

With such an education I developed obsessions through

the entire history of architecture though at certain times I'm more interested in some aspects than others.

Somewhere in the middle years at architecture school I had a passion for "stiff" Art Nouveau designers like Mackintosh and Hoffman, less so for their English equivalents such as Voysey and Baillie Scott. This interest was supplanted towards final year by Le Corbusier and the Italian rationalists.

As soon as I graduated and got to London in 1950, I set about visiting the bombed out churches of Hawksmoor. I was intrigued by English Baroque architects such as Archer, Vanburgh and Hawksmoor and admired the *ad hoc* technique which allowed them to design with elements of Roman, French and Gothic — sometimes in the same building.

Also during those early years in London I learned about the Russian Constructivists — about whom I knew nothing when studying in Liverpool. There were just no books on them, though they did have the book on Asplund which I devoured. However, my fascination with the modern movement never really got more recent than early Corbusier and the Constructivists, and in the early fifties I developed an interest in all things vernacular from the very small — farms, barns and village housing — to the very large — warehouses, industrial buildings, engineering structures, including the great railway and exhibition sheds.

Somewhere in the mid fifties (was it to do with finding a *genuine* brutalism?) I became interested in the stripey brick and tile Victorian architects like Butterfield, Street, and Scott, etc. and when I went to the US as a visiting critic I found the asymmetric "turn of the century" timber shingle houses of even a town like New Haven an eye-opener and more interesting than Saarinen or SOM — the current heroes, though I do confess I was impressed by a limited period of Frank Lloyd Wright's production — particularly the concrete block houses around Los Angeles. During my first visits to the United States I was also aware of the incredibly high finish and "way out" aspect of New York Art Deco buildings such as the Chrysler Tower. It seemed to me we had nothing to come near them.

I'd known the Soane Museum from the early fifties and later I became interested in Neoclassical architects like Soane, Gandy, Playfair and Goodridge. Their German counterparts — Gilly, Weinbrenner, Von Klenze, and Schinkel — seem to me to extend the process with a far greater juxtaposition of scales and materials. It is the transition from Neoclassical to Romantic in the first half of the 19th century which I find particularly interesting. The move from that sparse abstraction which somehow carried a maximum of emotive association to the break up of classicism with the incoming language of realism and naturalism was a fascinating circumstance which I think has parallels in architecture today.

I do not have time to go further. If I could I would surely refer to English castles and French chateaux, to Bavarian Rococo and Italian gardens, to Venetian palazzi and English country houses, and more. But now I should switch to our own limited production.

We are alas too well known for a small part of our output, namely the university buildings of the early sixties, particularly at Leicester and Cambridge, and recently I've heard the comment "Why has our work changed so much?" While I think change is healthy, I do not believe that our work has changed. Maybe what we do now is more like our earlier work, and that oscillating process is still continuing.

The Leicester, Cambridge and Oxford projects have been referred to as Expressionist, or Constructivist and even Futurist and, while this may be so, they also have more humble origins, such as Leicester's backward look to the typical prewar industrial estate factory where the office block is up front and the workshop behind. Cambridge refers to 19th-century public reading rooms with glass lantern roofs while the Oxford building tries hard to make connections with the courtyards of the Oxbridge College.

I think our projects have tended to come in series: brick buildings in the fifties, glass skin and tile buildings in the early sixties. Then there were buildings in precast concrete and in the later sixties "high-tech" buildings of prefabricated plastic. In the seventies there is the attempt to incorporate the more familiar appearance of public buildings in stone and render.

In 1971 we had the problem of designing in an historic/preservationist context, in the centre of old St. Andrews. We had to plan a gallery and studios alongside an 18th-century house by taking down adjoining properties and at the same time preserving the entrance lodges. With the forecourt solution we proposed a new outdoor room for the town — a transitional space between Town and Gown.

In 1975 we were invited to take part in two limited competitions in Germany — both in historic centres and both museums. In Germany many public buildings go to competition and recently there has been a tendency to invite foreigners — maybe some local politicians consider that German architecture is well built but lacking in imagination. At Düsseldorf there was concern to preserve existing buildings and façades, so we buried the new building in the centre of the city block but pulled out an entrance pavilion to represent and symbolise the whole museum. It also marks the start of the mandatory public footway crossing the site. These short-cut footpaths are a "democratic" requirement in many German competitions.

At Cologne (the second competition) the massing of new buildings either side of the Hohenzollern Bridge reinforces the axes of the railway crossing the Rhine on the axis of the Cathedral. The Museum is at its bulkiest farthest from the Cathedral and the ecclesiastical aspect of the entrance hall and other parts is also in deference to the Cathedral.

The next German competition in 1977 for the extension of the State Gallery and Theatre at Stuttgart we did win — it's now well on its way up. The old gallery is Neo-classical and U-shaped in plan. There is a semi-circular drive to the entrance and the mid-point of the forecourt was marked by a classical urn — later replaced by a man on a horse. Stuttgart was bombed out and even more destroyed by the reconstruction, so preservation of existing buildings was an important requirement of the competition.

The new building is also U-shaped in plan, but instead of a man on a horse it has a taxi drop-off pavilion; instead of a semi-circular forecourt it has a circular garden. The wing of the experimental theatre balances the wing of the existing gallery.

Referring to some notes from our report that went in with the competition:

Site Layout and Town Planning Objectives

1. "To bring the public moving diagonally on a new footpath into meaningful contact with the building" (again the requirement for a footpath across the site). "This footpath passes at high level around a circular court then down to the entrance terrace — and through the arch under the new theatre to the corner of the Eugenstrasse. It is hoped this routing will stimulate people to visit the Gallery."

The new building may be a collage of old and new elements, Egyptian cornices and Romanesque windows but also Constructivist canopies, ramps and flowing forms — a

Düsseldorf, Museum für Nordrhein Westfalen (with Michael Wilford), 1975, plan of the entrance level and longitudinal section

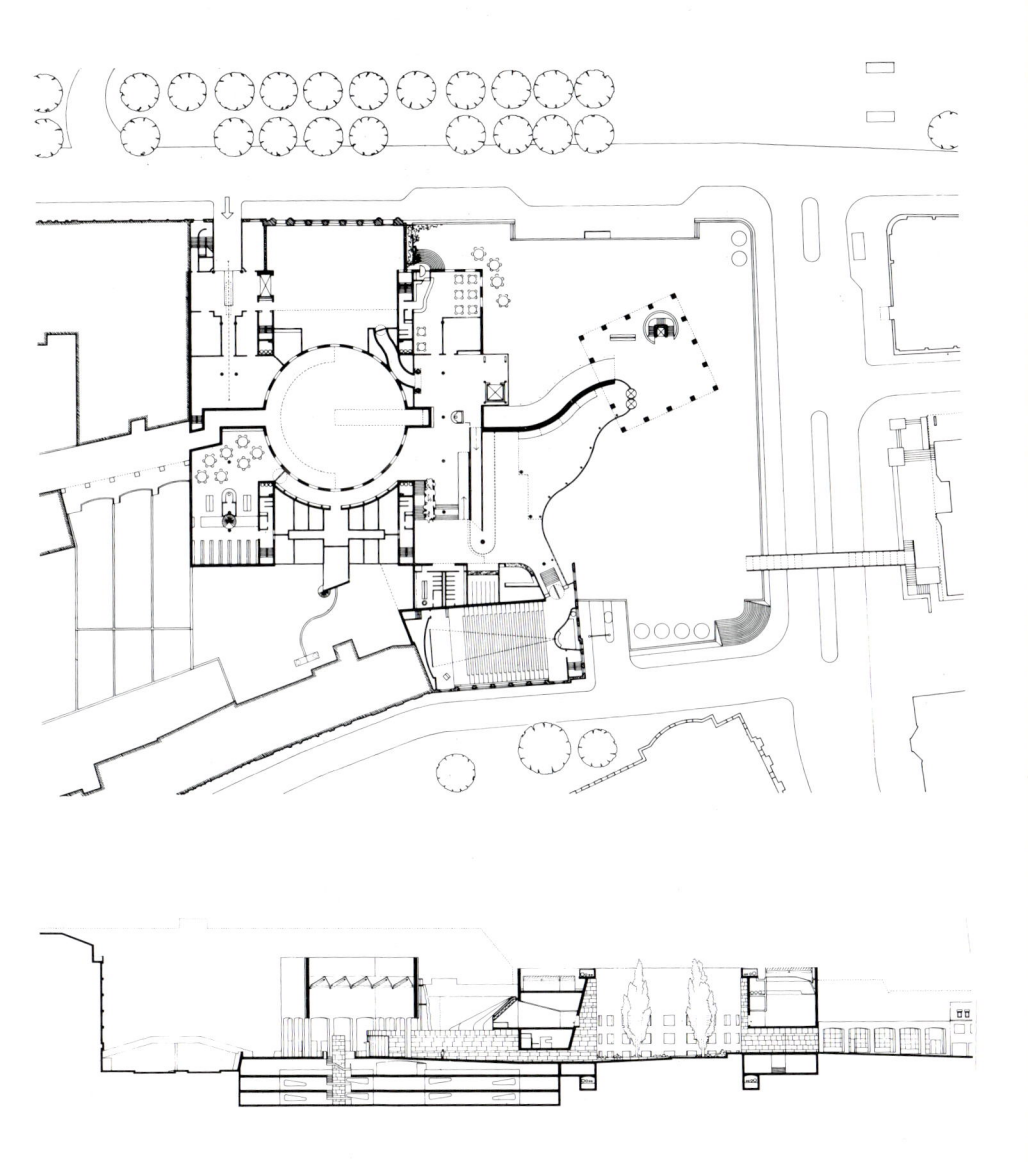

Düsseldorf, Museum für Nordrhein Westfalen (with Michael Wilford), 1975, axonometric view and distribution of the gallery spaces

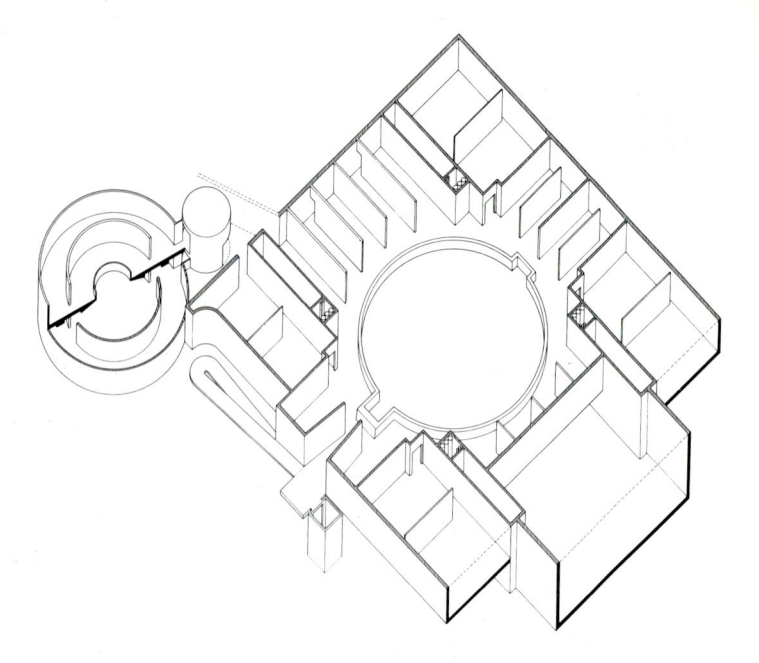

union of elements from the past and present. We are trying to evoke an association with museum and I find examples from the 19th century more convincing than examples from the 20th.

2. "To continue a three-metre high terrace with carparking under along Konrad Adenauerstrasse and allow the possibility for a footbridge across Eugenstrasse. Directly off this terrace are the public entrances to the Gallery and Theatre."

3. "By design of the new buildings, respect the axial/frontalising characteristics of the existing State Gallery and State Theatre and by siting of the new theatre wing allow the possibility for a public plaza on Eugenstrasse to develop." The theatre wing is set back from the street and we showed in the competition how a similar set-back could be made across the street when the adjoining site was developed. In

*Cologne, Wallraf
Richartz Museum
(with Michael Wilford),
1975, general planimetry
and longitudinal section*

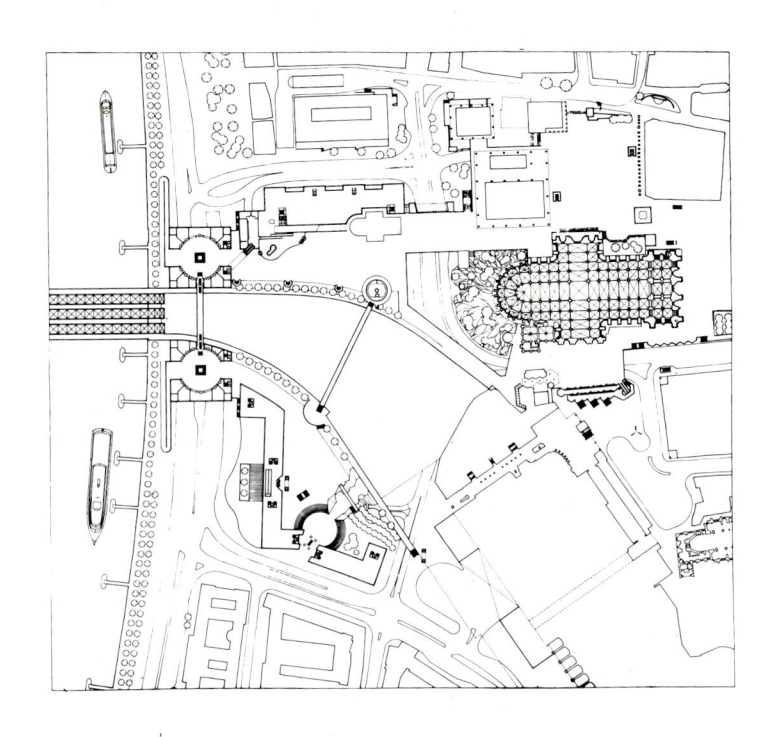

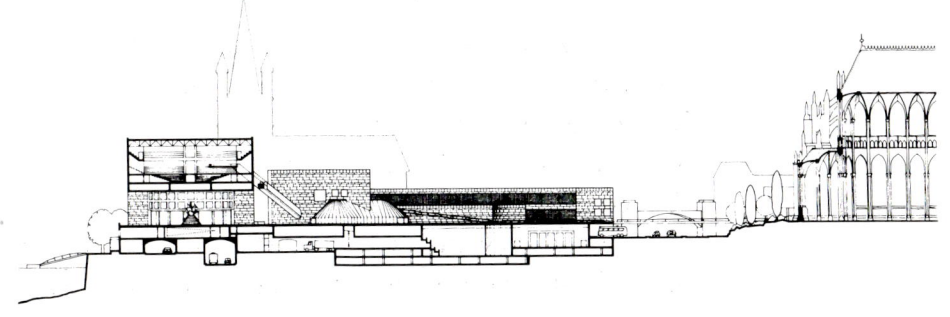

Stuttgart, Neue Staatsgalerie (with Michael Wilford), 1977–84, plan of the gallery level

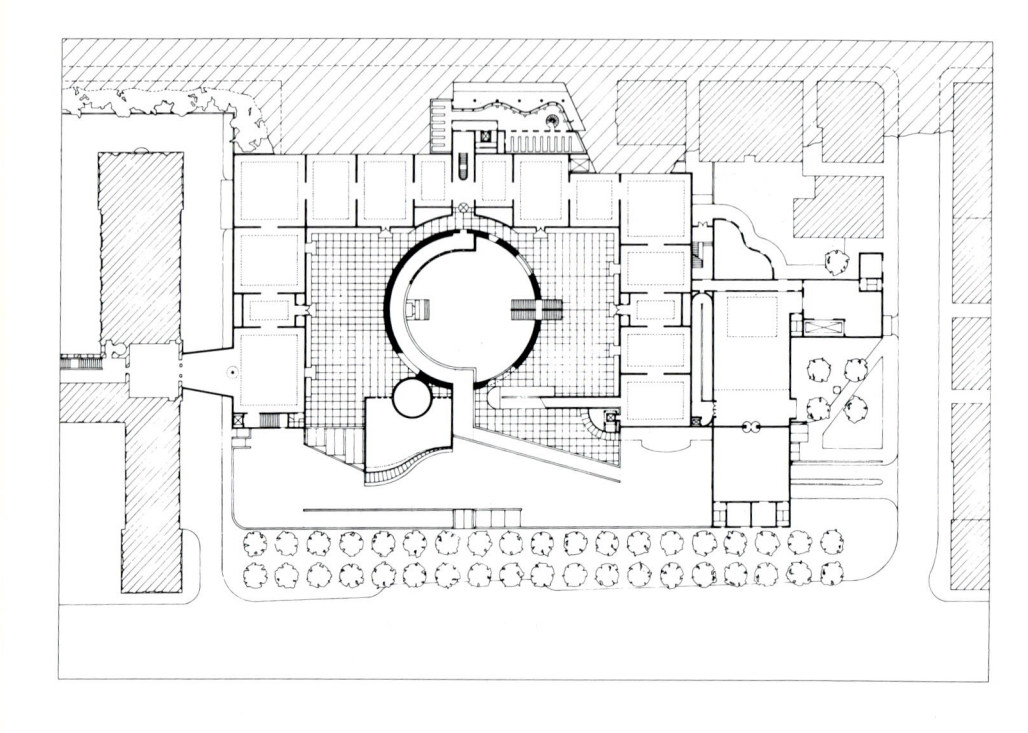

this way a new public plaza on the axis of the existing State Theatre could be planned.

4. "To reinforce the traditional relationship of buildings to street — by retaining *all* existing buildings on Urbanstrasse and Eugenstrasse thus maintaining the street character of this area."

Regarding the Gallery's objectives:

1. "To create a sequence of well-proportioned Gallery rooms, avoiding endless flexible space or gymnastic roof sections."

2. "To allow the public to flow without physical or psychological break between the new and old buildings, hence no change in floor level or awareness of crossing a bridge."

3. "The Administration offices are located in the upper levels of the building facing Urbanstrasse into which there is a separate non-public staff entrance."

There is a hierarchy in the entrance canopies — three modules over the gallery entrance, two over the theatre entrance and one over the staff entrance, also with windows.

The next German competition in 1979 we won and it has to be completed in 1984.

This is the upcoming 1985 Interbau where instead of concentrating all the new buildings in a single area as previously the idea this time is that they will be sited in different parts of Berlin where each can be beneficial, even remedial, to an immediate area. This building is for the Bonn Government and is really a Think Tank — but called a Science Centre — an Institute for deep thinking on matters of ecology, environment, sociology, management, etc. We also have to re-use the huge old Beaux-Arts building which somehow survived the war. Having destroyed so much with the post-war reconstruction they now want to hang onto everything which is old and remains.

Reading again from the competition report:
Objectives

1. "The primary need is for a great multitude of small offices and a particular concern was how to find an architectural and environmental solution for a programme composed of repetitive offices. The 'typical' office plan usually results in boring box-like buildings and the banality of these rationally produced offices may be the largest single factor contributing to the visual destruction of our cities in the post-war period."

So, I made an early decision that, whatever, we would break away from the office block stereotype and I said to those working on it: let's make a clustering of buildings — take for instance a long bar, a cruciform, a half circle and a square, and juggle them together, with the old building.

Quoting again from the report, "Our proposal is to use the three Institutes of the Centre (Management, Social and Environment) plus the element for future expansion to create a grouping of buildings, all of which are similar, but different, and the architectural form may relate to familiar building types with each Institute having its own identifying building."

2. "Each Institute has two directors with complementary staff, and a binary organisation seems fundamental. As the buildings have symmetrical planning, allocation of rooms should adapt to this dual organisation rather well."

3. "The new buildings cluster around an informal garden with the single large tree at the centre preserved. The loggias and arcades which overlook the garden also relate to the cafeteria, the conference facilities and the old building. Free standing is the Library tower with a reading room at ground level."

4. "We hope to make a friendly, unbureaucratic place —

the opposite of an 'institutional' environment, even accepting that the functional programme is for a repetition of offices in a single complex. Actually the whole can function as a single complex, as each building is joined at every level."

The irony is that while we have varied the building form we have retained an aspect of repetition in the wallpaper-like application of windows. A decision in regard to the typical office was that each would have a single centrally positioned window with flanking walls, for curtains, bookshelving, etc.

External walls are rendered in *putz* with alternating colour — pink and grey per floor.

I've been asked to make some observations about working in Germany — though our building experience there is very limited. Firstly, I've been surprised to find that it's the established architects who are the architectural critics — much more so than journalists or historians — the reverse of the situation here. We have been attacked by several well-known architects but at the same time we've had sympathetic, friendly and welcoming criticism from others. The professional critics seem to have a subdued role, maybe constrained by libel, whereas an established architect can say and print whatever he likes about another architect.

Secondly, I'm very impressed by the extremely high standard of building. Methods of insulation, thermal barriers, fixing of materials, and acoustics, are absolutely mandatory and cannot be adjusted in relation to a budget. This is a relief as it removes any temptation to juggle the cost of technical details with the cost of architectural input, something which I have often found a problem here, particularly with low cost budgets.

Thirdly, it does seem you should haggle over fees even though the percentages and ratings are set out in the documents. However, the documents do not refer to the continuous claiming process by which architects increase their entitlement and which seems normal practice. Unless you have been tipped off about this and other subtleties you can catch a very bad cold indeed.

There has been no problem in setting up an office in Germany and maybe that is to do with the Common Market though the bureaucracy seems even more rigid and inflexible than it is in the UK. Building sites appear incredibly clean and efficient, however building costs are maybe twice what they are here; surprisingly buildings do not seem to go up any faster — though as I have said they end up very well built.

In America our first project was for a developer who asked Richard Meier and ourselves to make separate schemes for luxury town housing on a street in the "posh" upper east side of New York. He thought that each house should have its own lift, and his requirement was for 11 houses with maybe some apartments. The whole was to be five stories and built over an underground parking garage which had included in its roof structure — at ground level — a row of structural beams on 18-foot centres to support the party walls of the houses to be built on top. We used this beam spacing to plan an 18-foot wide (thin man) house alternating with a 36-foot wide (fat man) house, the latter on three lower floors with an independent apartment on the two upper floors. We could therefore plan three varieties of dwelling.

The movement backwards and forwards of the street façade expresses the house within the terrace and the application of bay windows, studio glazing, and balconies indicate the more important spaces within. This is similar to surface projections of windows and entrances on traditional New York Townhouses and Brownstones.

*Design School,
Rice University
(with Michael Wilford),
1979–81, ground floor*

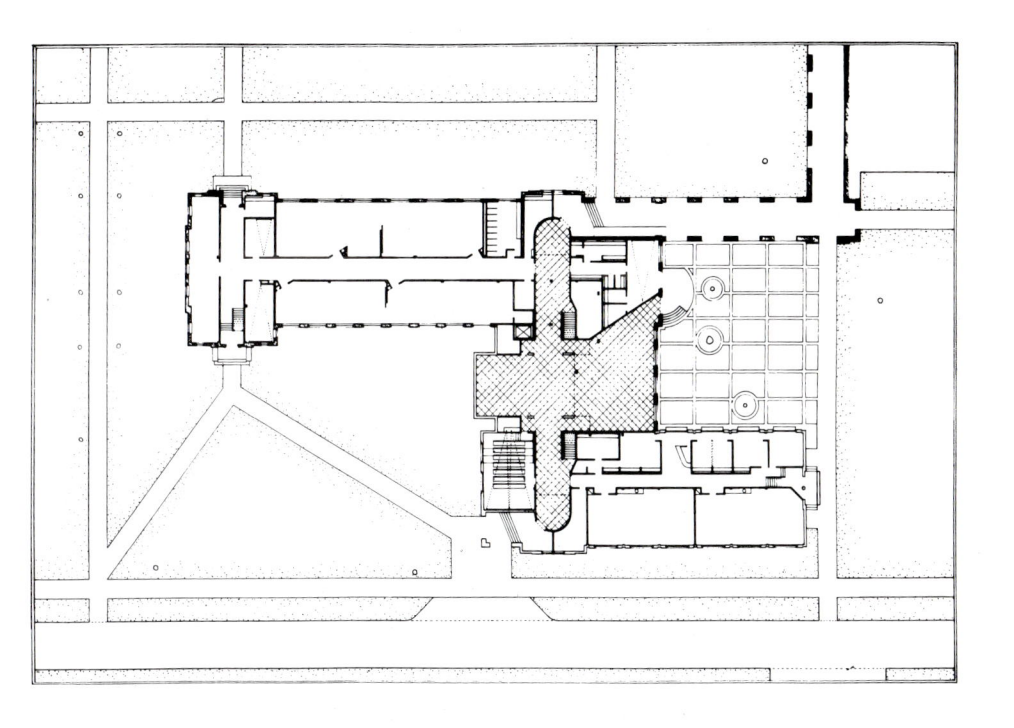

These dwellings would be for sale in the luxury market and are planned with utmost dollar per square foot utilisation of floor area. There is no vertical space and planning is quite dense. The small front garden set behind railings is also similar to sidewalk and basement areas in this part of New York.

In 1979 we were commissioned by Rice University in Texas, Columbia University in New York, and Harvard University for new buildings. Fortunately due to finalising building accommodation the phasing has slipped and we are able to design in sequence, not all at the same time. The new building for the Fogg Museum at Harvard is on the drawing boards and we are just starting with Columbia.

The last project is for extending the School of Architecture at Rice. The original campus by Cram, Goodhue and Ferguson is from the twenties in a sort of Venetian, Florentine, Art Deco and we were asked to work within a limited range of bricks, pantiles, and pitched roofs which is reasonable for this eccentric but elegant campus where there are many arcades, marble balconies and fancy spires.

The School of Architecture is an L-shaped building and we are extending it with another L-shaped piece. The interlock is joined by a surgical splint — a galleria of circulation core binding the pieces together and connecting the old entrance with a new entrance at opposite ends of the splint. These entrance areas are lit through glass spires on the roof. The galleria overlooks a new exhibition space on one side and a jury room on the other.

The existing building is connected with a colonnade to an adjoining building and the L-shaped extension creates a three-sided courtyard — a new sheltered garden in an otherwise very open campus.

It may be difficult to distinguish the façades of the new

building from the existing ones and for those who think this design is uncharacteristically quiet or conventional, I would point to the Mavrolean Houses, a project from the fifties, to indicate that reserve and restraint — like the formalism of other projects — is not a change in our work. Both extremes have always existed in our vocabulary; so if we have a future I see us going forward *oscillating*, as I did as a student, between the formal and the informal, between the restrained and the exuberant.

Thank you.

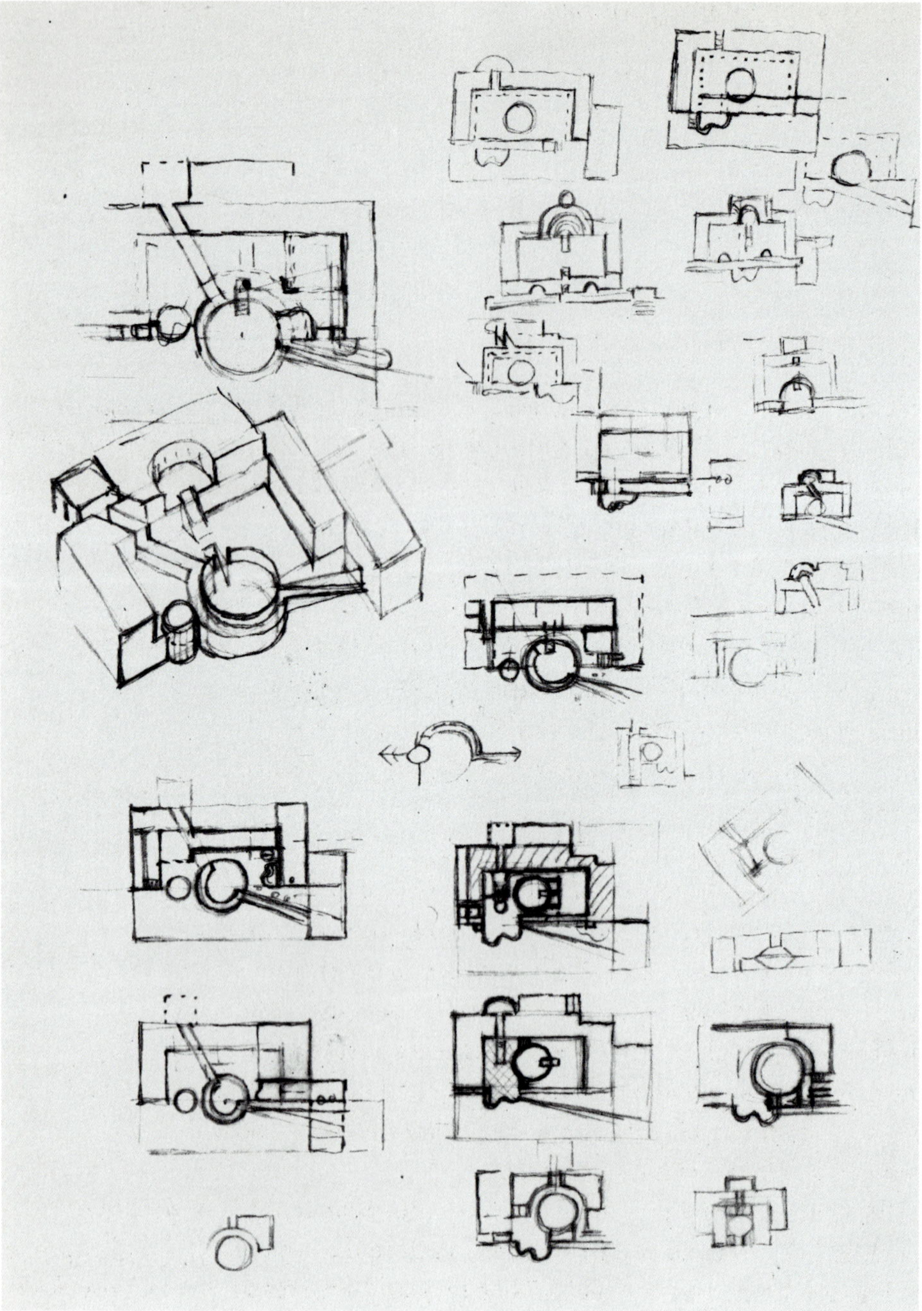

The Monumentally Informal

I would like to think that our work is not simple and that within the design of a building for every act there is a counteract. We hope the Staatsgalerie is monumental, because that is a tradition for public buildings but also we hope that it is informal and populist, hence the antimonumentalism of the meandering footway and the voided centre and much else including the colouring. I'd like also to think of our work in regard to the context, referring briefly to some of our earliest projects which I would categorise as either *Abstract* or *Representational*. "Abstract" being the style related to the modern movement and the language derived from Cubism, Constructivism, de Stijl and all the isms of the new architecture. "Representational" being related to tradition, vernacular, history, recognition of the familiar and generally the more timeless concerns of the architectural heritage. I would claim that both aspects have existed in our work since the beginning, with projects being in one category often to the exclusion of the other. More recently and particularly with the Staatsgalerie I think both aspects are contained and counter-balanced in the same building.

In our piece for *Roma Interrotta*[1] — (the architectural game of 1977 wherein twelve architects each re-did a piece of Rome as an update of Nolli's 1748 city plan) — we made

Comments on the Staatsgalerie, published in SD, No. 241, October 1984.

Stuttgart, Neue Staatsgalerie (with Michael Wilford), 1977–84, study sketch

a thesis of contextualism using our projects of the previous twenty-five years, integrated or juxtaposed, into and all over the Trastevere site.

"This contextual-associational method of planning is somehow akin to the historic process, albeit instant, whereby built form is directly influenced by the visual context and is a confirmation of, and a complement to, that which exists."

In 1950 I finished at architecture school. Projects which followed included a House (1951) which was unashamedly and totally "Abstract" — there was no reference in it to anything earlier than the 20th century: in those days we believed that modern architecture could do it all.

Whereas, and soon after, a Village Housing project (1955) was a study in how to extend the typical English Village, it was "Representational" that is, traditional, vernacular, and not dissimilar in appearance to High Street villages as they have existed since medieval times.

Similarly a project for a rich man's house in South Kensington (1957) was to have been built in an area of Edwardian mansions, it was influenced by the form and materials of that context and was "Representational" with coursed stone walls and copper roofs.

However, the early buildings which got built, such as the Engineering Building at Leicester University (1959), tended to be in the "Abstract" category where the surrounding context had little influence — maybe because the site was in the backyard of the University.

Our first design for a museum/gallery was for St. Andrews University, Scotland (1971). An 18th-century house and flanking lodges had to be preserved and converted to an Arts Centre. We added a gallery, theatre and studios, using high tech elements (lift up walls from Olivetti, Haslemere) combined with traditional rustic stone walling. High curved

[1] *Architectural Design*, vol. 49, No. 3-4, 1979.

walls connected the house to the lodges and the new accommodation and defined an outdoor room in the town. It was both *formal* and *contextual*.

In 1975 we were invited to take part in two limited competitions in West Germany, the first for a Museum in Düsseldorf. Both "Representational" and "Abstract" were present in this design where a Neo-classical type entrance pavilion is, as it were, pulled out from a circular void to symbolize and represent the whole museum, which to minimize its impact on the historic centre, was otherwise buried in the city block. "Neo-classical", as there were several such buildings nearby and because I think there is an identifying association still attaching to 19th-century museums. The main building may be "Abstract" but the entrance pavilion is more "Representational" related to tradition, history and familiarity, and maybe with archaeology and memory, as prior

Stuttgart, Neue Staatsgalerie (with Michael Wilford), 1977–84, detail of the inner courtyard

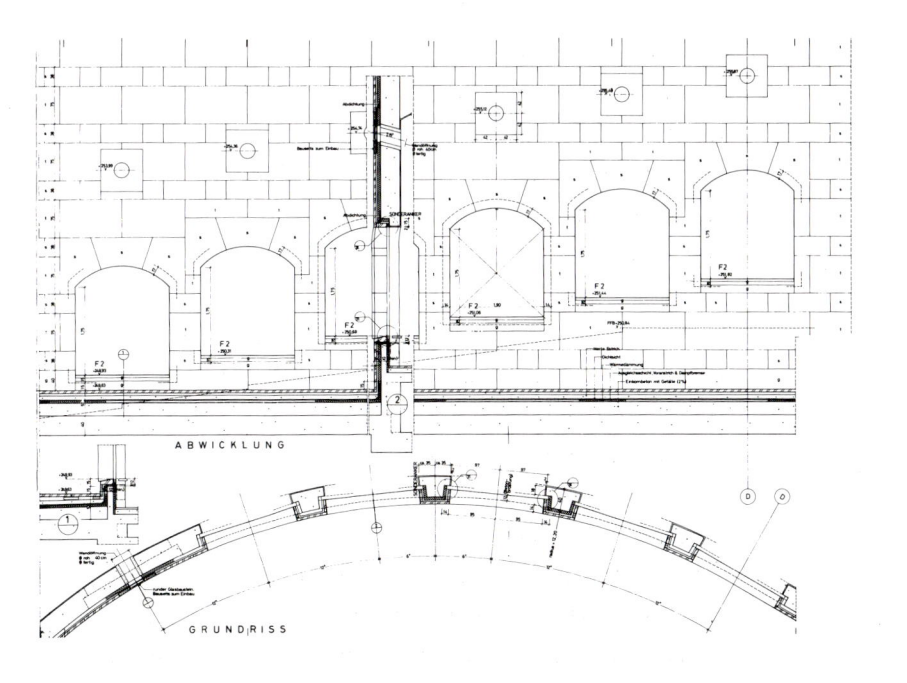

to the war a building of about the same size had stood in this place exhibiting the city's art treasures. I particularly regret we didn't build this project. It was the first in our German museum series — Düsseldorf/Cologne/Stuttgart. Similar to our earlier University series — Leicester/Cambridge/Oxford. I don't know why projects sometimes come in series, though this is a phenomenon for many Architects (i.e. Frank Lloyd Wright concrete block houses in Los Angeles and Le Corbusier's early studio houses in Paris).

The second competition in Germany was for a Museum in Cologne. "Representational/symbolical" and "Abstract/technical" aspects were combined and the peristyle entrance hall and sunken sculpture court were two symbolic elements which referred to the presence of the Cathedral. The free spanning enclosed escalators and mutli-flexible auditorium referred to engineering aspects of the adjoining railways and suspension bridges. The monumental and symmetrical grouping of new buildings reiterated the Cathedral towers on the axis of the Hohenzollern Bridge crossing the Rhine.

The third German competition we did win was the extension of the State Gallery and a New Theatre and Music School, Stuttgart 1977. Some interrelating characteristics of the old and new context are:[2]

a. Existing buildings were as much as possible retained, preserving the street character of the area. Stuttgart was bombed out and even more destroyed by post-war reconstruction, so preservation of buildings was an important aspect of the competition. Where new buildings come to the street, such as the theatre service wing on Eugenstrasse and the museum administration on Urbanstrasse, they have the scale, alignment and materials of adjoining buildings.

b. The old gallery (1837) was neo-classical, and U-shaped in plan. There is a semi-circular drive to the entrance and at

[2] From the competition report.

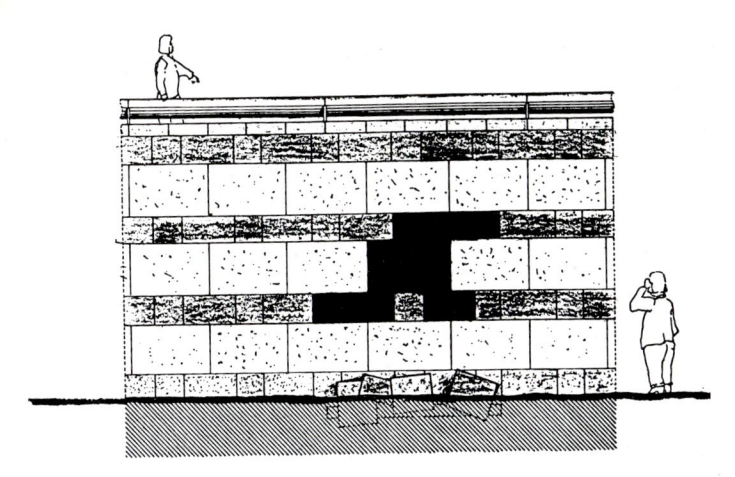

Stuttgart, Neue Staatsgalerie (with Michael Wilford), 1977–84, detail of the main front

mid point of the forecourt was a classical urn,[3] replaced in the 19th century by a man on a horse. The new building is also U-shaped, instead of the semi-circular drive there is a circular court. The man on a horse (with sword) is reiterated by a taxi drop-off pavilion (with banner) also on the axis of the plan.

c. The new theatre wing reiterates the wing of the old gallery (similar scale and materials). They both semi-contain forecourts with entrances that front onto the boulevard.

Mandatory to the competition was the inclusion of a three-metre high terrace fronting Konrad Adenauer Strasse containing a large carpark.

Also, a public footpath short-cutting across the site, a democratic request in many German competitions, which unfortunately may not help in maintaining the entity of a city block.

I hope this building will evoke an association of Museum, I'd like the visitor to feel it "looks like a museum" and as precedents I find 19th-century examples more evocative than the 20th. In its details it combines traditional and new elements, though traditional elements are used in a modern

[3] This urn has been rediscovered, repaired and resited in the forecourt garden of the New Theatre on Eugenstrasse.

way, for instance the histrionic coving is not a cornice used throughout, but only defining the sculpture terraces. Similarly there are assemblages of constructivist canopies which define a hierarchy of entrances, etc.

I would refer to Schinkel's Altes Museum as representative of the 19th-century Museum as a prototype. They have attributes which I find appealing, for instance an enfilade of rooms, as against freely flowing space and even when small they have a certain monumentalism — in the City it's essential to have landmarks: a city without monuments would be no place at all. For me, monumentalism is nothing to do with size or style, but entirely to do with *presence* — thus a chair could be monumental — I have several.

Of course it is no longer acceptable to do classicism straight and in this building the central pantheon, instead of being the culminating space is but a void — a room like a non space; instead of a dome — open to the sky. The plan is axial but frequently compromised, set piece rooms conjoin with the free plan and the public footpath meanders either side of the central axis — thus the casually monumental is diminished by the deliberately informal.

The ambivalence of the "front" corresponds to the ambiguity of the boulevard (Konrad Adenauer Strasse is more an *autobahn* than a street). Instead of a "façade" the front recedes, presenting a series of incidents adjacent to the walking movement, into, through and across the building. Some details which contribute to the "monumentally informal" are: the juxtaposition of stone walls and highly coloured metal assemblies — such as the entrance canopies, and fat tube parapet handrails and the S curving bay window to the entrance hall, also the taxi drop-off pavilion, air intake funnels, etc. These colourful elements counteract the possible appearance of a monumental stone quarry. Internally the green rub-

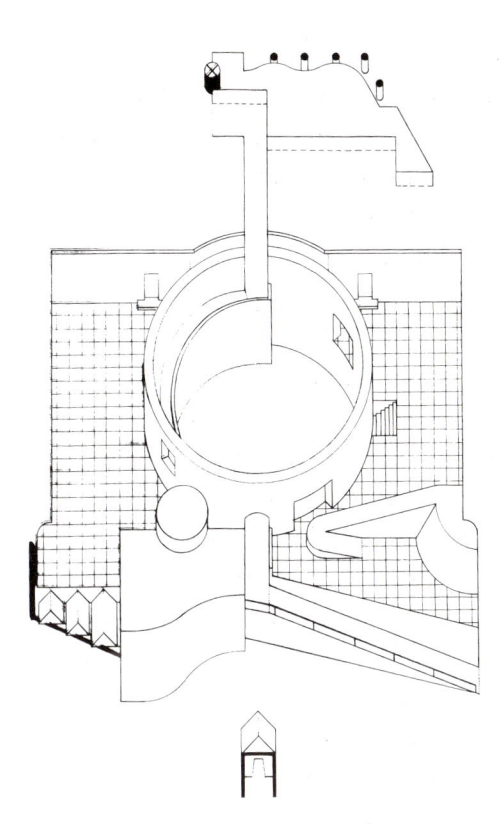

Stuttgart, Neue Staatsgalerie (with Michael Wilford), 1977–84, public path through the inner circular court

ber flooring (as alternative to the normal highly polished stone) reminds that Museums today are also places of popular entertainment — it seemed more appropriate as well as having an acoustic value. The brightly coloured open life assembly, and sunburst ceiling lighting, and the curved counter tops, etc., all contribute to the informal. The ceiling light grid of the Kunsthalle may remind us that like shopping malls there is today a market side to art and exhibitions — though here this association is juxtaposed with the monumental presence of the flared columns, and for the painstaking, there is much more innuendo to be discovered.

"Historically, the quality of the art in the architecture is remembered as the significant element. However, with the advent of modern architecture — sociological, functional and real estate values came into ascendancy. Ironically, coinciding with the recent loss of certainty in modern architecture, the conviction of welfare state and hardnosed commercial standards is also, I believe, declining and the more ancient desire, wherein a primary objective is for buildings to appear appropriate in their context, is returning — at least that's what our clients seem to want now. For many architects working with the abstract vocabulary of modern architecture — Bauhaus, International Style, call it what you will, this language has become repetitive, simplistic and too narrowly confining and I, for one, welcome the passing of the revolutionary phase of the modern movement. I think the mainstream of architecture is usually evolutionary and, though revolutions do occur along the way (and the modern movement was certainly one) nevertheless revolutions are minority occasions. Today we can look back and again regard the whole of architectural history as our background including, most certainly, the modern movement — high tech and all. Architects have always looked back in order to move forward and we should, like painters, musicians and sculptors, be able to include 'Representational', as well as 'Abstract' elements in our art... So, freed from the burden of utopia but with increased responsibility, particularly in the civic realm, we look to a more liberal future producing work perhaps richer in memory and association in the continuing evolution

Stuttgart, Neue Staatsgalerie (with Michael Wilford), 1977–84, longitudinal section

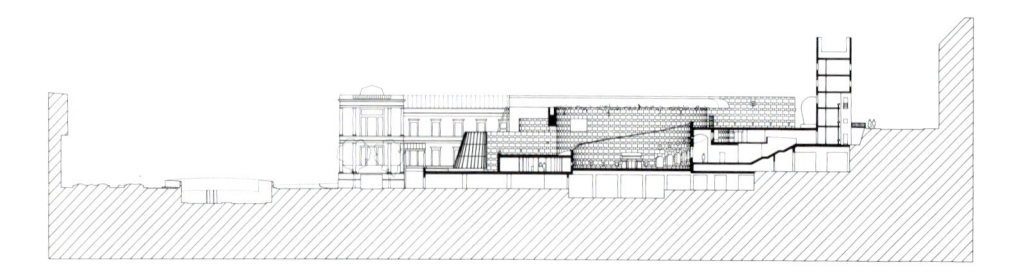

of a radical Architecture."[4] In addition to Representational *and* Abstract, this large complex I hope supports the Monumental *and* Informal; and the Traditional *and* High Tech.

It has been a pleasure to work on the Staatsgalerie where the budget seemed reasonable and the standards of workmanship have been the highest, where we have been able to use fine materials and achieve complex detailing and not be subjected to contractual hostilities. I would like to compliment everyone who has worked on this project.

[4] From a talk given at Rice School of Architecture, USA, in 1979.

*London, enlargement
of National Gallery
(with Michael Wilford),
1985, general view*

Architecture and Politics

Architects are among those who generate the cultural ambience, but the quality of their buildings can be directly related to the political environment — architects are both the victims and the beneficiaries of the political will. On the one hand, like Palladio and Ledoux, architects can spend time in prison, or they can become the pets of our political leaders and, like Speer and Chernyshev, have bestowed on them giant commissions.

This happened in history and in the twentieth century, and is still happening: we know the dubious building achievements in Germany and Russia during the dictatorships, and more recently we have seen the gross architecture produced in Romania under Ceaucescu. And if they go out of favour even the most successful architects can die worn out and in poverty: Sir Christopher Wren and Charles Rennie Mackintosh suffered this fate.

Since the second world war, we tend to believe that in the Western democracies political liberalism has resulted in the situation becoming more reasonable and logical for architects.

Unfortunately this is not necessarily so. Unlike the other arts which are produced relatively quickly, such as painting, poetry or writing, a new building takes time. From conception to completion — according to which country of West-

Published in RIBA Journal, *June 1981. James Stirling set out his ten points for political survival at an international conference on the cultural environment. Here is an extract from his speech.*

ern Europe or city of America — a major public building may require four to six years. This time period makes architects vulnerable to changing politics and fashion.

The intervals between government elections and financial budgets can be four to five years, so a change of local or central government or economic reversal is quite likely within the time frame of design and construction, though it is the two to three years prior to construction when architects are particularly vulnerable. Keep your fingers doubly crossed if there is a local or general election during that time.

It is the fashion these days among political, and in my country Royal circles, to make rules for the production of "good architecture". We know, for instance, of Prince Charles' ten rules for good design, which are aids towards a revival of Classical architecture at least two centuries after the event. In keeping with the vogue, architects — particularly those with international practices — should have guidelines pinned on their studio walls: guides to the realisation of our designs, safeguards from the hazards of politics and the swinging change of fashion.

So here are my ten rules to architectural/political survival, derived from my own experience:

1. Beware of the commission from a single political individual, particularly from abroad. It may be a public relations exercise, so check if there is an approved budget. If not it could be a self-promotional puff.

2. Make sure there is a commitment by both (or all) political parties to your commission. If not, you may lose it at the next election. Commitment by succeeding local governments to complete the buildings of their predecessors is the case with some Western countries, but not with others.

London, enlargement of National Gallery (with Michael Wilford), 1985, axonometric study

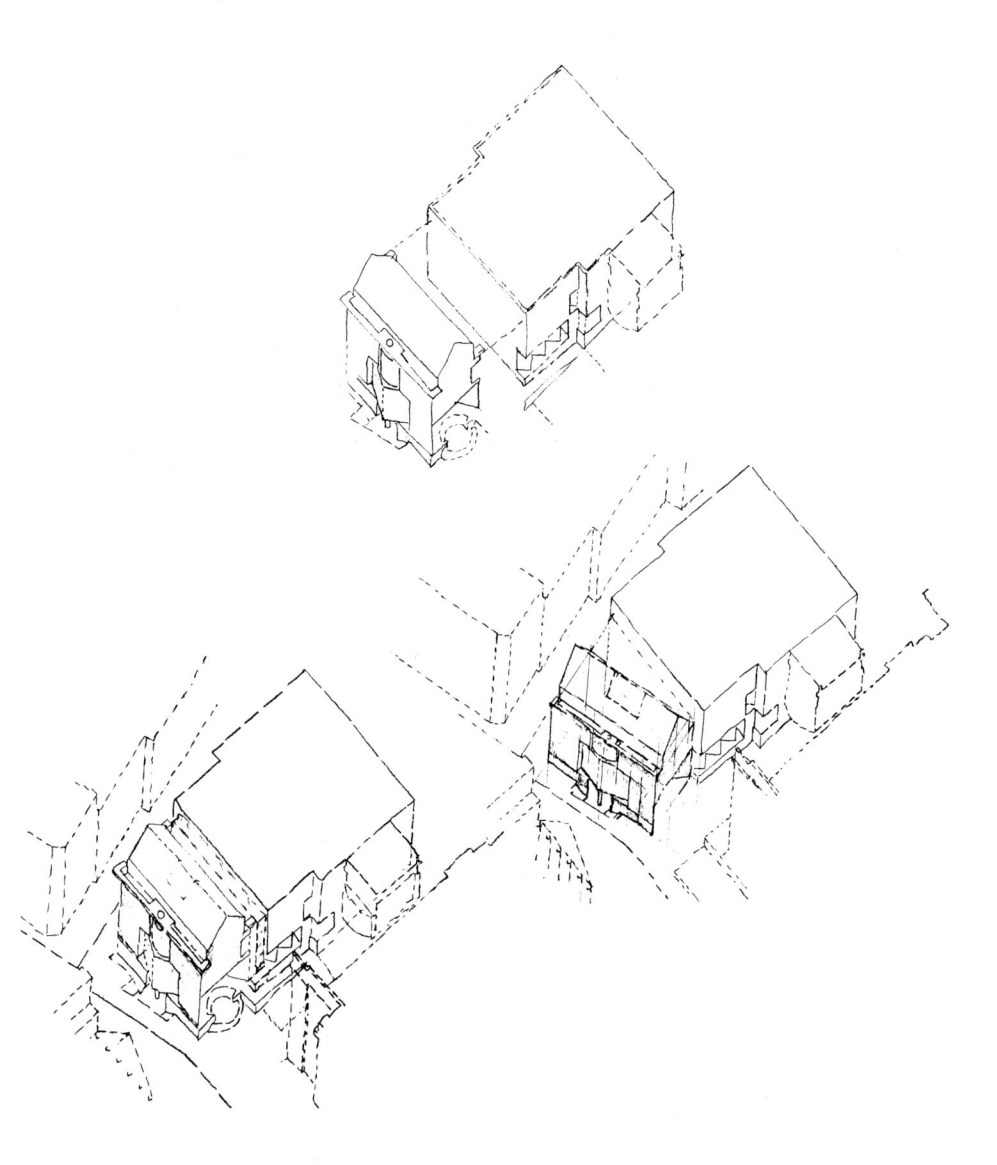

3. See if you can suss out the private life-style of your political client. If it is extravagant he or she may disappear in a scandal before you get your first fee payment.

4. Be careful about accepting a commission from a politician who is nearing the end of his or her term in office, it could become complicated if this period runs out before you get your building into the ground.

5. Be careful about the requirement for a sequence of phased buildings, where your design solution is dependent on repetition. The client and user requirements could radically change before you get beyond the first phase.

6. Beware of the prestigious international architectural competition. Try and ascertain beforehand if the final choice is going to be made by the national leader and not by the architectural judges — particularly important if you are not from the country of origin.

7. Try and ascertain if your client has a partner with either strong or fluctuating opinions about design. His and her views may not coincide. Ultimately you may lose out.

8. Make sure that your political client has agreement by the planning authorities to the commission *and* that these officials approve of his or her choice of architect.

9. Find out if you are being hired by a client from abroad because it allows him to avoid the infighting amongst the architects back home. If you are, the fighting may never die out.

10. Be wary of the Royal influence particularly when it is

supported by a sycophantic national press — a major problem in the United Kingdom where the Royal member, even though he has no legal power, is an extremely influential and indeed terminal arbiter of architectural taste.

So architects remain beholden to politics, though our problems nowadays derive as much from politicians or leaders who are not strong enough as from those who are over strong. Whilst we are happier when our politicians are less strong, and we would not have it otherwise, nevertheless the perception and understanding required for architectural success may be even more complicated than it used to be.

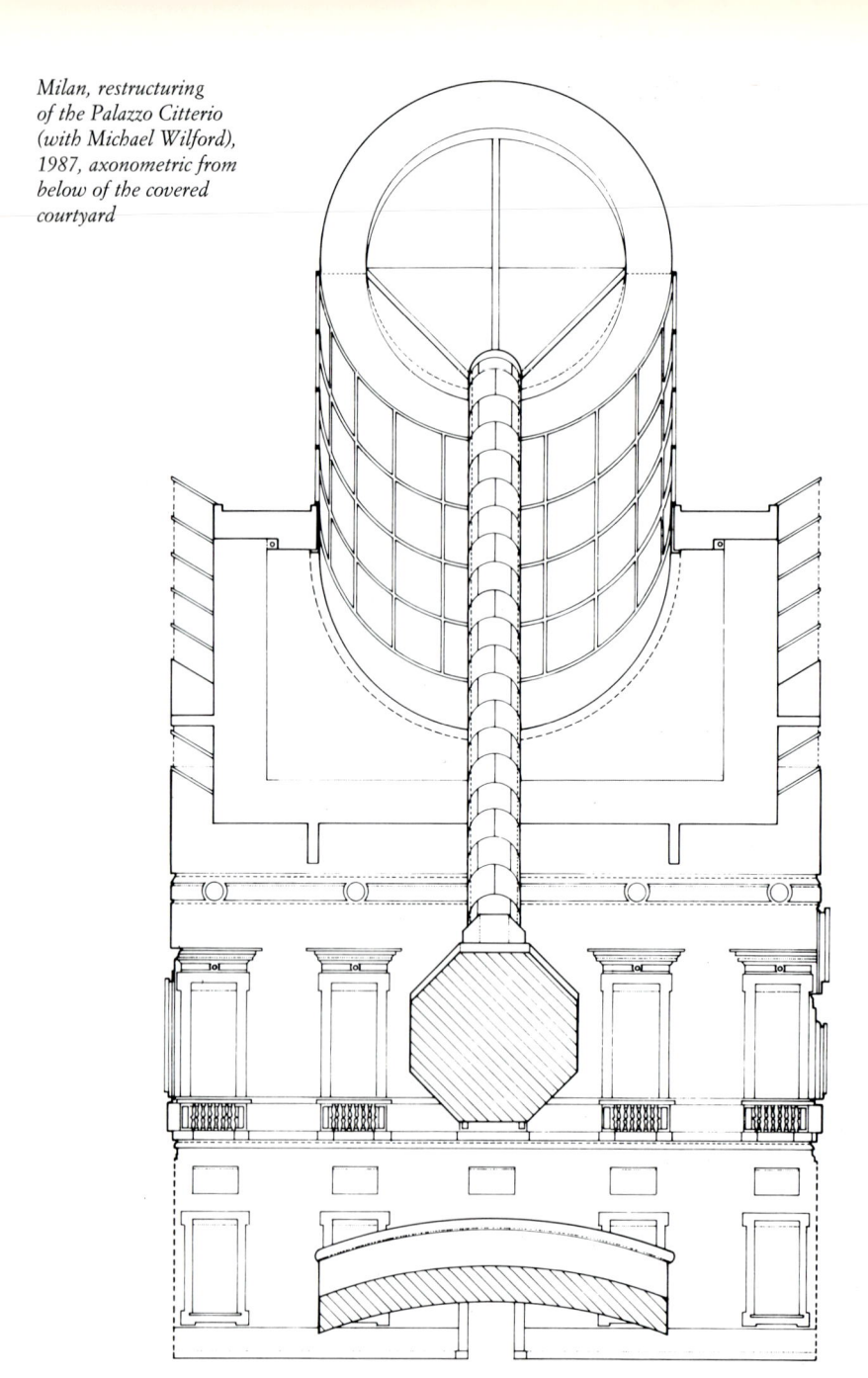

Milan, restructuring of the Palazzo Citterio (with Michael Wilford), 1987, axonometric from below of the covered courtyard

Restructuring of the Palazzo Citterio

Palazzo Citterio was built as an eighteenth-century Milanese patrician residence. During the 200 years of its life it has seen many transformations in taste and use: from Barocchetto to Neo-classicism and Neo-gothic; then the Novecento, and the post-war period. These led to internal and external modifications which, by 1970, when the building became owned by the Brera, had reached the condition of a "mish mash" — a superimposition of many successive interventions. In 1986, we were appointed by the "Friends of the Brera" to reorganize it as a museum of international stature, with emphasis on temporary and travelling exhibitions, and display of twentieth-century Italian art. The programme also required facilities normal for modern museums, including lecture-rooms, bookshops, a cafeteria, and also the restoration of the garden which allows visitors to walk through from Palazzo Citterio to Palazzo Brera — interconnecting the two museums as one.

Published in Domus, *February 1991.*

We amalgamate the historic remains of the palace with a series of new "pieces" inserted where the building had already been extensively modified. The most important are:

A *new building* to contain a library and archives and a cafeteria. The volume and footprint of this new wing was determined by an earlier Neo-classical addition that was demolished after 1970.

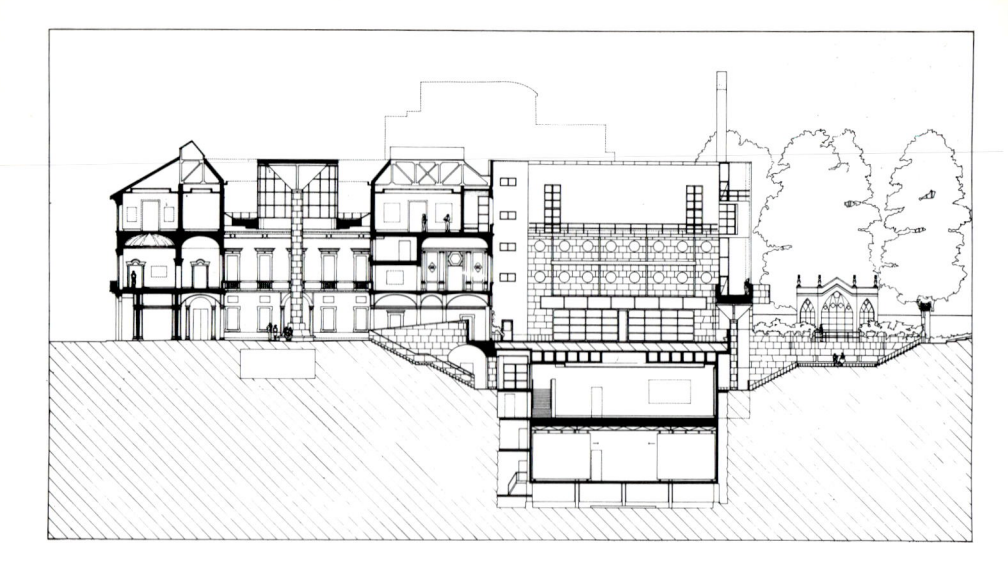

Milan, restructuring of the Palazzo Citterio (with Michael Wilford), 1987, longitudinal section

A *new public stair*, which we placed on the long axis of the courtyard. This provides direct access to the large exhibition room in the basement.

A new *core of lifts and stairs*, positioned on the cross-axis of the courtyard. A point of departure and return for circuits of exhibitions at *piano nobile* and second floor, as well as providing access to the exhibition galleries at ground and first floor and to the lecture and seminar rooms in the basement.

A *new roof* with glazed cupola covering the courtyard. This makes a visual separation between the lower levels of the courtyard façades (which are original), and the upper levels (which are a recent addition). This cupola/roof enables the courtyard to function as the entrance hall, providing access to all parts of the museum.

A new *open courtyard* flanked by the rear façade of the palace and by the new library wing and by a stair and bridge which are the beginning of a high-level connection to Palazzo Brera.

Milan, restructuring of the Palazzo Citterio (with Michael Wilford), 1987, axonometric of the new court and the garden

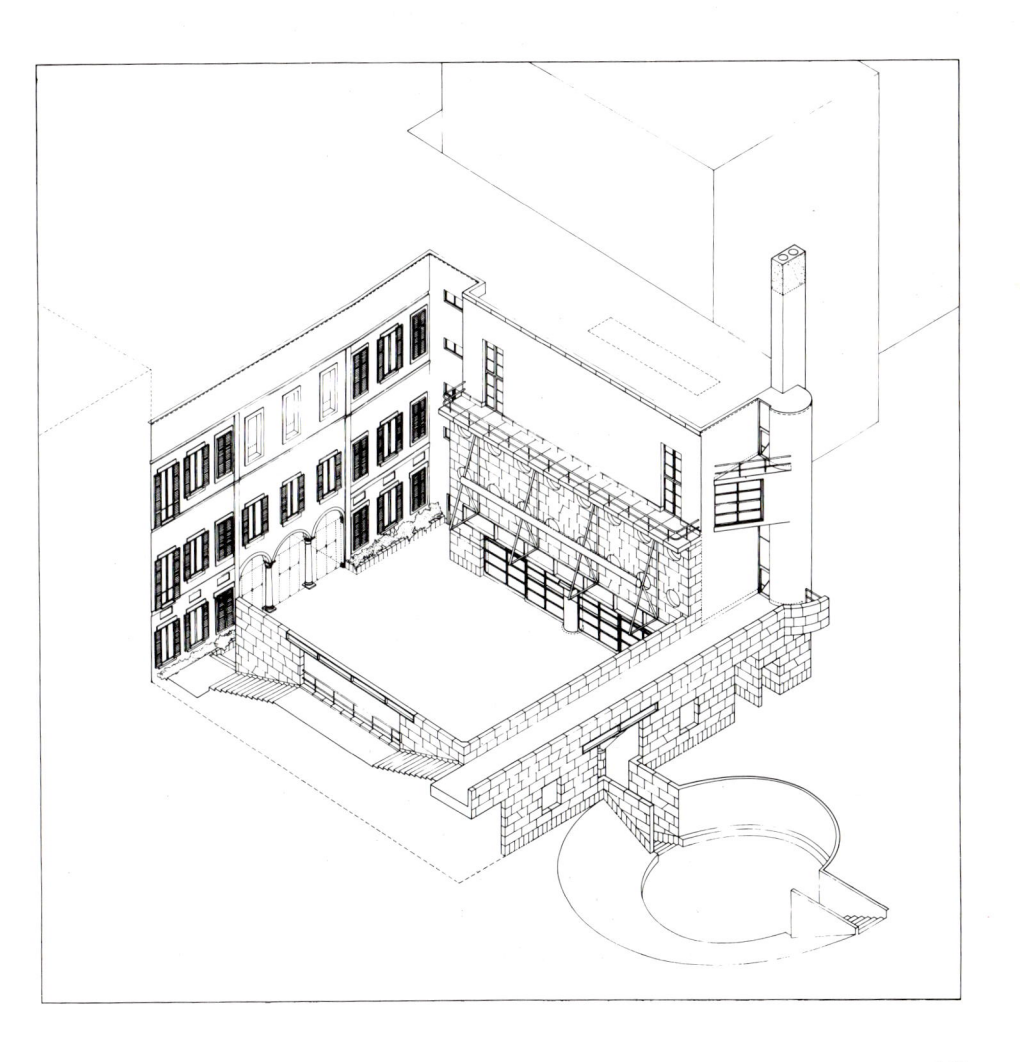

A new *open-air amphitheatre*, through which the public enroute from the basement exhibition gallery can rise into the garden.

These interventions will reinstate the palace and its gardens and enrich the entry from via Brera, into the covered courtyard; the sequence being through the open courtyard and amphitheatre, to the remains of the *giardino all'inglese* (complete with artificial romantic grotto) which will be repaired.

The street façade of Palazzo Citterio is articulated in three bays with two entrance archways. The principal archway leads into the covered courtyard; the second allows independent public access to the ground level exhibition hall.

The covered courtyard will be the focus of public arrival, meeting, and access to galleries. Existing openings are re-utilized and according to their degree of monumentality they lead to greater or lesser functions. The courtyard floor in contrasting bands of coloured cobbles in an octagonal pattern is typically Milanese and will be preserved.

The cafeteria is planned as a typical Milanese bar with some small tables for those who prefer to sit and a long counter serving drinks and snacks. The front wall is a glazed screen which in the mild season can be opened with tables and sunshades spreading into the courtyard.

Basement. The new stair descending from the entrance court arrives in a vaulted space from which a ramp leads back to the basement lecture theatre and seminar rooms. There is a wide balcony from which a double stair descends into the temporary exhibition hall which in turn has external doors allowing public access to the amphitheatre and gardens. The basement lecture theatre and seminar rooms can be used via the alternative entrance in the evenings and at times when the Museum is closed.

Piano nobile. The stair and lifts ascend to a wide landing with windows overlooking the entrance court. From here the public can visit the exhibition rooms or donations rooms which are *ensuite* behind the front and rear façades of the palace.

Second floor. The second floor area will be subdivided as exhibition rooms arranged in a circuit echoing the plan at first floor. Central on the garden façade is a sitting room where visitors can have a view of the garden.

The archive and library in the new wing can be reached from the entrance hall.

The library has a top-lit double-height reading room and mezzanine. A bay window overlooks the garden and a balcony allows outside reading in good weather. Construction of these works will start shortly. Maybe.

James Stirling, 1985

Acceptance Address for the Pritzker Prize

One of the continuities in the history of Architecture is that every now and again a new patron and benefactor appears, and on behalf of my profession, here and abroad, I would salute Jay Pritzker — a most generous friend to Architects.

Somehow I think it might have been easier for Philip Johnson who, on the first occasion of the Prize giving, talked about the importance of the new Prize to the Profession, and maybe easier for Luis Barragan, reviewing a lifetime's work. Perhaps it's more difficult for me — at any rate I feel it that way. I can't talk about the Prize as a new event and I hope I'm not at the end of my work, though I guess I'm somewhere past the midway.

It's always been difficult for me to see myself. I work very intuitively, I'm not even sure whether I'm an English Architect, a European or an International Architect. It is embarrassing to talk about myself and therefore I will quote from a recent article written by Robert Maxwell[1] especially about this 3rd Pritzker award. Maxwell was a fellow student at Liverpool School of Architecture in the forties and is now Professor of Architecture at London University:

"In England in particular there is a peculiar breath of scandal attaching to the pursuit of architecture as Art. Criti-

Published in the Official Brochure of the Hyatt Foundation, 1981.

[1] Robert Maxwell: "The Artist as Hero", in *Architectural Design*, May 1981 (newspages).

173

cism of architecture in the public mind is broadly associated with sociological or material failure, and these spectres haunt the practise of architecture. Yet when such faults occur they are not thought to be really scandalous except when associated with high architectural aspirations."

The "high architectural aspirations" achieved in some of our earlier projects were in a sense accidents — the clients were not necessarily expecting a work of art in addition to a well functioning building — but they got buildings which have ever since been overrun with hordes of architectural students pounding through, something the users didn't anticipate or now appreciate.

However, for me, right from the beginning the "art" of architecture has always been *the* priority. That's what I trained to do (and incidentally it's what students are still trained to do), so it's particularly gratifying to feel that the Pritzker Prize is being awarded annually to Architects who value the art as highest and who have at the same time achieved a consistent sequence of buildings.

I agree with Maxwell that by and large the UK situation is to rate artistic content as coming rather far down the line of priorities (or as something which, with a bit of luck, might just happen). So how do fine buildings get built in the UK? Often subversively, I suspect. Certainly in my earlier days it was never discussed that the buildings should also be beautiful. However, I'm pleased to say that this situation has changed and our Patrons in Germany and America and our single client in the UK have commissioned us because they particularly value high quality architecture.

Historically, the quality of the art in the architecture, both at time of building and in retrospect, is remembered as *the* significant element. However, with the advent of modern architecture in this century, sociological, function-

James Stirling, 1968

al and real estate values have come into ascendancy. Ironically with the loss of certainty in Modern Architecture, the influence of Welfare State and Hardnosed Commercial standards is also, I believe, declining and the more ancient desire to see buildings wherein a primary objective is for them to appear beautiful and appropriate in their context, is returning — at least that's what my clients seem to want now.

Having stressed the importance of the art perhaps I should say where I think it's at. For many of us working with the language of abstract modern architecture, Bauhaus, International Style — call it what you will — this language has become repetitive, simplistic and too narrowly confining and I for one welcome the passing of the revolutionary phase of the modern movement.

I think the mainstream of architecture is usually evolutionary and, though revolutions do occur along the way (and the modern movement was certainly one of them, as was the time of Brunelleschi), nevertheless they are minority occasions.

Today we can look back and regard the whole of architectural history as our spectrum — including most certainly the modern movement, high tech and all. Architects have always looked back in order to move forward and we should, like painters, musicians, and sculptors, also be able to include representational as well as abstract elements in our art.

To quote again from Maxwell:
"The risks which Stirling has been seen to take are paradoxically of two kinds, corresponding to two major phases of his career; at the beginning he was thought to be manipulating form in the name of modernity; and then, when that was finally accepted, he suddenly appeared to be manipulating it in the name of history... Modernity was never more to be a simple matter of only following function; it involved a necessary meditation on form, and on what I have called the two faces of form: the face that beckons on, and the face that looks back...

There is a new kind of search for the *locus* of modernity in a non-utopian future."

Actually, another critic writing on our work[2] has recently perceived that there are four phases — in fact both are wrong — there is only one[3] (though our parameters are wide) and what we do now is not very different from what we have done since the beginning, though maybe there are differences in scale and materials.

So, freed from the burden of utopia but with increased re-

---

[2] Martin Filler: "Architect for a Pluralist Age", in *Art in America*, April 1981.
[3] "Acceptance of 1980 Royal Gold Medal in Architecture — James Stirling", in *Architectural Design*, No. 7-8, 1980.

sponsibility, particularly in the urban and civic realm, I would like to look forward to a more liberal but equally committed professional future, producing work perhaps richer in memory and association in the continuing evolution of a radical Modern Architecture.

Melsungen, Braun headquarters (with Michael Wilford), 1986–92, axonometric view

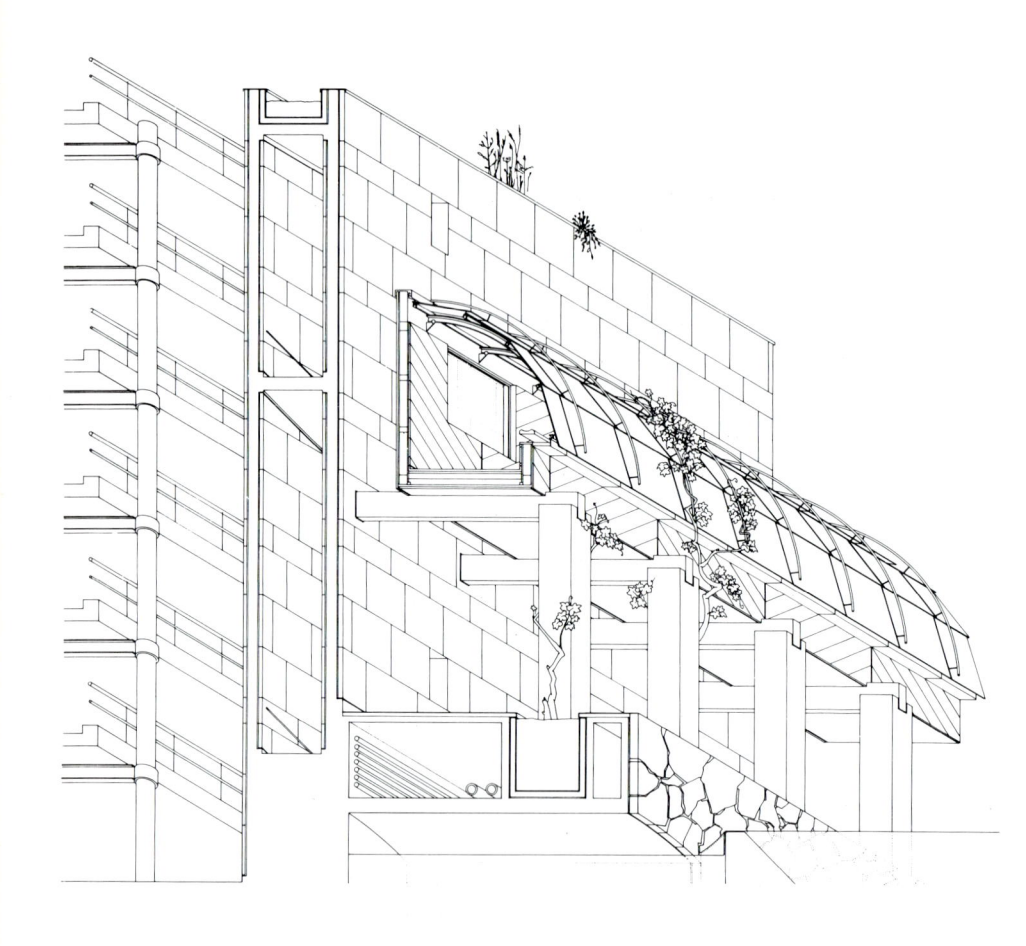

Speech at the Opening Ceremony of the Braun Headquarters at Melsungen

We have won several architectural competitions and some of our most successful buildings have been in Germany, including the extension to the State Gallery in Stuttgart — the Neue Staatsgalerie — and our building for the Wissenschaftszentrum in Berlin, close to Mies van der Rohe's Gallery, which was when we set up the Berlin office in 1979.

The Braun factory at Melsungen was also obliquely obtained through architectural competition — though here the buildings are in a green field arcadian site and not in the centre of an historic city. These headquarters and production buildings for Braun originated in 1986 as a limited competition of eleven architects. Though we were not the winners the Braun Company nevertheless decided to build our design, which we did with Walter Nägeli and our Berlin office.

We are indeed indebted to the vision and self confidence of Ludwig George Braun and his colleagues who have constructed the first phase of our competition proposal which is being officially opened today. Braun are manufacturers of medical equipment and they required most of their buildings be constructed in phases.

I might like to think that the design of these buildings was influenced by nothing — and certainly not influenced by his-

27 May 1992.

toric buildings. But nothing is conceived in a void. So if I'm looking for precedents, it might be from those of the "functional tradition" — which makes a connection back to the beginnings of the modern movement in architecture — and its rejection of history, which for some was like throwing out the baby with the bath water. The fluctuation between modernity and tradition which has been so characteristic of this century is echoed in microcosm in the oscillation between functional abstraction and historic association in our own work. Here we hope we have achieved an unmonumental lightness of being.

This site is near the town of Melsungen, though the factory is already larger than the medieval centre of that town. We thought our design, if anything, should respond to those man-made objects in the *campagna* — elements in the landscape such as viaducts and bridges, canals and embankments. Also avenues of trees and the straight edges of forests against fields. This 45-hectare site extends from the southern slope of a valley to the top of a small hill which, although only 10-metre higher than its surroundings, forms a visual interruption between the lower part of the site and the town, and on this hill we positioned the administration building — the first object to be seen when coming from Melsungen. Which has been referred to as a dinosaur's brain relative to the size of the animal.

It was required we park over 1300 cars, but surface parking would have consumed a large area of the site, with long walks in the open from car to work place; and car parking had to be outside of security. The valley shape suggested two levels of circulation and we proposed a large multi-storey car park in the middle of the site, accessible via an enclosed footbridge to the edges of the terrain and linking important parts of the factory. Which makes an architectural image for the place, like those modern road viaducts which contrast with the landscape and complement it in a dramatic way; there are many of them to be seen in this part of Hesse. Seven levels of car parking are connected to the footbridge by staircases inside a 250-metre-long double wall that geographically divides the site into front and back zones.

Through this wall the stairs discharge into the footbridge which like a giant centipede marches across the site.

The front zone is designed as an open *jardin anglais* with a tree-lined canal in the form of a river cascade, a bubbling lake, and stepped terraces and "tree henges".

The main entrance has three entry roads. Before the entrance pavilion a service road turns left along the outer edge of the canal up to the multi-level car park, which is outside security. A second (VIP) road goes past the entrance pavilion then turns left, parallel with the first road but separated by the canal; this leads to the administration building which bridges the first road, thereby keeping security zones unconnected. A third road goes straight ahead to the production building and further on to sterilization and the goods distribution centre; this is mainly for industrial traffic and forms a "traffic spine" perpendicular to the "pedestrian spine" of the elevated footbridge.

The back zone of the site has a large service *plateau* flanked by a green scaly monster with many mouths, the elliptical goods distribution centre. The long curved wall of this ellipse allows many lorries to dock simultaneously.

Construction started in 1988 and the first phase (costing 180m DM) has been completed. 81,000 square metres of buildings are being officially opened today.

I hope all who come to work in these new buildings will find them as easy to occupy as those families of falcons which have taken so readily to living in the bird houses we placed on top of the highest building. On behalf of Michael Wilford and Walter Nägeli and all who have worked on this project I thank you for the good working relationship we have had and for the trust and support you Mr. Braun have given to us — you are indeed the ideal client.

Opening Speech for the Clore Gallery

Most of the voyage had been quite stormy and it's been difficult to bring this small ship safely into harbour. But now that it's finally docked I hope it does not suffer from the same fate as Rainbow Warrior — sunk in harbour — by those who think they know what's good for us.

I'm certainly relieved to see that neither strawberry mousse nor porridge are included in tonight's menu — and incidentally I would like to thank the Tate for this splendid dinner this evening — which so many of our friends have come to.

There are many I should thank — firstly of course Vivien Duffield who made the whole thing possible. Then our office, and Michael Wilford and Russell Bevington in particular. Also the Trustees, the Director and those Curators of the Tate who supported the project.

The belching of the critics — particularly the architectural journalists who seem to have reached new heights of lewdness. "Mixed" is hardly the word to describe their reactions to this building. It's amazing to me that this small and modest building can be so controversial — at least nobody is ignoring it.

We're lucky indeed to have most of our work in other countries, and like Turner I spend large chunks of time in

183

*London, Clore Gallery,
Turner Collection,
Tate Gallery
(with Michael Wilford),
1980–86, axonometric
of the two main fronts*

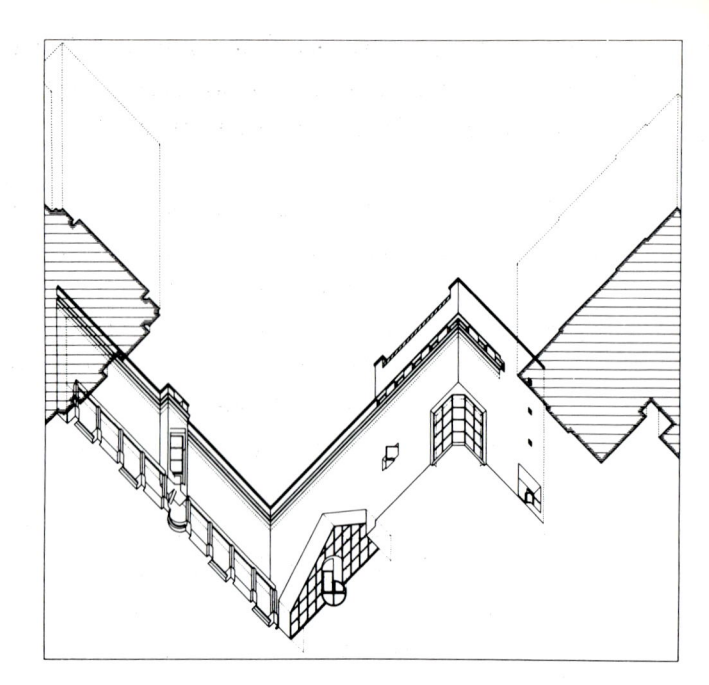

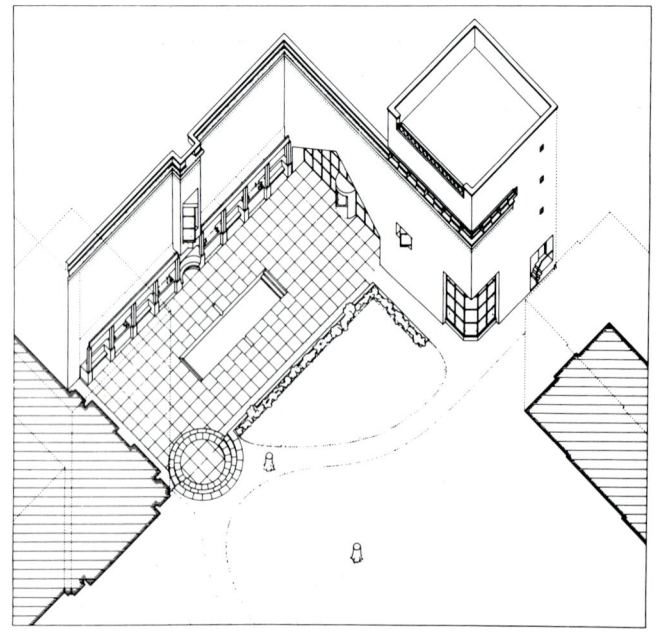

other places, but I *now* know, that *if*, we do another building in this country, it should be colourless, perhaps grey or *brown* — preferably the latter — or better still maybe just invisible.

I remember there was something of a controversy when our Gallery at Stuttgart opened — though not to the same pitch of hysteria, and then after six months everything changed, and within a year it became the most popular new Gallery in West Germany. And though many of the architectural journalists may never like the Clore Gallery — I'm sure I'm right in believing that the Clore will become a most popular building with the public.

I think Mr. Turner would like his new galleries and know why they are not a replica of his studio. He would appreciate that today's viewers who are younger and more informal would enjoy galleries that are lighter in feeling than his studio — indeed just like many of his paintings – more atmospheric and open — and so I welcome home Mr. Turner.

Thank you.

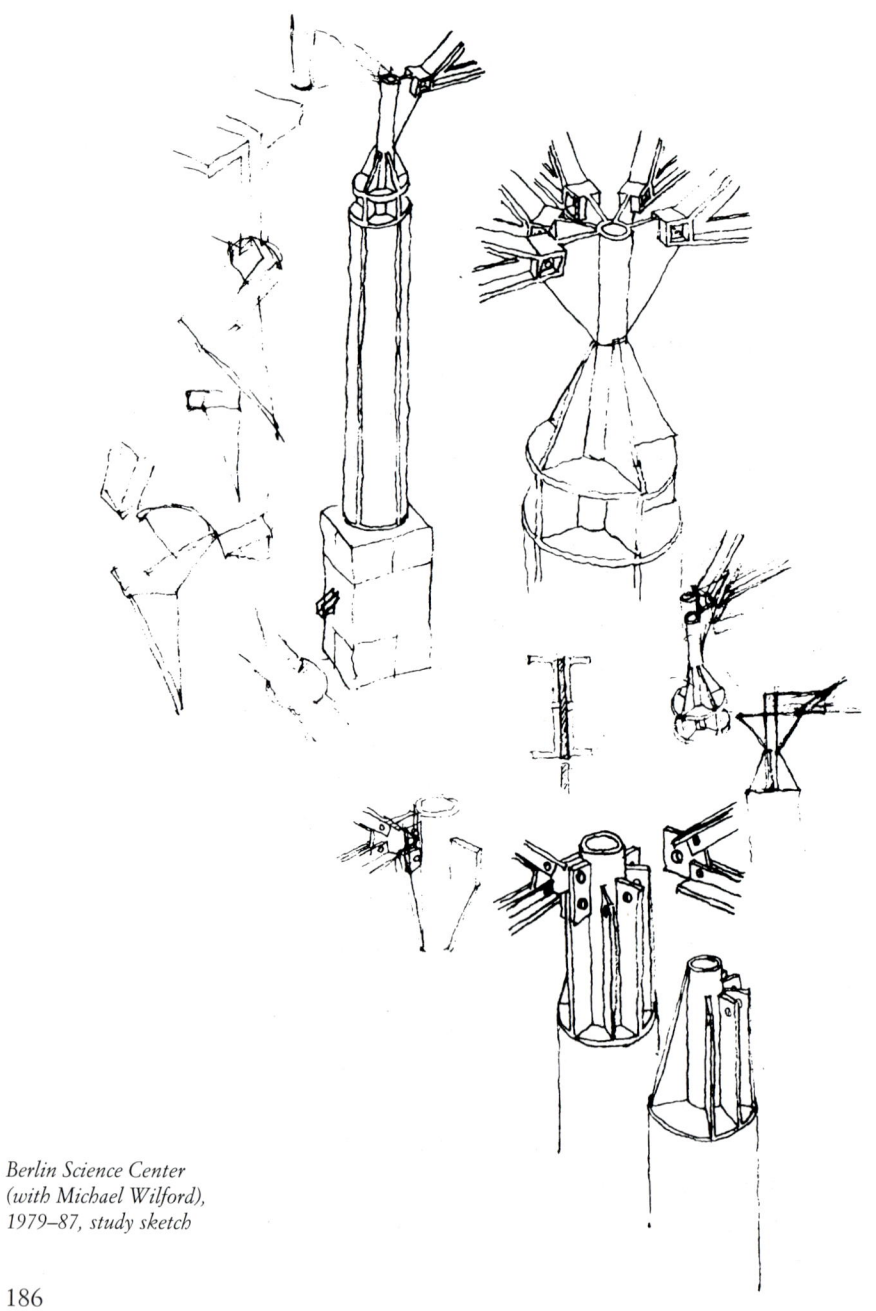

*Berlin Science Center
(with Michael Wilford),
1979–87, study sketch*

Inauguration of Berlin Science Centre

Our Stuttgart office moved to Berlin when the Staatsgalerie was completed, and though not quite finished the building was officially opened on the 9th May 1988. The Wissenschaftszentrum — which means Science Center — is really a Think Tank, a government institute for deep thinking on matters of environment, sociology and management, and almost everything except military.

The old Beaux-Arts building on the site (by the same architect who built the Reichstag) which somehow survived the war, had to be preserved and we have converted it for Secretariat and Conference facilities. In the entrance hall we have removed the fountain which was opposite the entrance and have made an opening with a few steps down leading to a newly formed colonnade in the back of the old building. The visitor thus walks directly through the old building into the garden from which there are separate entrances to the new buildings.

The primary requirement was for a large number of cellular offices and we were concerned to find an architectural and environmental solution from a programme which was almost entirely of repetitive small rooms. Simplistically we could have considered it as just another office building and the design of office buildings has frequently resulted in banal box-like modern buildings — perhaps too many architects delight in expressing the appearance of simple repetitiveness.

Our competition design used the three departments; of environment, sociology and management, plus the element for future expansion, plus the library/archive (in the tower) to create a grouping of five buildings juggled together with the old building. Within this architectural ensemble each department has its own identifying building. Though as each building connects with its neighbour at every floor level, the whole can function as a single institution.

It is perhaps an irony that whilst we greatly varied the form of buildings, the windows are applied like wallpaper on each building. Each room has a centrally positioned window allowing flanking wall surface for curtains, bookshelving, etc. The windows are framed with projecting stone architraves giving the illusion of a thick external wall and a secure (cosy) feeling inside the room.

The old and new buildings cluster around a garden, and glass-roofed loggias are incorporated in the stoa and arena buildings. Colonnades are formed within the old building and in the end of the cruciform building; in all there are four arcades around the garden. We hope to make a friendly unbureaucratic place — the opposite of an "institutional" environment.

Although there is stone cladding at the base of the buildings — similar to the veneered stone walls at Stuttgart — the primary surface is stucco (known as putz), with each floor level of alternating colour. We used stucco at Stuttgart on the exterior of the administrative building and Chamber Theatre. Berlin is full of stuccoed buildings but they are usually grey — dark grey — dirty grey, and they need not be grey — stucco can be any colour. We were probably influenced

Berlin Science Center (with Michael Wilford), 1979–87, general plan

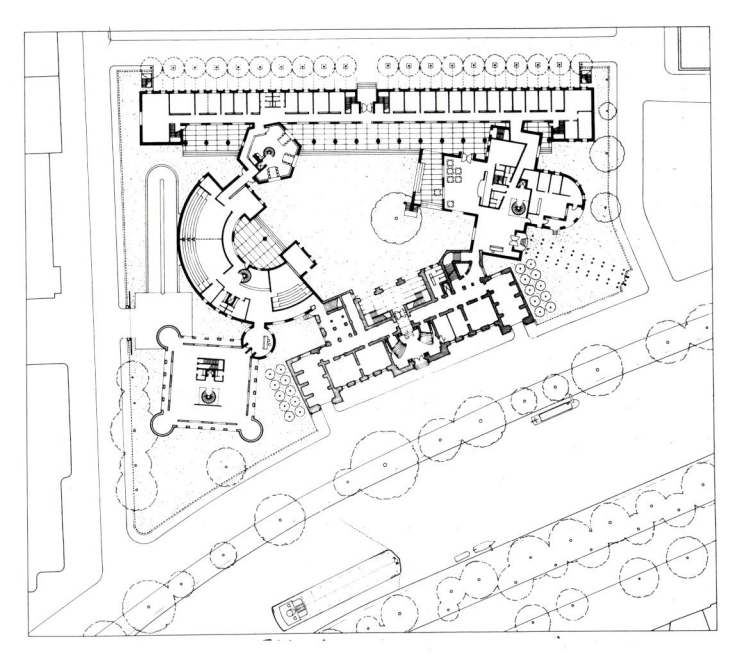

by the Neo-classical buildings of Helsinki and St. Petersburg where bright colours are used — ice blues and turquoise greens, also by buildings in Italy that are rust and burnt amber and almost orange.

Our problem was how to get putz onto the exterior without consistency — a difficult thing to achieve in Germany. We couldn't get the contractor to stop being ever so even and consistent; until I found two old men at the back of the Charlottenburg Palace repairing the stucco to match the antique. We got them to come to our building for a week and teach our men how to do it — so a technique was passed on.

The loggia columns are precast concrete and triangular in plan. The tops of the columns support firstly the gutters and secondly the roof trusses. The base of the column is a stonework drum. Rainwater pipes routed down the center of the columns are separately tuned like organ pipes to make a musical sound when a heavy downpour of water is flowing through them. So when the weather's really depressing a metaphysical sound — a bit like Japanese music — should be heard coming from the loggias.

But the opening day was a beautiful day and there was a huge party in the garden with bands and dancing and eating and drinking; and speeches — many speeches. So to conclude I include the short speech I was asked to give.

The Opening Day (9th May 1988)

Sehr geehrter Herr Bundesminister, sehr geehrter Herr Parlamentarischer Staatssekretaer, sehr geehrte Mitglieder des Deutschen Bundestages sowie des Berliner Abgeordnetenhauses, sehr geehrter Herr Praesident, Ladies and Gentlemen.

Many people are involved in a project of this size, and we are grateful for their different contributions. For example, the institutional support we had from the Bauaustellung — the IBA, and the financial support we had from the Berlin and Bonn governments. Also we are grateful for the organisational and supervising work required in building the Wissenschaftszentrum and, of course, the skilled professional work on site. Nevertheless we hope the building can be finished soon and everything made neat and tidy.

Berlin Science Center (with Michael Wilford), 1979–87, main front

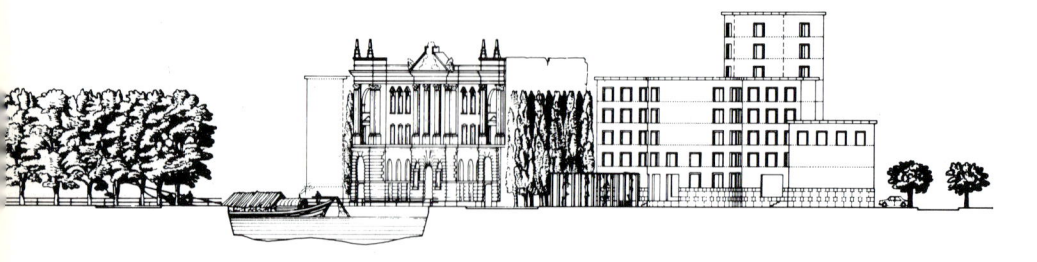

One of the good experiences for us in Germany is the high quality of modern craftsmanship we have come to expect, which we had with the Staatsgalerie and which we have experienced here. Craftsmanship today cannot be compared with the kind you find in old buildings, but what you see here is a great achievement — although I am told that what you see is not always quite as we've drawn it.

Which reminds me of an early experience with Palladio's villas. When I was a young architect I admired his buildings but only knew them from drawings and photographs. I imagined them to be made of the finest materials — marble and other stones. Only later when visiting did I discover that the beautifully formed columns were in fact made of stucco on brick or sometimes just stucco on rubble.

There was an essential contribution I'd like to thank especially, that of Professor Meinholf Dierkes (the Director for most of the time the building was in construction): his neverending enthusiasm and energy ultimately made the building possible. I think the Wissenschaftszentrum will be forever in his debt.

It's a memorable day for everyone involved in this project, and it's a happy day for the City of Berlin. We are adding a colourful new animal — perhaps a zebra — to the distinguished architectural zoo of Berlin's "cultural forum".

Berlin Science Center (with Michael Wilford), 1979–87, longitudinal section

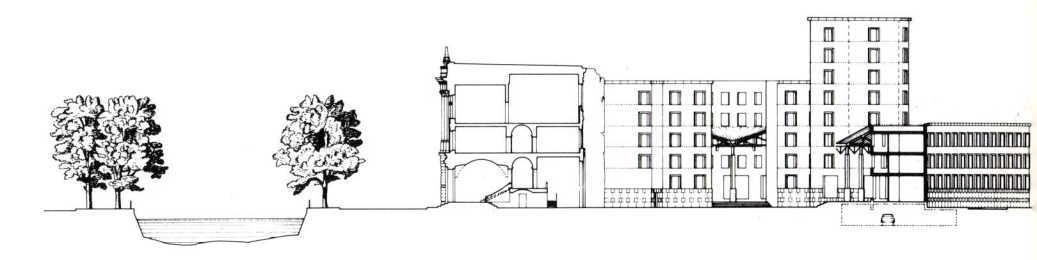

Berlin has long been an important place for architects, not only because of Schinkel and Stuler and the other Prussian architects, but also because of its significant role in the development of the modern movement — for example the distinguished housing schemes of the twenties by the Taut brothers.

Many architectural styles and periods are found in this city, and there are representatives from the two extremes of modernist thought in post-war Germany. Nearby is Hans Scharoun with his marvellous Philharmonie, and even closer is Mies van der Rohe's marvellous National Gallery. Somewhere in between (and lying just behind us) is the more cautious but elegant modernism of Emil Fahrenkamp's thirties building (Shell House).

We are happy that our design, which we won in competition, has finally become a reality; and can be judged not just from the drawings. Now that the building is finished I am sure that some critical comment will have to be revised. I have in mind those critics who likened the plan to a collection of historic buildings — whereas we always knew that three-dimensionally it would appear quite different; more as the panorama of an informal continuous building around a space — which is not a classical space but more akin to a college garden.

I remember the first journalists who wrote about the Staatsgalerie in Stuttgart (also before it was completed) were mostly negative — then within a year almost everything written about Stuttgart became very positive; I am sure the same will happen here and it will become one of the interesting modern landmarks in Berlin.

We of course, would like to see the upper floors added to the building above the cafeteria. In the meantime we have to be content with this fragment which reminds me of the incomplete single-storey palazzo in Venice which houses the Peggy Guggenheim collection, though ours is more like a folly in a garden than a folly on a canal — though it might have become so if Hans Hollein had pursued his idea of flooding the back of our site. Our folly does have the advantage of providing built-in foundations for the Wissenschaftszentrum to expand onto when it needs additional space.

The WZB does not look like the ubiquitous shoe-box post-war office block we are all too familiar with. Here we tried to create a rich social and architectural environment in contrast to the "repetitiveness" of 300 or so individual office rooms which is the basis of the building programme.

I hope those who come to live in the building will find the time to leave their rooms and from time to time stroll around the gardens and through the buildings, finding a place for contemplation — in contrast with the evermore efficient computerised reality of the working day.

This contrast (maybe anachronism) could become the main quality of your new home and a major contribution to strengthening the identity of the Wissenschaftszentrum.

I am told the building appears to some as a wedding cake — so on this happy occasion I would like to thank all of you who have come to the celebration.

Thank you.

*Milton Keynes,
Olivetti headquarters
and distribution centre,
1971, general view*

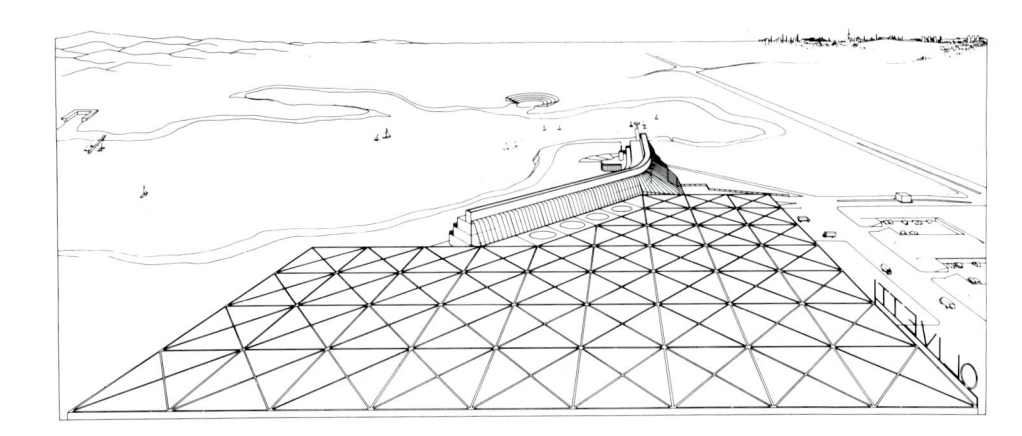

James Stirling in Tokyo
Interviewed by Arata Isozaki

Arata Isozaki: Our time is too limited tonight to discuss the problems of modern architecture or the mass of your work, and so perhaps it would be best to limit ourselves to your personal involvement with architecture and your feelings about Japan and Japanese architecture.

I'd like to know the purpose of your current visit to Japan and your reactions to Tokyo. At the same time, I'd also like to ask you about your situation ten or fifteen years ago. I'm not very well acquainted with the Independent Group in London, but I think they must be of your generation or perhaps a little older.

James Stirling: Yes, the generation of the Independent Group is my generation. It arose around 1951 or 1952 and continued until about 1956. The ICA (Institute of Contemporary Art) had just started functioning in 1949 or 1950 and it naturally drew people to it. London after the war was rather bereft of cultural places, which of course is not the case now, but at the time the ICA had a certain attraction for people of my generation. Another thing was, though, that the people who came to form the Independent Group were all people who knew each other already. I don't really know how it happened, but we were mainly architects, with some painters and some sculptors, some graphics people, some

Published in A+U, *August 1971.*

musical people, and historians, and I suppose we had all come out of university five or six years before. The Independent Group was never a formal club. It existed because we were a group of friends, and the architects were the main people in it. It did have meetings at the ICA, and people would show slides and discuss what they were doing. There were also some exhibitions put on. But I really do want to stress the fact that the group consisted of people who were actually friends outside the ICA. There was an Italian, Toni del Renzio, who was sort of the social centre of the group and who made it his business to organize everybody into meeting at the ICA every month, but in fact the ideas that were exchanged by the members of the group were really exchanged outside the ICA building in the daily context of their work. In those days the Smithsons talked to everybody; now they only talk to a few people. I know that people like Alan Colquhoun, Sandy Wilson, Arthur Baker, Edward Reynolds, who are architects, Richard Hamilton, who's a painter, critics like Lawrence Alloway, everyone was interested in what later was called "pop culture". What we talked about was what appeared in *Life* magazine and *Look* magazine, the quality of photography, American styling as it appeared in cars and the like. There was a post-war excitement and enthusiasm for American styling. This no longer exists, and most people are very much turned off by it, but it held great attractive power at the time. Everyone was very much against established culture. There was the National Gallery and the Tate Gallery. The establishment was disseminating the orthodox, unthinking, bland point of view. In some ways the establishment has changed for the better, like the Tate, but in the post-war days we were all rather fed up with the establishment. At the time, the Smithsons were going to the CIAM meetings and invited their friends, which at the time included me, although it wouldn't now, to do some work that was to be taken to Aix-en-Provence, and we all did some work because we were all doing projects for competitions and things. That was sort of the beginning of my break with the Smithsons. I heard from people at the meetings, people from abroad, that is, that we were being represented as people and work from the school of the Smithsons. This was completely untrue. We were all a bunch of friends at that time, and it was somehow this misrepresentation that first began to make one sort of suspicious of the Smithsons and tread warily. Since then it has developed into a sort of definite break. They can't tolerate anyone unless they're in a sort of guru situation, with people sitting at their feet. It's really a pity, because there could have been a real British group, but they're not capable of that. I think it's been the Smithsons' attempt to dominate Team 10, architects from all over, that has led to the demise of that group, too. I suppose it's just a personality problem.

AI: I am of the same generation as the Metabolics Group, but I've never been in that group. Some of our tendencies are the same, but somehow I always feel different. I've never become a member.

JS: You say member, and that makes it sound as if it were a small club with membership and tickets and membership cards. Was that the case? With the Independent Group we were all just a bunch of friends. I suppose when you read about it in the books and magazines and papers it must sound like a club, but then it never really was.

AI: When did you establish your own office?

JS: In 1956. I was working for a firm called Lyons, Israel, and Ellis, who built the Polytechnic Building in London quite recently. I was their design senior assistant. James Gowan was the technical senior assistant. I was teaching part time at the AA, too. I had a stroke of luck. The father of one of my students turned out to be a rather rich developer, and the student introduced me to his father as being the architect to do Ham Common, and that's how I got my first commission. When I had the plan accepted by the developer, I was able to open an office. It was a small job, but I thought it would be enough to keep the office going for a couple of years. At the time I felt a little deficient in technical contract organization and the aspects of private practice, so I went into partnership with James Gowan. We had both quit Lyons, Israel, and Ellis. They were rather upset, losing two of their senior assistants, but we set up practice. Two years later, when Ham Common was completed, we had no work, and to stay alive we taught in schools of architecture. Our next commission came from Lyons, Israel, and Ellis. They were very generous — after all, we had left them — and asked us to do a housing scheme in Preston in North Lancashire. They didn't want to do it, because it was a very low cost project and too small for them. We were able to do less teaching and carry on with the next job. There have been two or three times when our practice has just about gone out of existence for lack of work, but on each occasion I've been able to keep going by doing some teaching in the London schools of architecture. There are three architecture schools in London, and all three have the system of keeping a lot of part-time teachers, young people who have just started their practices. It's been a very good system because it's managed to keep young practices going and because, in addition to the older teachers, it's succeeded in bringing young, outside practitioners into contact with the students.

*Milton Keynes,
Olivetti headquarters
and distribution centre,
1971, perspective
of the main hall*

AI: This is also true in Japan. I've had similar experiences. Did you get the Leicester University commission by competition?

JS: No. Leicester was our third project, the one after we'd finished the housing in Preston. We started getting invited to participate in competitions at that point, because you only needed a little reputation at the national level. We did a competition for Churchill College at Cambridge. We didn't win it, but we were among the last four contestants, and that helped our reputation also. At about that time, Sir Leslie Martin, who's a friend of mine, although of an older generation, and who is probably the most enlightened of the pre-war generation of architects in England, now a professor of architecture at the Cambridge School of Architecture, befriended us as architects. I had known him since I first came to London, because during the early days of the Independent Group we tried to make contact with the very few older, pre-war architects we admired. Leslie Martin was one of

199

the very few in this category. As a result of the fact that we had begun to acquire something of a reputation, and as a result of the fact that I knew him, he suggested to Leicester University that we might be the architects for the job. At the time he was the consulting planner to the university and I suppose that when the university approached him about architects to do the Engineering Building he suggested us. We had an interview and got the job. That was really rather remarkable, because Leicester Engineering was a much bigger building than anything we'd ever built. We'd actually only built two or three small jobs. The Engineering Building was a much bigger, more complicated building than we'd ever done before. We had to do it in a rush, because the university had a commitment to have the building built by a certain date, so we had to do the design and the working drawings in nine months and then get the contractor started. The contractor took longer to do the work than he should have, but eventually the building was done. I suppose that brought us an international reputation. Between 1956 and the early sixties we built up an international reputation rather quickly, and I suppose that it was because of the Engineering Building that a lot of our recent work has come in, although I'm not really sure of that. The History Building, which was the next work we did, also came to us because of a recommendation from Leslie Martin, who had by that time become a professor at the architecture school of Cambridge. He suggested a limited competition for the History Building, and the university put together a group of architects, including us. We were in the group, though, because of the introduction of Leslie Martin. We have benefited from the patronage of an older person. I suppose it happens everywhere. Kenzo Tange must also help younger people here in Japan.

AI: Yes, sometimes Tange will do it. But in England today, is it difficult to get architectural work?

JS: Well, in England today there's a depression like there is in America, and a lot of the smaller firms are going out of business. The larger firms are doing all right. You have a situation where the larger firms can survive because they can lose a few jobs and get rid of some of their staff; but the smaller firms, who don't have the ballast to dispense with, are in a very vulnerable position. It's a very bad time for architecture in England. I think there is not only a shortage of work but also a feeling of national guilt about architecture, that architecture is a guilty profession, that making a building is somehow sinful or that spending so much money is somehow evil. I don't contribute to this, but certainly a lot of the magazines are putting out a sort of guilty line, and a lot of architects are sort of contributing to the situation. It's a sort of dog-eat-dog situation, where architects write articles about other architects and the profession is in a sort of mean and nasty mood. I suppose that it's because there's so little work around. There are too many architects and not enough work to be done.

AI: In Japan, architectural firms are changing their organization. There are a very few large firms, and the large construction companies are hiring many architects. They are designing and producing many buildings. At the same time there are many small offices with two, three, and sometimes as many as ten architects. But as in England, it's very difficult for these small firms to get jobs.

JS: We have this phenomenon in the extreme, I would say. The larger offices in England are now staffed by several hundred people. I suppose it's like American style, the American style of the forties, which of course is not anything like the

American style of doing things now at all. At any rate, they're running these huge organizations, sort of empires that just keep getting bigger and bigger and swallow up the smaller people. But I also think you have to distinguish between commercial and non-commercial architecture. Non-commercial architecture, which in England is perhaps only one percent of the total architectural work being done, is mainly being done by the smaller firms, and commercial architecture is being done by these enormous established firms. It may not be the case in Japan, but in England there's a tremendous amount of commercial building being done, which has no architectural value at all. It's just done in the name of modern architecture. Unfortunately, the public image of modern architecture is entirely based upon these bland, boring commercial buildings. In that respect, "modern architecture" is a dreadful bore, because all the buildings are worthless in terms of design. It's no wonder that people sort of despise modern architecture, because it's so dreadfully boring. But the few people who do good work are so rare, doing one building here and another there, that it's not understood that that's really what modern architecture is. There's just not enough building done by these people to make an adequate impression.

AI: People know your later work from magazines, so let's change the subject. Have you visited any traditional Japanese buildings?

JS: No, the only thing I have visited is the Meiji Shrine, although I am going to Kyoto. I understand that the Meiji Shrine is only fifty years old, although it's built in a very old, traditional style. I think the Japanese must have an entirely different sense of time with regard to architecture. Would you consider the Meiji Shrine an "old building" even though it was only built fifty years ago? Would you regard it as bogus or phoney because it's only fifty instead of five hundred years old?

AI: Emotionally I can accept and appreciate older buildings, buildings, that is, built in the old style and with old techniques. The only thing is that now styles and techniques have changed and the design and architectural techniques observable in buildings like the Meiji Shrine are really of no use to us. Over the past fifty or sixty years, there has been a great debate in Japanese architectural circles, and a very simple theory was established. It was decided that building style had to be Japanese while techniques had to be modern. We built buildings that just looked Japanese while they were constructed out of concrete.

JS: Yes, but the Meiji Shrine is constructed of wood in the style of a building 300 years old. Take the nineteenth century in England, our greatest period of building ever. There were millions of things built in Medieval this, Roman that, or Renaissance the other. It was a whole century of fake building. I don't think the Japanese feel this way about their architecture. Traditional Japanese architecture probably originated five or six centuries ago. The very fact that you built the Meiji Shrine only fifty years ago would, to English eyes, make it appear a fake.

AI: No, it's not a fake for Japanese, because tradition has come to transcend change. Take for example the Ise Shrine, the oldest shrine in Japan. There are two sites, and every twenty years the shrine is rebuilt on the alternate site and the gods are moved there. In this way, new buildings are built without there ever being a change in design or architecture, and change is accomplished without change.

Milton Keynes, Olivetti headquarters and distribution centre, 1971, perspective of the main gallery

JS: That's an entirely different attitude toward the past than we have in England. It is very different from the attitude toward time and history that we have in England or in Western culture. Western culture is much more vitriolic. In one century there's one style and another style in the next.

AI: In Japanese history we have no tradition of denying an old style in favour of a new one. The tradition has been, rather, to take an old style as it is and preserve it. Change, when it has taken place at all, has been very gradual. This was the case up until the war, although changes were made in some areas.

JS: Yes, I know. But in European buildings, it's impossible to replace them piece by piece. If you take a piece out, the building is likely to collapse, so we haven't the tradition of replacing a building as it wears away. In Japan, on the other hand, old buildings are always being manicured. As a piece wears away, it's replaced. If you take an "old" building in Japan and analyse it piece by piece, you'd probably find that it wasn't old at all. We haven't this tradition in Europe. In a sense it's a great pity, because this attitude suggests a great respect for buildings that I don't think we have. You see, we have a view of history as a series of events. There was the Norman period. It was then replaced by another period with its own style and the buildings of the older period were left to rot. This process has left us with a whole sandwich of old buildings, kind of rotting away, representing various centuries. It's quite a profound difference. I wonder, therefore, how modern architecture comes to Japan. What will you do with your modern buildings as they wear out? Will you replace them bit by bit?

AI: I don't believe so. Wooden buildings can be renovat-

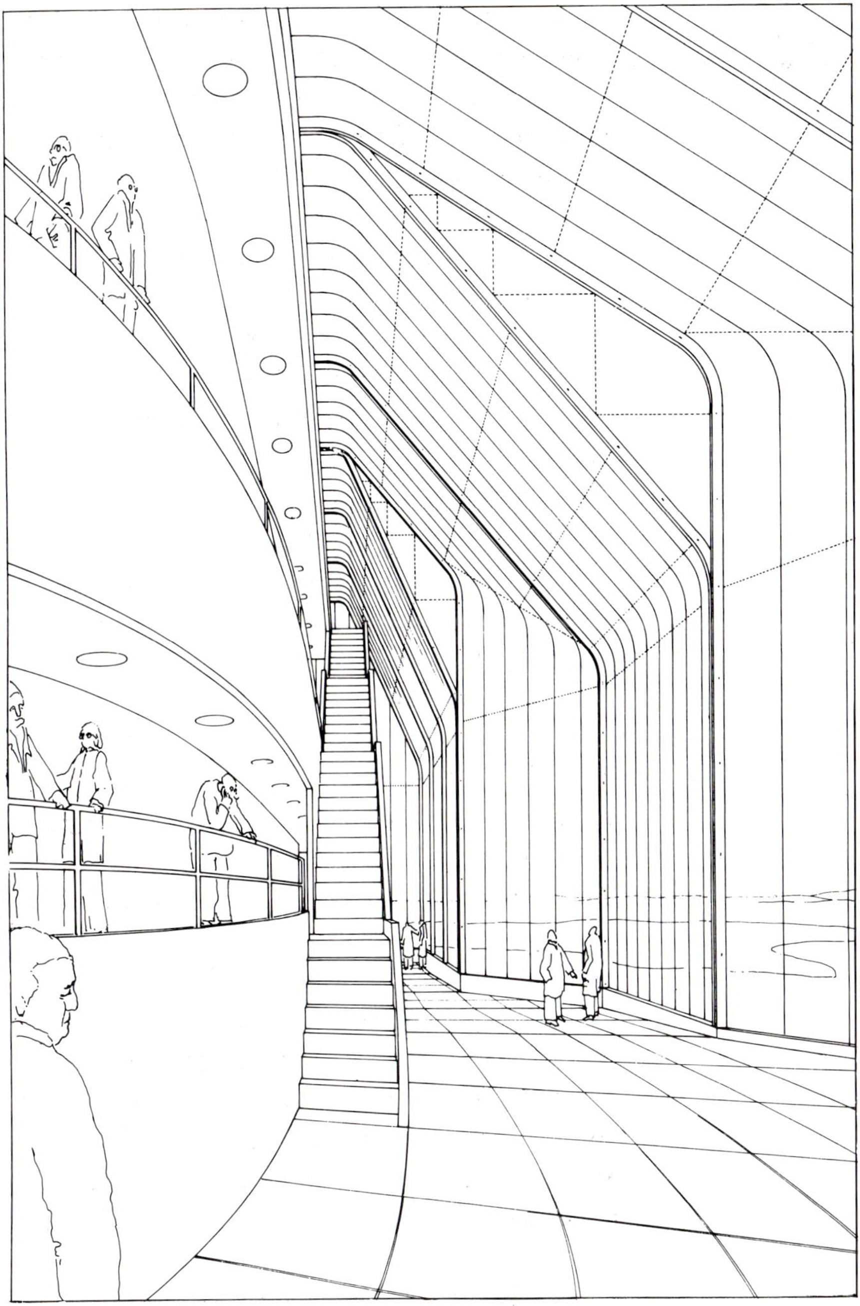

St. Andrews University, Art Centre (with Michael Wilford), 1971, perspective of the main gallery

ed because they can be moved and replaced. Let's suppose you want to have a Japanese tea house. In two or three months it can be built and shipped to England, where it can be set up in a matter of days. It's very strange, but this is the traditional Japanese system. In Europe there is a tradition of stone and brick, but in Japan we have only had wood.

JS: I don't think that it's been a lack of technological know-how that has prevented the same thing from happening in England, rather it's been a lack of a sort of national desire to repair and reconstruct old buildings. Our attitude is much more wanton. As soon as a building is finished it is doomed. It's a very philistine attitude. You build a building and then leave it. It's partly due to lack of money, of course, but it's also a matter of national character. The English are simply not interested in old buildings. There is a great English interest in literature and theatre, but it's mainly the field of literature that we excel at and not the plastic arts and certainly not architecture. We lack a respect for buildings. I suspect that in Japan you have a very respectful attitude toward the plastic arts.

AI: Today, though, things are changing. Perhaps it would be better to continue this discussion after you've returned from Kyoto. During your stay in Kyoto you'll find that traditional Japanese buildings are of very light construction. This, however, requires a great deal of preventive maintenance and upkeep. The tatami mats have to be recovered every year. Paper doors and screens also have to be entirely redone yearly. Wooden floors have to be polished every day. A great deal of money and a great deal of labour are required merely to maintain the human environment.

JS: Much as I am an admirer of Corbusier, I began to get turned off by his later buildings, like the buildings in India,

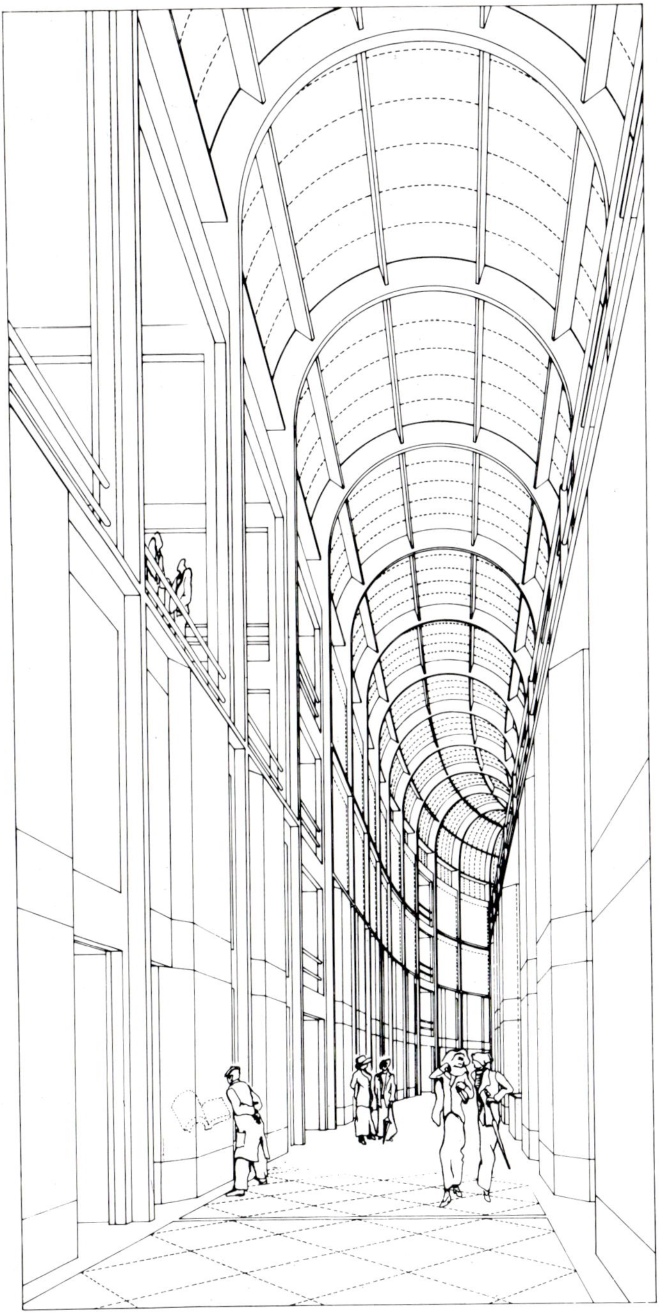

for instance, where ha made a massive use of concrete. He was trying to build buildings that could withstand the elements without the constant attention required by Japanese buildings. That seemed to me, however, very much alien to the spirit of modern architecture. I began to question the whole idea of using concrete as a modern building method. It seems to me a very massive and antiquated method. I began to think that buildings constructed out of a thin membrane, buildings that could be built with assemblage methods instead of more Egyptian methods of construction, were much more in the spirit of the modern age. I've always regretted that last period of Corbusier's work.

AI: After the war in Japan, the building situation was very bad, and the massive concrete method of construction was the least expensive. Steel and glass were very expensive at the time. Japan immediately after the war shares a great deal with the situation in India. The situation is changing now in Japan, because the cost of labour is getting higher and we have many prefabrication factories. In the next few years we may have many more buildings with glass walls. I want to point out, however, that today the situation centres largely on specific factors of economy and technique and materials and not so much upon what you have called national characteristics.

JS: Yes, we have a similar situation in England now. We are approaching a sort of American situation, where labour costs are high. The situation is indeed probably quite different from that in India, but I suppose that it was more the spirit of the thing that turns me off, where buildings are turned into sort of massive concrete sculptured pieces. I don't know how it is in Japan, but we've been able to get away with thin glass buildings in England. But then we have a more moderate climate than you: we don't have the same heat or the same cold that you have. Our climate doesn't vary in its extremes as it does here. Now we're actually doing buildings in plastics. We're now doing a building for Olivetti in plastics. It's sort of designed as a whole clip-together, glossy assemblage of polyester units. We were going to fly the pieces into the site, which is a heavily wooded area on the top of a hill. One of the notions was to fly the pieces in by helicopter, but it's turned out in fact to be cheaper to put in a rough road. This again is a clip-together, fast assemblage type of building that's light years away from the battleship method of massive concrete construction.

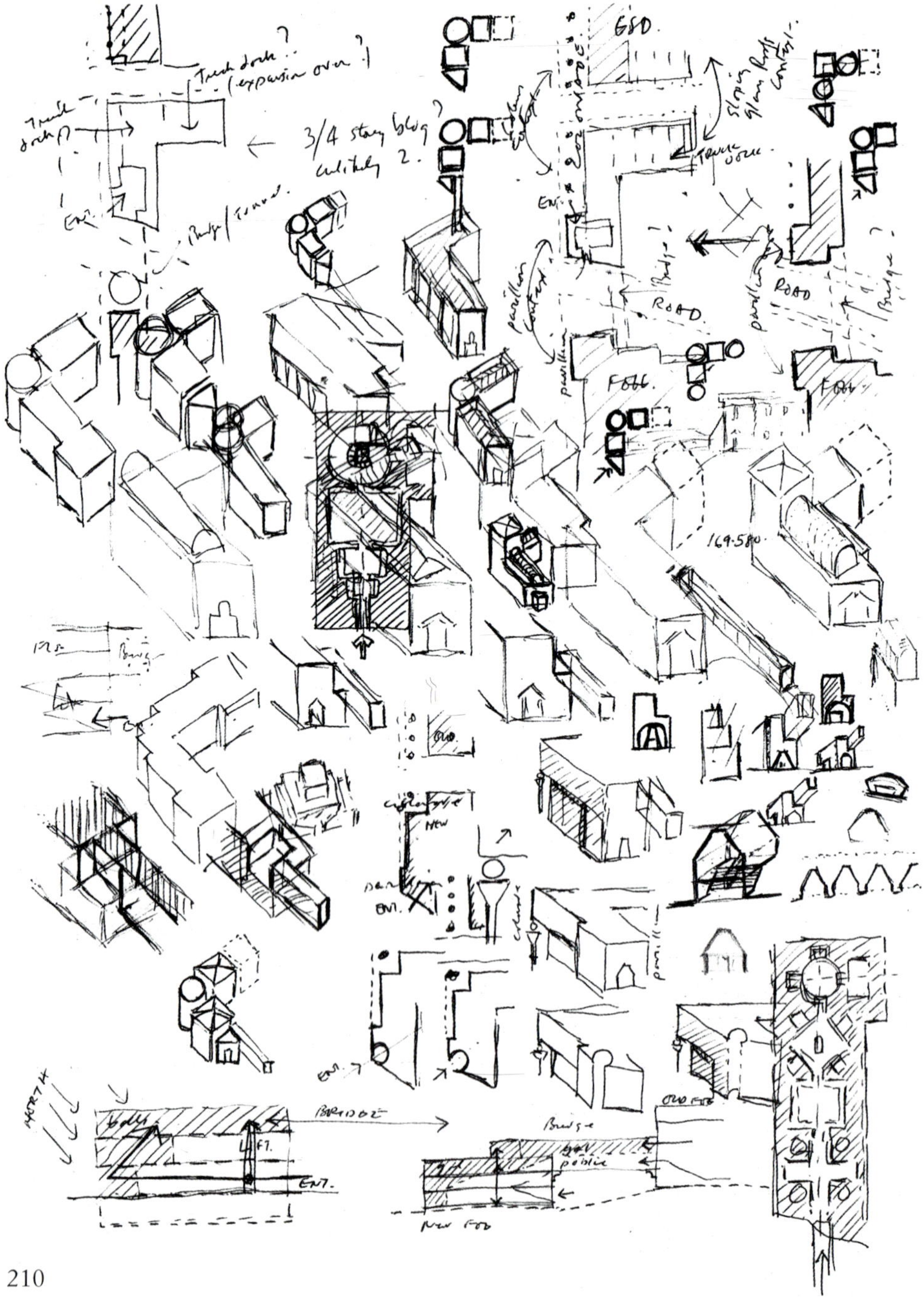

GSD.
3/4 story bldg?
ROAD
ROAD
ENT.
169.580
NORTH
BRIDGE
ENT.

James Stirling and Michael Dennis.
Notes from an Informal Discussion

Michael Dennis: Your work to date has been involved with juxtapositions, contradictions, and collage: early buildings seem consistently "modern" in their materials and formal cacophony, whereas your recent work includes more "traditional" ideas in its juxtapositions. This is especially true of the museum projects: Düsseldorf, Cologne, Stuttgart, the Tate, and the Sackler. They are all "contextual" projects, and all utilize traditional typologies and materials. Yet among these projects the Sackler is unique: it is small; it is a teaching museum; and it fills the available envelope of the site, becoming as much urban fabric as monument.

As a teaching museum, the building seems elegantly and functionally arranged, and the public sequence of *entry hall*, *grand stair* and *galleries* is a powerful idea. Some planning decisions seem especially crucial, however: for instance, why are offices on the outside and galleries on the inside? And other decisions about the types of internal spaces also seem important: why are the galleries traditional rooms, and why is the stair abstract, unresolved as it ends, and treated as an outside space?

James Stirling: To respond to your question about the stair "that doesn't go anywhere", usually one thinks of the grand stair as a feature in a continuous sequence. But I prefer to

Cambridge, Massachusetts, 17 May 1985. From the Official Brochure at the opening of the Sackler Museum, Harvard University, 1985.

Cambridge, Massachusetts, Arthur M. Sackler Museum (with Michael Wilford), 1979–84, study sketch

211

think of this staircase as an event in itself. The circulation flow in the Sackler is interrupted by a series of contra axes and stop movements as you move from the entry hall and up the stair to the top-floor galleries. The in-between transitional elements normally found in Baroque ensembles, such as vestibules and ante-rooms, are here excluded, making for an abrupt juxtaposition of basic elements. The staircase is therefore more a picturesque and less a sequential element in the spatial whole.

MD: Harvard has several good traditional rooms, and it has one very beautiful space — a room "inside out" almost — in the Carpenter Centre. But to the best of my knowledge, there are no grand modern rooms on campus, so the presence of your entry hall is a gift. I also agree that the stair is a place in its own right. However, you wouldn't deny that it is part of a grand sequence of large *entry hall, grand stair,* and *galleries* above, with an implicit connection back to the Fogg Museum. In your mind there is the connection, and the interior courtyard of the Fogg is very much a part of your conception. I would further argue that you can't understand the Sackler unless you know the Fogg.

JS: Absolutely. When you arrive at the big window, having gone through all the galleries, you're confronted with the Fogg and with the desire to make the crossing, as it were, ideally, of course, through a long gallery connecting the two museums.

I hope that visitors moving through the Sackler will experience a succession of minor shocks or jolts. Firstly, they have to go down instead of up to enter the building. Then, entering through the glass lobby between the columns, the cross axis of the entrance hall immediately creates a stop movement: across the hall the staircase reverts to the axis on which they entered and, when the gallery at the top is reached its axis is again at right angles and so on. In a short *staccato* walk the reorientation of stop/go axis changes is a substitute for the transitional vestibules in a Baroque sequence.

MD: This also fits with the idea of the stair's being, in a sense, an outside space. On one side of the stair the galleries are traditional or representational in the nineteenth-century sense — large, simple rooms arranged in enfilade. On the other side are staff and curatorial offices planned with the windows in the centre of each room. Embedded between these traditional arrangements is the staircase, repeating the stripes from the exterior and making it quite abstract, like the outside of the building.

JS: The staircase has been likened to a Neapolitan street. But I tend to think of it as a steeply inclined bazaar with overlooking windows, people talking and flanking activities. There will be the traffic of students *en route* to class rooms and the flow of the public visiting the galleries; it could be quite active, a sort of mini-bazaar.

MD: Last fall, we had our beginning architecture students analyse the entry spaces of the Sackler. It was interesting because the most successful drawings were frontal axonometrics; perspectives did not yield the same sense of the building. The students were initially perplexed, trying to figure out the absence of resolution of the joints — resolution in the classic sense — and the lack of exact alignment of the parts.

JS: You're right, perspective drawings might not do too much for you in the Sackler except depict an atmosphere. In some parts I hope there is the quality of ambiguity that you sometimes see in Soane (who devised ceilings that float and introduced light from mysterious sources). [Referring to the architect Sir John Soane, 1753–1837.] For instance, in the Ancient Greek gallery, when looking back to where you entered from the staircase, you cannot see the recessed door. People will just appear in the gallery, as it were from the mist of the wall; alternatively, one moment they will be there and, when you look again, they will have disappeared without a trace.

MD: Much of your work seems to involve the juxtaposition of ideas, both in concept and in detail. People generally notice, I think, small things like the bright green trim on the exterior and the different hand rails on either side of the main stair, but the "shocking" or surprising aspects of the building are there at a larger and at a more conceptual level as well.

JS: I see the building in some ways as very *un*shocking; for instance, the conventional arrangement of the staff/curatorial rooms and corridors. The galleries are intended to have a more public though not monumental persona, to have an ambience verging on the domestic, especially when the ancient, Islamic and oriental objects are installed in the galleries, and if arranged with the charm and slightly idiosyncratic layout I associate with the Fogg, the domestic character should be reinforced. The galleries will, I hope, be more personal, more like those annex rooms of grand houses which display the owner's private collection than galleries in a public institution.

MD: Fifteen or twenty years ago, there was a great polemic about flexibility and open-plan exhibition spaces. Louis Kahn, for example, made an open-plan museum at Yale. But nowadays, there has been something of a return to the idea of traditional rooms, and your preference for that type of exhibition space represents this change in attitude.

JS: Well, the Sackler does have rooms, but not always with an axial relationship to each other; some have two openings per wall, so you may experience some ambiguity as to the type of room you are in. The final gallery with the big window is parallel with the first gallery but the in-between spaces may seem somewhat like a maze.

MD: Nevertheless, they do have a rather impressive sequence and a distinct regularity.

JS: Only the galleries on the middle floor are in enfilade — although you enter them obliquely — where openings line up with a dead-ahead relationship of room to room. However, on the top floor where there is daylighting, the nature of the spaces and the route through may be less obvious.

MD: Can we talk about the idea of literal or phenomenal connection to the Fogg?

JS: Yes. Do you mean the bridge in the mind or the bridge in reality?

MD: I realize you had to allow for the possibilities of both, but do you think that the bridge is crucial — not to the functioning of the museum, but to the sequential idea of the two buildings, or the two buildings becoming one building?

JS: I don't think the bridge is fundamental to the existence of the Sackler. However, if it was there as a long gallery and not an airport glass tube, it would be very practical and beneficial to both museums. But I don't think it's necessary as a formal or aesthetic element. In a way the gesture is made, the flanking columns support an imagined structure and the entrance focuses towards the Fogg. The big window suggests in the mind where you would make the leap, and I think the termination of the galleries at that window is how you connect back, not only to the Fogg, but to Harvard itself.

MD: And you know in your mind that the completion, or perhaps the beginning, is the courtyard of the Fogg itself?
JS: That's right.

MD: I find myself in a dilemma about that because, functionally, the bridge would be a great asset; on the other hand, it would drastically alter the façade. To come out of the Yard into the enclosed space in front of Sever Hall, facing the Fogg, and to see two modern buildings — Le Corbusier's and yours, on the diagonal right and left of the Fogg — is a strong scenographic idea. The fact that your façade is facing that ensemble is no accident, I'm sure.
JS: There are precedents. In London the Gibbs Church faces sideways overlooking the front of the National Gallery, and a proposed extension to the National Gallery (with linking bridge) on the opposite corner of Trafalgar Square could also face sideways towards the Gallery.

MD: Harvard seems to favour representation and decorum on the outside, and to keep any abstraction or oddity well concealed on the inside. Your building is almost the reverse: traditional ideas are found on the inside — the grand entry hall, the galleries as rooms — while the building is primarily abstract and differentiated on the outside. It is hard to tell how much is due to intent, and how much to evolution based on logical planning, humane considerations and so on.
JS: Well, nowadays one can draw equally, without guilt, from the abstract style of modern design and the multiple

*Cambridge,
Massachusetts, Arthur
M. Sackler Museum
(with Michael Wilford),
1979–84, section
of the main stairway*

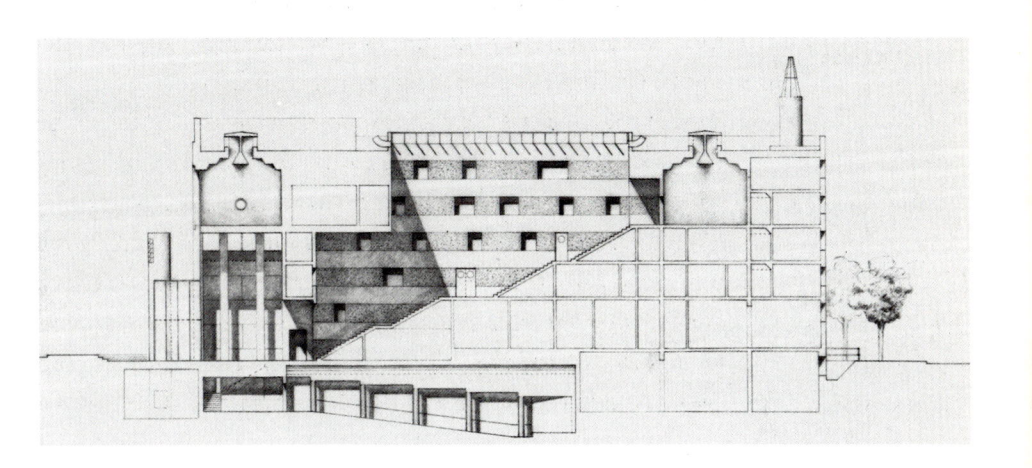

layers of historical precedent. Here we are combining the abstract repetitiveness of the long façade with the more representational character of the entrance façade which is larger in scale and where there is a cyclopean focus on the oblique.

MD: You might not like the fine-grained distinction, but I find it curious that you use the word "façade" to describe both those conditions. I would prefer "elevations" as a basic description, and to say that there is a representational façade with abstract elevations on the other sides.

JS: I think your distinction is correct, though some people may have a problem comparing the entrance façade with the side elevations because they look so different. We made the decision to put the staff/teaching rooms on Quincy and Cambridge Streets which has the effect of demonumentalizing the building and producing an almost residential appearance to the street. Unlike the Wissenschaftszentrum in Berlin, where they required more than three hundred staff/seminar rooms, here no two rooms seemed to be of the same size or function. The planning programme had produced something very unique in that respect, and we tried to recognize this complication in the seemingly random positioning and size of windows. Which appearance, I thought, had to be counterbalanced by the completely different appearance of the entrance.

MD: I've been through the building, including all the service zones, and it's certainly impeccably planned. The private realm seems very well served from the planning and the conceptual points of view, but I do have concerns about the relationship of the institution to the public realm. I think the decision to put the staff/teaching rooms on the outside, so that people in the offices overlook the street, rather than the courtyard space, created a problem.

JS: It was our feeling that these rooms should have a view of the street and an involvement with campus activities around the building. On the other side they would have overlooked the service yard — which might have been rather insensitive, especially as the galleries could not have windows. Maybe I prefer doing the obvious and then designing a way out of the problems it creates. So the galleries became wrapped by the offices and were not exposed to the street. They rely on the interior and the staircase for their presence, which relates to the problem of where to put the public entrance. The notion of having the entrance face forwards onto the back of the fire station always seemed a bit crazy to me. There were really only two possibilities: either on Gund corner looking towards Memorial Hall, or the other corner looking towards the Yard and the Fogg, which we chose. An entrance by Gund Hall would have been too far from the Fogg and in the wrong direction for the centre of Harvard. Then, having concealed the museum behind a wall of academic rooms, we had to announce on a short elevation that, within, this was a public museum.

MD: For me the most beautiful façade is on the inside facing the service yard, the one with the galleries and the protruding box for the little Asian rock garden. That wall facing the apartment houses is a tough, taut, and beautiful design.

JS: But it's a straight... one might almost say... fifties' functional façade. It's almost like Walter Gropius at that point.

MD: Oh, I don't agree; to me it's not just a simple wall. It actually has a presence as a wall and as a façade; it's both abstract and representational. However, I do find the abstraction of the two street elevations a bit at odds with the urban role of the building. At Rice University, and in the German museums — both at Düsseldorf and at Stuttgart — you had a certain flexibility — "room to maneuver". Façade issues were not critical. With the Sackler the constraints of programme and site meant the buildable envelope had to be filled, thus defining and enclosing the street. Didn't this demand a representational façade, not an abstract elevation?

JS: I think one sets up certain stresses which have then to be corrected. There's a danger in throwing the gestures so far apart, as it depends on one's skill in bringing them back together again. In this building, we hope it is achieved by the experience of the entrance hall and staircase; it's essential to enter, otherwise the building may not be entirely understood. I think the entrance façade is respectful to the Fogg (and to Harvard) and I think the Cambridge Street elevation is supportive of Gund. All the movement of Gund Hall is horizontal, and I think our elevation to Cambridge Street makes a stop-end to this movement, giving the architecture school an urban stability it previously didn't have.

MD: There is an interesting phenomenon on the Harvard campus *vis-a-vis* the use of brick. To the best of my knowledge there have been three cases where the material conventions of the Yard have been interrupted or violated. The first was Bulfinch's University Hall, a grey stone building built in contrast to the brick buildings that existed because it was opposite the main gate. The next was Richardson's Sever Hall, which is a very beautiful, odd, and almost perverse building on the outside. He built it in brick even though the other buildings it the time were in grey stone — the old chapel and library. The logical thing would have been to make a stone building so that there would have been a brick

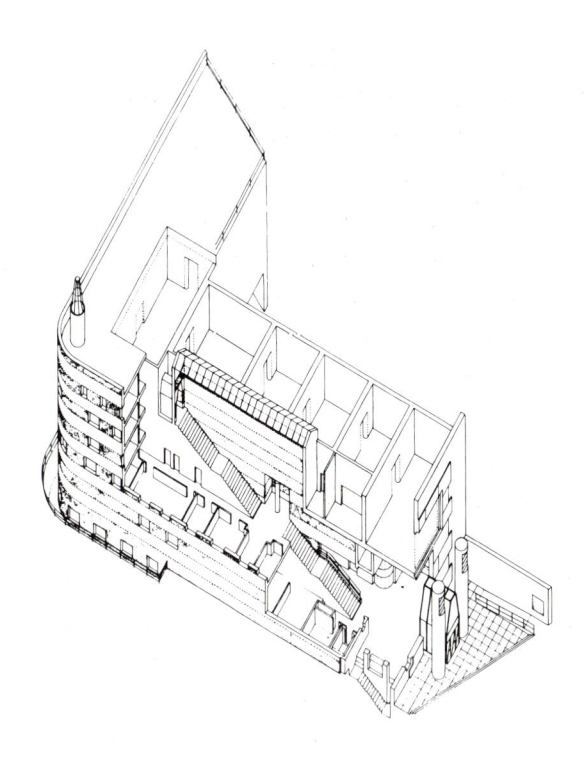

Cambridge, Massachusetts, Arthur M. Sackler Museum (with Michael Wilford), 1979–84, axonometric view and internal distribution

quad and a stone quad. But Richardson went against the grain and made a different kind of building. Then, when the chapel and library were rebuilt, they were built in red brick — to unify the whole. The next violation of convention (both type and material) was the Carpenter Centre for the Visual Arts designed by Le Corbusier. He did not want to make a brick building, but rather to relate back to the idea of a unique building such as University Hall. Your building seems to be the fourth in this series of "violations". It is unique not only in its abstraction but also in the materials, and the colour of its materials.

JS: We could have tried for a balancing act either side of the Fogg, with Carpenter Centre on its right in concrete, and the Sackler on the left also in concrete — two modern concrete pavilions either side of a Georgian brick Fogg. Corbusier was able to make a pavilion of Carpenter Centre but that was never likely with the Sackler due to programme requirements and site limitations. Furthermore, Gund Hall is in concrete, and if we had also built in concrete, it might have overwhelmed the character of the street, changing Quincy Street from a brick promenade into a concrete alley. My greatest respect is for Sever Hall and I would have preferred the horizontal bands of the Sackler to have the hard metallic resonance of Sever, but we just couldn't get those bricks or have them made within the budget constraints.

MD: What about the stripes going around the corner, not the stripes themselves, but the actual corner? Why did you leave the building as a continuous façade, not articulating the two sides?

JS: Well, the speedy corner is meant as a deference in passing to Memorial Hall. With a small building you can't play all the stops out at the same time. Instead of trying to be everywhere original, it's necessary to have neutral areas offsetting the unique and particular, to have both high pitches and low notes.

MD: We know that the programme required the building to fill the site envelope. Is this why the steps go down into the entrance rather than up?

JS: Maybe it's like stepping into an archaeological dig; here the up flight of steps associated with a monumental building is reversed. Lately I have begun to feel it's equally monumental to go down as to go up. But the functional answer is that we wanted the bridge overhead to connect the Sackler and Fogg galleries at the same floor level, but then when the required programme was fitted underneath, the entrance level was more into the ground than out of it.

MD: We didn't talk earlier about what the façade represents.

JS: Well, there's a big cleft or opening, an entrance; or there's a head with a face, a visage overlooking the campus. Maybe it has a slightly — I hate to say it — eastern or antique gaze, ambiguous as to its origin, not exactly a Western face. Perhaps I was trying to make a face which was, shall I say, not British.

London, enlargement of Tate Gallery (with Michael Wilford), 1985, central court

Stirling Stuff. Conversation with Sunand Prasad and Satish Grover

Humanistic Considerations

Sunand Prasad: Talking about the project for Dorman Long[1] in 1969, you said that, "as buildings get larger and more complicated, the structural content in architecture is likely to increase." You went on to say that, "however, it will be even more necessary for architects not to rely merely on the question of technique for an architectural solution. Humanistic considerations should remain the primary logic on which the design evolves." Do you still hold to that?

James Stirling: Yes, very much. I think the comment was made in the context of the then developing type of modern architecture which has since been called "hi-tech" in European and English circles. While we have done buildings with technological aspects which you can call formal (like the Dorman Long project), I was stating a reservation that if an architecture becomes entirely expressive of technology — structure, plumbing and servicing — then it is really more like industrial design than a humanist architecture. What I was really saying was, "beware of hi-tech!" And even though Dorman Long itself was in a sense a kind of hi tech building, it was not as extravagant as hi-tech has since become.

Published in Architecture and Design *(New Delhi), No. 5, July-August 1987.*

[1] Dorman Long Headquarters (1965) are England's largest producers of rolled steel columns and beams. The headquarters site has steel mills at one end and "is surrounded by the symbols of heavy industry — slag mountains, cooling towers, flaming chimneys, etc." The building is 14-storeys high and almost 1.000 feet long.

SP: What exactly did you mean by humanistic considerations?

JS: The expression of the building should be related to what the building is all about — its major spaces, how they relate to each other, the way people enter the building, how they move through it and how they use the building. Now hi-tech solutions are often expressive of structure and services, not really of the people within, and how they relate to the types of spaces within.

SP: What is the method by which such expression is conveyed? On the one hand the word "hi-tech" denotes actual surface and texture, whereas humanistic considerations, on the other hand, denote organization.

JS: That's right. If you look at the Stuttgart Museum[2], it is an assemblage of recognizable elements: a public footpath that goes through the building, a central garden, the entrance hall which is expressed as a huge bay window, the galleries which have a kind of linear wall-like quality to them. In other words, the total building is made up of recognizable functional spaces even as perceived from the exterior.

SP: Bits of the actual programme...

JS: That's right! Our reliance on the actual programme is not in any way on structure or techique. Externally, for example, the Staatsgalerie has some sentimental touches, but it has no basic reliance on structure or technique.

SP: That's a nice way of putting it: "sentimental touches".

JS: Well, they're meant to be little references to what I would consider to be the past of hi-tech.

SP: One very sentimental and poignant building to me is

[2] Staatsgalerie, New Building and Chamber Theatre (1977–83) in Stuttgart, Germany. The project designed by Stirling and Michael Wilford was won in a limited competition.

the Olivetti Training School at Haslemere[3], where you have the two ramps and flared gallery, and in between there's a little fragment of a balustrade; like a balustrade which has been sawn off.

JS: Well, you've got to chop down hi-tech — not let it get too important. And perhaps the comment I made about the Dorman Long project was because I was feeling a little bit guilty about it... getting a little bit worried that perhaps I'd gone too far in that direction!

SP: You were asked to, in that project, weren't you?

JS: Yes, we were. The clients wanted an expression of the main product which is steel beams and girders. Of course it's really a repetitive office space building, a boring programme, with the one idea of expressing their own structural elements. They built the Sydney Harbour bridge too, as well as many other important civil engineering structures. So that's why we used the idea of the externalized frame, which I think has become something of a *cliché* since then.

Satish Grover: When you talk about humanism, you refer to the kinds of functions that take place within the building. Is that enough to define humanism, or is there also a contemporary context to humanism that you are searching for?

JS: I think it's essential to make a building that's both familiar and striking to the public. The public at large are not greatly knowledgeable about the modern movement, particularly in England. And when they encounter a new piece of architecture, they look for things that they can identify with, which they find familiar, and so enjoy. Unless the public is enjoying the building, I think there's something not quite right. On the other hand, some buildings are public buildings and some are not. For example, the architecture of a re-

[3] Olivetti Training School, Haslemere, Surrey (1969–72), is sited in the 42-acre wooded grounds of an Edwardian estate. The country house has been converted into a residence for trainees. The new building provides classrooms and a multispace for teaching and social interaction. Classroom wings are connected to the old house by a glass enclosed link.

search centre would have to allow for a wired fence around it and the public would not come into contact with the building. That's a different issue. But when you are the architect of a building, like a museum or a gallery or the Indira Gandhi National Centre for Art, then the clientele for that building is the public.

SP: Would you include university buildings in this?

JS: Oh yes, I would in a way, but they're half and half.

SP: There is a reason for asking that, because there seems to be a change in your position. There's the Stirling that we knew up to the mid-seventies, from the red brick buildings, the engineering brick buildings, and maybe Dorman Long, and then there were the German projects with very important antecedents, like the little St. Andrews scheme[4] or the Derby scheme,[5] and that seems to be a new period, a significant period.

JS: A lot of people say there's been a change, but I would say that if you were to look back to before the university buildings, you would find projects for housing — both low-cost and housing for rich people — which were quite vernacular in their expression; perhaps grander, in the case of rich people. In other words, the expression is always relevant to what the building is about. And I think the university buildings — Leicester, Cambridge, Oxford[6] — were a period I went through, and so they have a similarity to each other.

SP: Do they stand the test that people should be able to recognize elements?

JS: I hope so. The Engineering Building at Leicester, if you look at its parts, is expressive of its usages — the ramps leading into the entrances, and the places where people go up

[4] Arts Centre, St. Andrews University (1971) designed with Michael Wilford. Housed in St. Katherine's, an 18th-century house in the centre of town which was to be preserved, the additions include an art gallery, theatre workshop, a reading room, a seminar room and a studio space for painting and sculpture. Stirling had also designed a residential expansion scheme for St. Andrews (1964–68).

[5] Derby Civic Centre (1970). The architect's intention was to re-establish the market square, the Medieval centre of Derby as the focal point of town. The plan includes re-siting of the Assembly Hall façade, a public arena, an auditorium, a shopping arcade, art gallery, offices, etc.

[6] Leicester University Engineering Building (1959–63), designed with James Gowan. Owing to the smallness of the site, the University was allowed, for the first time, to build upwards beyond three storeys. The building overlooks the municipal park. The building expresses a vertical ensemble of lecture theatres, workshops, office and laboratory towers, staircase shafts, and

and down. There is a kind of descriptive flow of the students and people through the building.

SP: I don't think you can argue that it's accessible to the man in the street, the public, as opposed to the people who have cultivated a taste for the modern movement. Do you think that people relate to it in the way they might relate to the Staatsgalerie?

JS: Like the other two university buildings, Leicester is a semi-public building, inasmuch as sometimes these have been so inundated by visitors, that a sign had to be put up, saying, "don't come in unless you have a right to be here!" And at Oxford the same thing happened. But it was somehow always meant by me, that the buildings should be an expression of a semi-public nature. There's a difference between that and buildings of a completely public nature.

Use of the Vernacular

SG: You've used one word which is creating a great deal of debate in India today — vernacular — which has different interpretations. What did *you* mean by it?

JS: I used it with reference to the English situation. Vernacular buildings were built right through the medieval period, but particularly in the nineteenth century. They were very often anonymous, and were either village houses or warehouse buildings or early industrial buildings. There may not even have been an architect. Their design was always very expressive of their function and scale-wise they fitted into the context for which they were created. They were always built of local materials, never by sophisticated means, and all this gave them a kind of "fitting-in-ness" to their location, which is what makes vernacular buildings always very comfortable.

a large water tank to be supported 100 feet above the ground. Churchill College (1958), and the History Faculty Building (1964), also with James Gowan, are Stirling's well-known Cambridge University projects. The former comprises a group of buildings for a residential college creating an internal atmosphere of privacy and enclosure. The latter provides multi-directional approaches to the History Faculty. Four entrances have been provided to allow for cross-campus circulation. Queens College (1966–71) at Oxford is a students' hostel of single-room apartments. The two-faced site is adapted to an asphalted municipal car park on one side, and a landscape of river, trees, meadows, and the towers of Oxford on the other.

229

SG: Is there any justification for an architect today consciously making an attempt to be vernacular?

JS: I think if he understands what vernacular buildings are, and how they came about, there's no reason why he shouldn't...

SG: Have you any specific projects in which you actually attempted to do that?

JS: It could be said that nearly all our projects are vernacular, though there are exceptions, like the Olivetti Training School which is made of plastic. You could actually say that the Staatsgalerie was vernacular in its relationship to other historic museums in Germany in the context of Stuttgart, the materials used and so on. You might say it had a kind of vernacular relationship to the Neo-classical buildings which abound in that part of Germany. Again, you might say that the projects we did for village schemes in England were greatly influenced by the traditional English village.

SG: In that context how would you defend yourself against the insinuation of being Fascist which many people have implied, particularly after your German projects?

JS: Oh yes, the Germans particularly have implied this — in fact only the Germans!

SG: Well, how do you relate this Fascism to the vernacular, to humanism — can they all be put together?

JS: Fascism is a German label really. Because of their recent history, the Germans are now so democratic that they react violently to anything that has the slightest association with recent history. But, of course, this is stupidity — it's like throwing a baby out with the bath water. Architects have always used stone and used classical proportions in forms, and produced great architecture with it. It's particularly the older generation of German architects who can't accommodate these references now, but all the younger German architects I know, don't have this problem.

History

SP: Do you think that there is a fundamentally new sensibility regarding history and the critique of the modern movement, not only in your work, but also at large?

JS: Yes, I think so, mainly as a reaction to the first half of this century.

SG: How would you place yourself in relationship to people like Venturi and Michael Graves?

JS: I don't think you can put Venturi and Michael Graves together, but there is a connection inasmuch as both of them have always been very interested in history. Both have written about it and it is evident in their work. I could be critical and say that it's not always used successfully in their projects, but I must say I'm glad to be in their company because these are architects with an awareness and knowledge of history which they try to utilize. There are some architects who take it much too far — just freak out on pastiche — and I would not like to be associated with that.

SP: So the study of history is important to you?

JS: Always has been. Fortunately, when I was at architectural school, I had teachers like Colin Rowe who taught us the parallels between modern and historic architecture. That was my education. I never had the Bauhaus type of education.

SP: Whereas the same cannot be said of the so-called postmodern architects?

JS: I don't know. I think this comparative study of contemporary architecture with history and tradition was almost invented by Colin Rowe. There were others also, like Vincent Scully at Yale. Today, there is a far greater understanding of the relationship between modern architecture and history than there was in the Bauhaus period or the early years after the war.

SG: In the history of Indian architecture, there are very few examples of so-called secular architecture because of our historic traditions in which secular architecture was always impermanent in relation to religious architecture. Fifteen years ago, the study of history concentrated on temples, mosques, etc., and these are the buildings which have survived. When you talk of relating aspects of history to the contemporary situation, how would you deal with this problem?

JS: In India, particularly, there's a lot to be learnt from the temples and tombs and so on, from their architectonic forms and from the sheer quality of their buildings — scale, proportion, materials — India's very rich in that. I had a look at three tombs in Srinagar recently which are made of granite; I think they're very simple in their boldness of form and sparseness of ornament. I don't see too much difference in the way they were trying to handle surfaces in those tombs to the way in which we were trying to handle surfaces in Stuttgart — surface and corners and composition and basic relationships of vertical/horizontal forms; one of the tombs was in a courtyard which had a purely geometric square surrounded by out-buildings.

SP: As a counterbalance to the lack of very old secular architecture, is it not true that in Indian history, traditions were alive until much more recently than in the West. (Fergusson wrote only about 100 years ago that the very principles by which Greek and Roman architects practised still existed here where craftsmen and master masons worked closely together.) In our cities there are buried *havelis* which may only be sixty to seventy years old, but these legitimately are of as great historical importance as anything older; not only *havelis*, there are *dharamsalas*, workshops, markets — what I'm saying is that we do have the material, waiting to be discovered.

The City and Architecture

SP: This business about the return of history, in a way also implies a re-embrace of the city, an acknowledgement of the urban space which a large section of the modern movement had really lost.

JS: Not so much a re-embrace, more a nostalgia. In Europe it's a nostalgia for the cities, because one realized that between the bombs and the reconstruction we had destroyed them to a large extent. And while bombs were a human frailty, reconstruction was a human error of equal dimension, although of quite a different motivation. One was destructive and the other was meant to be constructive, and both have contributed to the decline of very great cities, decline so incredible that it totally destroyed them. Of course, we've had a tremendous growth in preservation societies, but they've come too late. They should have been operating full belt when the post-war reconstruction was taking place. When instead, the combination of politicians and town planners resulted in the creation of urban motorways which cut right through the cities; when terrace housing was destroyed and tower blocks built instead. That was the time when the preservation societies should have been around, not now. I hope you don't make this same mistake. While I was up at Srinagar, I was alarmed at the suburbanization of the lake. If it goes on, in another few years you're going to lose a colossal landscape element; it will be a disaster.

SP: Is it not a tragedy that town planning and architecture are regarded as two separate hermetic entities nowadays?

JS: Yes. It has been a disaster, particularly in England where town planning came into existence as a goodwill notion in the post-war era. What happened was that we trained a whole lot of town planners who immediately became employed by the central or state local authorities almost without exception, and as such, became their handmaidens. They put into effect the local politician's desire for progress, and hence took us down the paths of urban motorways and tower blocks, and then, by sending the industry out there, they initiated the process of disintegration of the unity of the city. The whole town planning profession should be shot dead to a man! I think architects should have been made responsible for the putting together of cities. You see, I actually have done buildings in cities under the auspices I'm criticizing, but it always seems to me that the local politicians and town planners have deemed that on this plot of land such and such will be achieved with buildings not more than so many storeys high, with a matrix of a two or three bedrooms, one unit ratio. It all comes down to you as a mathematical equation. In England it's always been political — every ruling political party wants to say they've built up more houses than the previous government. And that being the basis of both housing and school buildings, both have suffered enormously from this political game.

SG: Charles Correa talks of the concept of disaggregating the numbers. At the same time, even by doing this he cannot produce the quantum that is needed. He's not really able to spell out a different approach to building.

JS: At least Correa is making warning sounds about the so-called rational way of doing things. Though I don't think the quality of urbanization of the environment has anything to do with numbers. I'm not sure, however, if the instincts of architects would not produce better results than the logistics of the other profession. Though I do think we architects should come out better by virtue of our design solutions for particular environments.

SG: Does the same conflict regarding leadership exist between architects and engineers in England, as it does here in India?

JS: The lead person has always been the client whether he's in the form of a public authority or a developer.

SG: Through whom does the client lead — through the engineer or through the architect, because the client himself could be a layman?

JS: Oh no, the client is never a layman. He is always an expert and is aided and abetted in the case of the local authority by a team of experts. And if he is a developer who is also a person with a lot of expertise and a single-minded view point, he too is aided by other experts.

SG: So the client in England has always been able to mobilize enough support and there isn't this conflict between the architect and the engineer, unlike India where we've been left this legacy by the British?

JS: No, this is not the case in England, though, of course, the problem is to get a developer or client who is enlightened and has belief in architecture, and these are very rare anywhere in the world. I hope their numbers will grow.

SG: Is that why you're building so much outside England?
JS: Probably.

SP: Would you like to be building in India?
JS: I would love to.

On India and the Role of Symbolism

SG: Do you agree that the volume of work being done in India today is incomparable to any other time or any other place?

JS: I really do confess that I'm not knowledgeable. The Indian architects who come to England are always the same and I do know three or four of them well — but beyond them I don't really know the work of the less internationally reputed Indian architects who are probably doing the vast majority of the new building works. I have a feel of the work being done here, which has to do with taste. But there's such an exuberance in India. All human life is here. I sometimes feel it's a little bit out of control. And the quality of architectural taste suffers in trying to accommodate this difficult situation (but that's a view from the West). This is particularly so with contemporary architecture, which is often exuberant but is not contained within the parameters that historical architecture in India was.

That's why I used the word *taste*, which is a funny word, but it connotes a kind of subconscious quality, which I'm not sure is here. What you need in architecture is refined thought, hard intellect and two or three other things to produce quality.

SP: Alberti!

JS: Yes, this sounds like Alberti. I find that exuberance in India is so bubbling that it's not very concerned with quality.

SG: So you are saying that there's a certain kind of maturity that we have yet to achieve in this framework of contemporary architecture and that we haven't absorbed enough of history to achieve this?

JS: Possibly. It's patronizing of me, but that might be a way of saying that there is a kind of effervescence here which is not exactly mature — like the difference between champagne and soda!

SP: How did you prepare yourself for judging the IGNCA [Indira Ghandi National Centre for the Arts] competition?

JS: I read the programme three or four times. It must have been quite a feat for the people who put it all together. I read it and realized what a huge problematical task it was and I was looking for a very high architectural solution. I think the project gives an awful lot of emphasis to social interactions (because all human life is here, in all aspects) and it also, in a way, underlines a bureaucratic aspect of India which sometimes worries me. One seems to be compiling archive upon archive, and centre upon centre, and then needing someone on top of that to organize it all. So I think the bureaucratic, the social, the exuberant and the mystical aspects of India are very well covered in that document, but I'm not so sure about the architectural aspects.

SG: May I add one other word, symbolism. In Indian architecture it has always been a more important objective than the architecture itself. And in the brief for the IGNCA, symbolism is also mentioned. How important a role does this play in Western architecture?

JS: Yes, the IGNCA does underline that aspect as important, and no doubt that I can find lots of symbolism in historic Indian architecture as well as in Western architecture.

There are certain commonalities between Indian and Western architectures which have to do with ordinary things like doors, windows, roofs, as well as ornamentation, decoration, proportion and so on.

Architectural Education

SG: One of your books said you're a man who wants to get on with the work rather than spend time in teaching or being too theoretical.

JS: Well, I have taught, you know. I taught for a long time in America, and I still do teach in Germany. I've always combined teaching with practice, though I have never been a full-time academic... I've always been a visiting teacher.

SP: What do you think they should teach in schools of architecture?

JS: Well, I'm biased. I think they should teach history of architecture — an understanding of how cities evolve through historical precedent — and this includes the modern movement. I don't think they should teach through engineering; I don't think they should teach that to make a design you have to understand structure and economics in combination, and perhaps also the logistics of the functional programme and say that from this the solution will emerge. Structure and economics should be put in the background.

SP: What about subjects like sociology?

JS: In England I would not teach sociology. I'm not so sure about the situation in India. Sociology in England is all around you — the way you live, the way you perceive people.

On His Own Work

SG: Mr. Stirling, you have been described as being somewhat like a magician, who pulls something new out of the hat all the time; in every project there's a surprise. Is that intentional, or is it because you get bored with yourself?

JS: Yes, one does get bored. There's a kind of myth in the twentieth century that an architect should go on repeating himself till he's dead. But I think that's a fallacy. Mies van der Rohe did this very elegantly and Walter Gropius did it not so interestingly. In times prior to the twentieth century it was not considered that an architect should repeat himself throughout his life. What happened in the first half of the twentieth century was therefore rather unique in that sense, and now, of course, we have a kind of over-the-shoulder view of that period. I would claim to be going back to a more traditional architect's point of view, which is that architects evolve and change as they grow older. They have phases, and Lutyens, of course, had several phases. Frank Lloyd Wright certainly had many periods of expression.

SG: But I thought Frank Lloyd Wright belonged to the same family as Gropius...

JS: Not really. I would say earlier. He was really a nineteenth-century architect. He had the spirit of that period and he hadn't got into the machine-age trap.

SG: Apart from your magician-like quality, I find that the one other consistency in your work is the very crisp detailing. Is that a common British trait?

JS: I wouldn't say that was true in my case. Other people like Norman Forster and Richard Rogers are much more meticulous in their detailing than I am. I think in a building, certain parts should be meticulously detailed; perhaps the part where you enter the building, or where interaction with the public is involved. I think there ought to be a gradation between highly thought out and detailed spaces, to spaces which are very unthought out and not so detailed, because by so doing, you are trying to express the importance and non-importance of the different parts.

SG: How would you define these in Leicester College?

JS: The tower was well articulated as a tower: in it were the academic rooms, the major lecture theatres and the entrances. The workshop areas behind — which I regard as secondary — came under the same roof which goes front to back, and so the space inside gets subdivided; so you have a very articulated place and a very unplanned or unarticulated place, under the same roof.

SP: Do you have some favourite projects of your own?

JS: Well, it's always the most recent project... The Turner Museum at the Tate Gallery is just finishing. [The Clore Gallery housing the Tate Gallery's collection of J.M.W. Turner's work was opened on 1 April, 1987.] I also have the Cornell Art Centre under construction in America. The Tate Gallery is based on a somewhat similar kind of solution as the Staatsgalerie. The latter is an extension to an old museum built around 1829. This old museum has a certain U-shaped form, and it is frontalized on to the avenue which has since degenerated into an *autobahn*. It also has a symmetry. The extension is about twice the size of the old building. I essentially wanted to keep to the same symmetry and U-shaped form, but certain dimensions were added to the building. I thought that a public thoroughway across the building site would be socially advantageous. So we exploited that by making a circular garden through which one could walk. The materials of the new building are similar to those of the old — sandstone, stucco — and the height of the new building is exactly the same as that of the old. One has also been very influenced by the surrounding context, not only of the original gallery but also of some of the buildings on the other side of the town, even if the reference has been more intellectually contextual, as in the administration building which stands on the highest part of the site. This corresponds exactly with a hill on the other side of the city, on which the Weissenhof[7] housing project was built in the thirties, and which includes buildings by Corbusier, Mies van der Rohe and Scharounn. The administration building has a kind of visual reference to the Weissenhof which you can actually see from the top of it. The problem with the Tate Gallery lay in the fact that the existing gallery is a monumental Edwardian building facing the river with a monumental flight of steps in the foreground, unlike the Staatsgalerie building which is U-shaped and had the idea of a garden in its forecourt even though it was not very well developed. When we came to making the addition to the Tate, we withdrew from trying to make a parallel at all, and decided instead to make a wing behind the corner of the existing Tate and tucked it behind a lodge which had been preserved. Even the approach to it is through a sunken garden, and to get into this new building you go down, about one metre — exactly the reverse of the steps going up to the existing building. The existing Tate is equally contextually influential but in a reverse way. Now why does one do these things? One has to make value judgements about what one is doing. In the case of the Staatsgalerie, one is in a sense replicating the form of the original gallery. In the case of the Clore, the extension to the Tate, one was actually producing something which was the reverse of replicating.

SG: So there's a lot of intellectual exercise involved?
JS: With me no... I think it's largely intuitive. I go through

[7] The Weissenhof-siedlung at Stuttgart was a showpiece collection of 33 houses designed by outstanding modern architects from Behrens to Le Corbusier.

241

a thought process and make doodles of different possibilities. Then, when one begins to understand what one is actually aiming for, one begins to intellectualize about it. It's a combination of what's coming out of the ends of my fingers and what I'm thinking of at the same time. I generally do that in office, sometimes at home, sometimes in aeroplanes. First I do that alone, then I talk to people about it and ask them to take the concepts and continue with the process — it becomes interactive.

SP: Does the idea that the business of thinking about buildings and actually making them be united under one head engage you at all? There was a very different organization of the building activity in the periods of architecture we admire so much, from what it is today.
JS: I don't think I've ever thought it possible that the architect can actually go and physically help make buildings.

SP: You say that you're going back to the more traditional view of the architect; in those times I think there was a much closer involvement between designing and making buildings — people who built them often did a lot of the detailing as well.
JS: I don't think that was so in the Classical or Neo-classical or Victorian times. It was so in Medieval times certainly.

SP: Take Alberti or Michelangelo — they certainly knew about it: the geometries of detailing, the designs and the moulding that they used were something perfectly understood by the craftsmen.
JS: That's right. Now that you put the question that way, one does regret that today the craftsmen don't understand what you are aiming at. That's partly where the change lies

from Medieval or even Classical times... when you see the drawings which were prepared by the architect for the builders to make, you realize that architects had a wonderful time; they prepared some beautiful drawings of elevations, etc., and from these drawings the building could be achieved. That's not possible any longer.

SG: Is there any one architect, contemporary or otherwise, that you can point out as being a person you wholeheartedly admire?

JS: There may be several: Le Corbusier, for one, who built several buildings in this country, and you mentioned Michael Graves and Venturi, though I have some reservations about them. I would also mention Isozaki and Fumihiko Maki. I admire the work of all these people. About Corbusier, it's a bit like what you said about me (and I'm very flattered by that), that in every project of his you can find something new, sparkling and different. In a way, I like all periods of architecture, but at different times one has liked different periods. When we were doing the Clore Gallery I was somehow very interested in the idea of garden architecture; architecture which was really background, and architecture which was essentially a wall. I was wanting to be deferential to the existing Tate and not destroy its symmetry, or compete with its entrance. So I got very interested in a garden wall, a traditional wall — the kind you find in English Edwardian buildings or in the work of people like Ashbee... I think it's something to do with the project you're working on; the projects as they start to evolve between your fingers and your head, and begin to suggest a kind of parallel in history. You then start looking at those things in history to see what they can tell you about what you're trying to produce.

*London, Clore Gallery,
Turner Collection,
Tate Gallery
(with Michael Wilford),
1980–86, axonometric
from below of a detail
of the garden front*

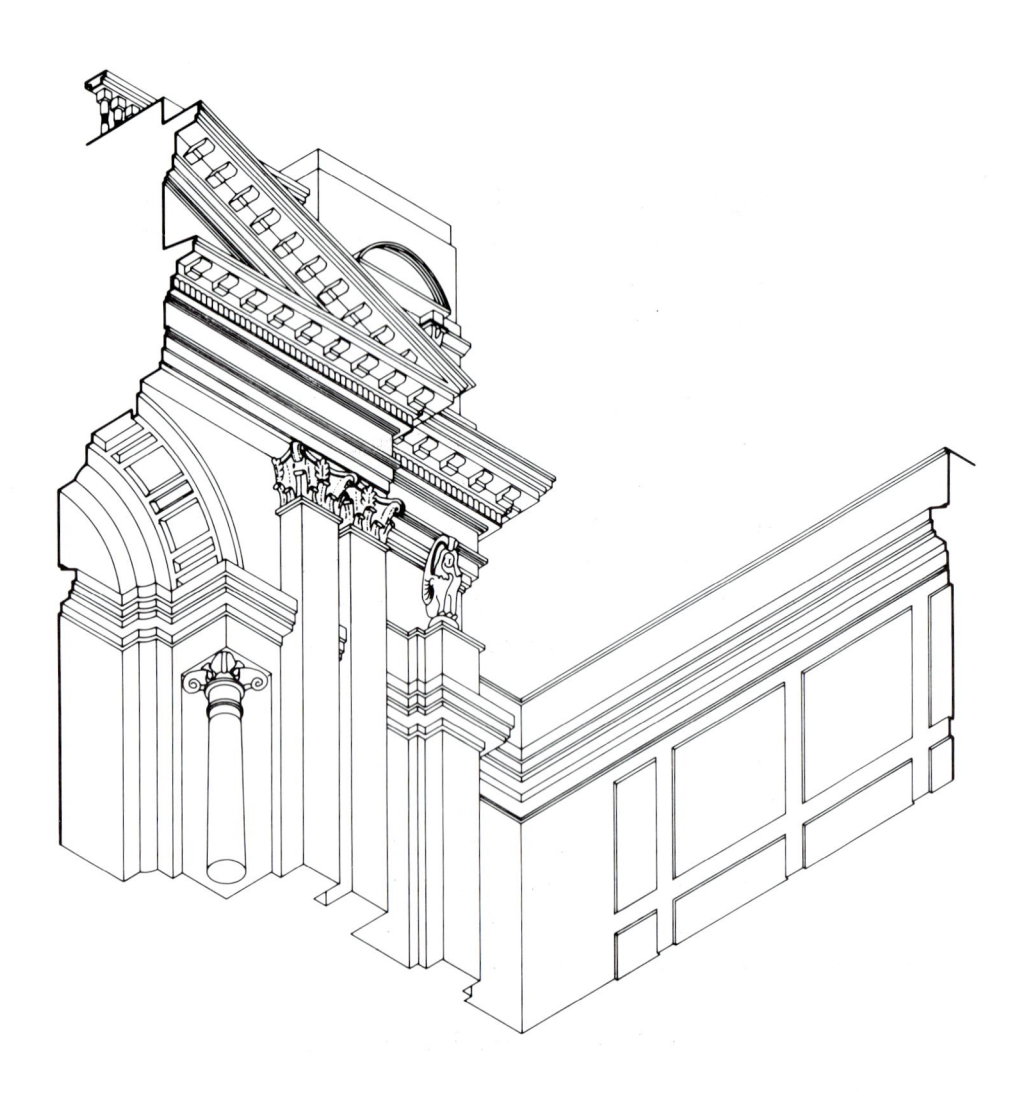

The Clore Gallery.
Interview with Charles Jencks

Charles Jencks: The Clore Gallery will be unique as your building is some kind of memorial to J.M.W. Turner. The gallery spaces are contextualism to him whereas the outside is a quixotic contextualism to things around it — so you have two different contextualisms.

James Stirling: I would hope there were more than two. As you come through the Entrance Hall and up to the galleries the interior may have a slightly sepulchral atmosphere. The exterior relates to the gardens in front of the Tate and there are service elevations to the back which are very different in character. There are three or four different types of elevations on this small building, and each makes specific response to its context.

CJ: What about Turner's work?

JS: I like late Romantic pictures — painters like C. D. Friedrich in Germany and Turner in England — the transition between Neo-classicism and Romanticism. I think transitional periods are rather exotic, more so than periods which have settled down and become rather fixed in their output.

CJ: You were asked to provide a traditional background to his paintings.

Published in A+U, *September 1987*

[1] The principle of reflecting indirect daylight into gallery rooms was first used by us at the Sackler Museum, 1979–84 (extension to the Fogg Museum — Harvard University) where also it was intended to use louvres to balance daylight across the room. The louvres however were omitted when the differing effects of morning and afternoon light were observed by the curators. The Sackler contains mainly objects (i.e. antique sculpture, large Chinese jades) and the lighting of them from different directions was, in a teaching museum, considered an asset. Steensen, Varming and Mulcahy — the services consultants at the Clore Gallery, were involved in transforming the rather elementary scheme for the Fogg into the sophisticated solution for the Clore, particularly with their proposals for curved light scoops and the precise calculation of light levels and the mechanics and controls of the louvring system to achieve a balance of daylighting. The stepped form of ceilings was also used at the Sackler, though here they did not integrate the artificial lighting as do the soffits at the Clore. JS

JS: We created a neutral wall zone, on which the paintings are hung. At the top of this picture zone there is a non functional picture rail, a division between the picture wall and the angled ceiling above which goes on upwards, becoming a light scoop down which daylight is bounced onto the picture wall. The centre of rooms should be slightly darker than the walls and we hope this will be an ideal atmosphere for looking at pictures.[1]

CJ: And the light scoops allow you to have very nice sculptural shapes in the ceilings.

JS: Which may contribute to the feeling of a slightly mysterious light source, like Soane's interiors, where he reflects daylight down walls and you're not quite sure where it's coming from.

CJ: At the main gallery level you have nine different rooms which correspond to different phases of Turner's work, so there's the possibility of taking visitors through in some kind of sequence. But there's a paradox, because you have two entrances — so that you could enter through the end of his life...

JS: This paradox has existed in most of our galleries. At the Staatsgalerie we also made an extension to an existing building and it's turned out that most people now enter the old building through the new one. However it's unlikely to be the same with the Clore which, unlike the Staatsgalerie is small compared to the original building. Nevertheless, we have to plan for the public coming from both directions and this may present a problem for the curators as to how they hang their pictures.

CJ: Your room shapes are classical and axial, with a minor shift off axis in one room where you can have a view to the outside.

JS: That's because the bay window, where visitors can sit down with a view to the river, is central on the external wall and the shift is caused by relating two axes — the axis of the exterior and the axis of the opening into the gallery.

CJ: I see, perfectly logical, but it looks arbitrary.

JS: I'm not sure that, with nine rooms where door openings are all centrally placed, to have something which is shifted off axis isn't a relief. The same happens with the internal entrance from the Tate, it's also off axis though it's on the central axis of the room within the Tate.

CJ: Summerson made the remark that Soane would have enjoyed the deep slotted entrance space of your building and so would Soane's friend Turner. And he (Summerson) says it's all a bit mad like the Soane Museum. I think its funny madness comes in this illogical logic; what at first looks arbitrary turns out on further investigation to be so straightforward that you could call it a kind of wilful logic.

JS: It's the combination of logic and non logic; instead of trying to be consistent I prefer to have them exist side by side. I think Soane worked this way when he made a new house in an existing terrace, using all the constraints of that site in a very productive way. We have similar constraints of entrances and levels and appearances (of existing buildings) that produce a combination of logical/non logical solutions which I think are always interesting.

CJ: In a way it's very underplayed but it ends up looking odd because it fits into both the art and the urban context so rigorously; you provide in this little *tempietto* a kind of relief from the art. It's the one place you get away from art and from architecture and it ends in this prow-shape bay window which is repeated on another façade. Both seem to be exceptions to the logic and the understatement.

JS: They're both places where we're trying to bring visitors into sight of the gardens and the river. We would have liked more of these interfaces but it was a compromise with what the curators would accept. The form of these openings is sharp prowed and pointed; it's as if — with some difficulty — the interior space has penetrated to the exterior.

CJ: Breaking through the skin... I'll suppress the metaphor. The entrance hall which crowds enter through a cut-out pediment into a low room — at first low, which then explodes upwards with the staircase into a slot of space, reminds one of historical stairs such as the Scala Regia and lots of mannerist stairs which are very high and thin — it also reminds one of Le Corbusier. Going up these stairs you then turn and go along another eroded slot of space, so you go from low to extremely high back to low again and that sequence is very dynamic and full of contrasts.

JS: We wanted to exploit the promenade through the entrance hall as a prelude to the galleries and bring people through on a zig-zag path backwards and forwards across the central axis from the sunken garden. On entering you make a deflect left to the information desk, then you make a deflect right to go up the stairs, then you make a left to come back along the balcony towards the galleries, then you make a joggle in behind the arched window which brings you back onto the cross-axis of the entrance hall. You're also entering from light to darkness and then into light (the roof light) and then into darkness (the balcony) before finally getting to the galleries — it's also a contrasting sequence of light. So the

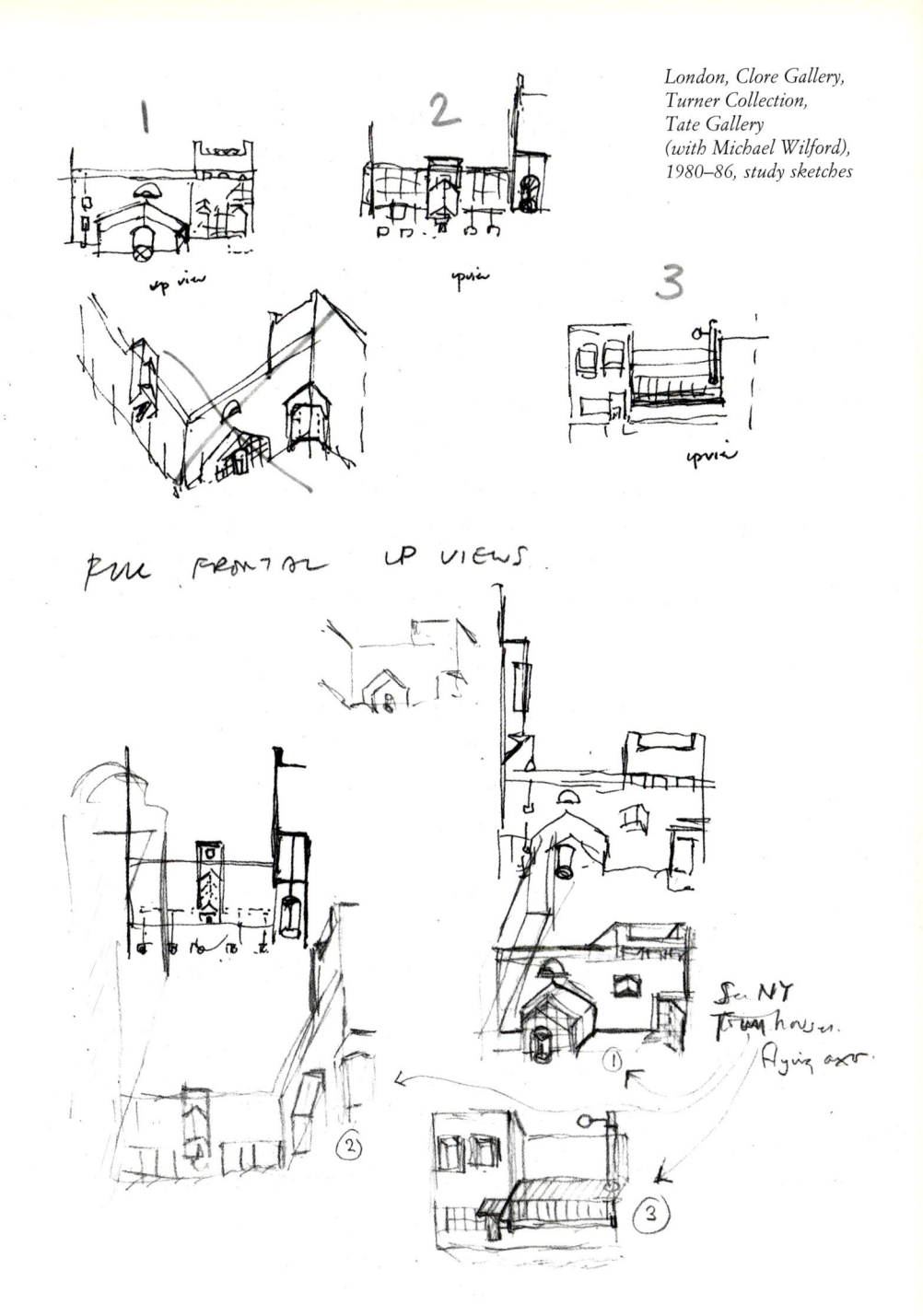

London, Clore Gallery,
Turner Collection,
Tate Gallery
(*with Michael Wilford*),
1980–86, study sketches

public are taking an extended walk through a relatively small space which should make for an interesting entrance sequence; or how with a small space to maximise the event.

CJ: Which is very traditional to Chinese gardens, they do precisely what you describe... because they believe the devil travels in straight lines, so they place a spirit wall behind the entrance so the devil can't get through, then they place zigzag bridges so that he can't travel in a straight line and whenever you have a tight small space they make it complex precisely for the reasons you say to lengthen the walk and make it more dynamic.

JS: At one point in our sequence the public are actually going in the wrong direction for the galleries. So, when they get to the top of the stair, there has to be a strong signal which tells them that the galleries lie in the opposite direction; you are signalled by the large arched opening that you have to return along the balcony to enter the galleries through the arch — except that you don't go through it, you sidestep in behind it. The arched opening is a message, but it's also not quite the normal way to use it.

CJ: It's a symbol of a door *à la* Venturi without even being a door. Is there any sequence of space historically that is similar?

JS: You mention the Scala Regia which does make a return on itself. It's got that long stretch and then instead of getting to a destination at the end (as you do with the Sackler) you have to make a return with another third of the trip to go.

CJ: Aside from the peach/apricot, pink handrails, turquoise/ultramarine, which are wonderfully dissonant, if you look at the surface articulations they're equally mannerist: all your triangles push up against horizontals and you erode your grid — your square order — off the wall and let it slide back to the balcony wall. In detail, colour and space it all reinforces mannerist notions of tension and contrast.

JS: Some of the architects in history I most admire must have been mannerist architects. Certainly it is intended that there are balances of symmetries and asymmetries as well as continuities and discontinuities. The gridding on the staircase wall confronts the visitor head on but isn't echoed symmetrically up the slot. One side is completely blank, an off white wall, which turns under and becomes the ceiling over the lower part of the hall. So the asymmetry in form is reinforced by the wall colouring. The gridding of the staircase wall is a reference to the panelling of the exterior where some walls are a combination of Portland stone and stucco.

CJ: What about the vexed question of colour, the dissonance in colours?

JS: There are two basic colours for non gallery interiors. One is called (I hate these commercial names) "Fragrance" and the other "Peach". They're an off white and a kind of... orangey beige. They occur in the entrance hall, the auditorium and the lounge, a suite of rooms which can be used in the evenings independent of the galleries (which may be closed) when there is a lecture or film show, etc. Drinks and cucumber sandwiches could be served in the lounge and people overflow into entrance hall. In the hall and some other places there are special colours — i.e. the turquoise/ultramarine lining of the arch, and the pink (illuminated) handrail. These vibrant colours are really trying to give you messages — this is the staircase you go up — follow the pink diagonal line; the outlining of the arch in turquoise/ultramarine is meant to increase the signal — that through this arch is where the galleries are.

CJ: So like at Stuttgart you use dissonant colours to indicate arrival and direction. But still, they could have been less acid and dayglo... Aren't they very "sixties"?
JS: You might say the arch colours are very "Regency" but I don't really associate colours with any particular period. Though I'm continually amazed that there are only eight basic colours in the spectrum and I have a problem as I tend to run out of colours.

CJ: I think you ought to read Adolph Loos again on ornament and crime — where he starts off on how different cultures don't see blue, and pink and purple because they don't have names for them.
JS: I see colours in terms of intensities and I believe there has to be a minimum of two. There are reduced colours, and there are colours which are stable and static and then there are colours which vibrate. According to overall combinations you get different messages.

CJ: So there is a philosophy which is reasonable. However, the particular choices may be a problem for some. Haven't you been through several here?
JS: The colours of "Peach" and "Fragrance" and turquoise/ultramarine were presented to the Trustees and accepted by them. I would have preferred to use made up (more subtle) non standard colours but cost and control would not allow.

CJ: I'm being the devil's advocate, partly as I like your colours on second glance — specially true of Stuttgart,

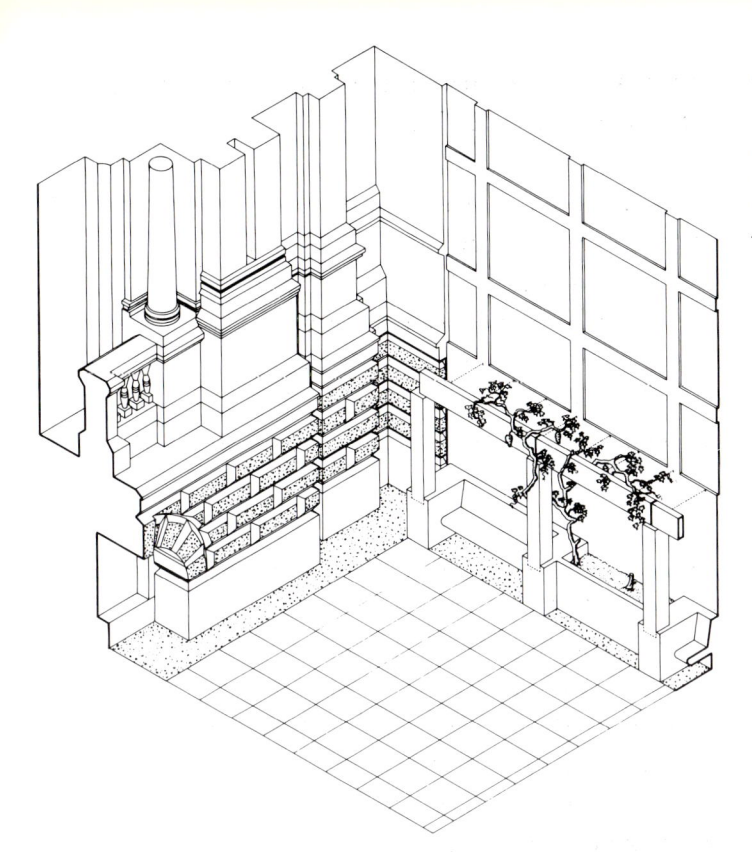

London, Clore Gallery, Turner Collection, Tate Gallery (with Michael Wilford), 1980–86, axonometric of a detail of the garden front

where I was shocked, and put off at first and it took me perhaps an hour to get used to them. After the second hour I was positively interested and after the third or fourth, I tried to take them away in my mind and I found the building dull without them. But I feel with the Clore there's going to be a period of shock and I think you can't deny it.

JS: It may take a year or so to settle down. Then I think it will be more acceptable and the building will have a certain identity and memory for the public and they will expect to see these colours when they come again.

CJ: Obviously architecture should stimulate and provoke at first and then achieve harmony afterwards. A slight provocation always is to be enjoyed and sought. I mean there are parts of the old Tate which simply put you to sleep.

JS: I think the public coming into the building might be somewhat startled but finally when they reach the galleries, all will be calm and bathed in diffused light. The mood will be very different and I think visitors will appreciate the changes as they come from outside, eventually through to the galleries where the paintings will take over and dominate the space.[2]

CJ: The brief said, "The Clore should express a sense of its own architectural identity although it will be bound to the Tate in certain ways." You were asked, in a sense, to contrast with the Tate. Some, traditionalists particularly, but also modernists, will feel that the building contrasts too much with the old Tate.

JS: I don't think so and the real situation was that we had to get the building through several types of approvals. I felt that deferences had to be made to the existing Tate, and connections, like stone courses and parapet heights, and materials like Portland stone had to be repeated. So the building comes out from the side of the Tate, turns round a corner and comes in behind the lodge — which I thought should be preserved as it maintains a symmetrical balance with a similar building on the other side of the Tate. But as the new building moves away from the Tate it becomes different and more eccentric and begins to express its own personality.

CJ: Well, I think it's a chameleon building fitting into several different environments which for me is very exciting and a new idea, taking contextualism to a new level. I mean you have joined up the parts, not on the edges where other ar-

---

[2] I think Mr. Turner would like his galleries at the Clore and understand why they are not a replica of his dark and overcrowded studio. He would appreciate that today's viewers are younger and more informal and would prefer galleries that are lighter and less claustrophobic — hopefully like his later paintings, more spatial, atmospheric and open. *JS*

chitects would have done it, but sometimes a quarter way down the façade and then you've overlapped them too. A classicist or a 19th-century eclectic architect would change style at the corners and make a front and a back. St. Pancras Station has a classic schizophrenia between railroad shed on one side and fantasy hotel on the other. That dualism, like the mews versus the classical terrace, is the normal way.

JS: I don't think you can make junctions on corners because if you do, the transition is too strong — it becomes a break... In the Clore, the transition from just Portland stone to stucco panels happens some way from the corner and, likewise, the change from brick panels to an entirely brick wall is away from the corners.

CJ: You've introduced a new rule here, which is very interesting but like the colours it will raise eyebrows and some will see it as wilful. You not only wrap the square brick panels round the outside corner but you slide the brick and stucco panels up at a diagonal. It's a new rule for contextualism. No one to my knowledge has ever slid up a building like that...

JS: I don't see it as wilful because to make a disjunction on a corner is too strong. What I want is disjunctions which are also transitions. It could make an interesting drawing to take the façades of the Clore and make a straightened out strip elevation, you wouldn't be able to see where the corners are.

CJ: Well, from a classical viewpoint you would be criticised for not making grammatical the lengths and proportions of this long sentence, which has been divided into parts that do not have obvious harmonic and scaled steps.

JS: Maybe it's a different way of thinking about façades: instead of being related to North-South orientations it's a continuous thing which can be bent at different places — not necessarily at a particular place.

CJ: Yes, but you know that comparison Leon Krier makes between the sentence "I love my mother" which has the regular grammar of subject, verb, predicate and is broken up into discrete parts and is opposed to the modernist version "Ilovemymother", which is a run-on sentence like a megastructure. Although your building is beautifully cut into discrete scaled parts, the parts are not necessarily grammatical in a traditional sense. I would argue you've got a new grammar here because, not only do you have three different languages, but you've added a fourth which is your own and that is the square neutral order, if you like, of stone pilaster and stucco or brick infills, which is a very interesting order because it allows you to relate to two different types of classicism without mimicking either. I wonder how you come to this new Esperanto or new order.

JS: Well, in regard to this particular context, we have the Portland stone Tate on one side and the brick lodge on the other and our garden façade is trying to mediate between the two. I think if we'd made this façade only of Portland stone and/or red brick we wouldn't have been able to make the transition between the two buildings in a sensitive enough way, so we introduced a third element, which is the panelled stucco/stone, and this allows one to soften and weld the conjunctions and transitions between the Tate and the lodge.

CJ: But why did you come to the square motif and its particular relation with the square pilaster systems?
JS: I felt it could produce more stable vertical/horizontal surfaces. It was less directional and allowed you to make transitions diagonally.

CJ: Yes, but classicists are going to have troubles with this building... Let's go back to Alberti and Brunelleschi where the pilaster system of rectangular bays on the outside represented a mental order and, perhaps, a real structural order on the inside. In your case you have this square grid on the outside which is repeated on parts of the inside, but it does not correspond to anything in particular, does it?

JS: I think when Alberti and Brunelleschi and others were setting up the orders of the Renaissance they were doing it in a more abstract way. They were proposing orders and proportions for a movement in general. What we're trying to do here is to find a solution in particular... How do you make an extension to this symmetrical/classical building? What we've done here we wouldn't necessarily do elsewhere. We might re-use the principle, but not in exactly the same way. You would probably have different circumstances... I found it a necessary transitional device and would point out that the grid disappears when you get round to the service elevation at the back but reappears on the fifth façade, which will eventually be the wall of a sculpture garden. So we are making distinctions between public façades and the service (functional) elevations, which you might describe here as low-cost high tech.

CJ: You speak of it as a garden building, hence its informality, hence the trellis, the pergola and lilypond. But is it a garden building in another way? What generic type did you have in mind?

JS: Well, it's also a garden wall containing the gardens of the Tate, and you will approach the new entrance by walking through these gardens. Moreover we wanted to make an entrance which was not competitive with the existing entrance of the Tate where you go up steps and through a central portico — symmetrical and monumental. So we turned our entrance side-on to the Tate, deferential to the established entrance. Instead of being monumental ours is downscaled like the entrance to a garden building, such as an orangery when it is an extension to the country house. We also wanted to have the galleries in the new building at the same level as those in the Tate so that the public could go from one to the other without awareness of change, which principle we follow at Stuttgart and at the Sackler (when they build the bridge). It means however that the accommodation below, in this case the entrance hall, auditorium, lounge, etc., is pushed down below ground level. So we designed a sunken paved forecourt as a transition or doorstep to the new building; instead of going up monumental steps you go down into a paved garden.

CJ: Nevertheless, some of the public are going to have trouble with some of the allusions which are all of such a generic nature that you can't say the building is immediately reminiscent of anything. The only thing it reminds me of is a previous set of buildings you've done, except that is the voided entrance pediment reminiscent of Mycenae; John Summerson finds this and the lunette window above like Newgate Jail, reminiscent to him of Dance.

JS: These elements relate to the immediate context and are up/down reversals of what happens on the adjoining corner of the Tate, where there is a pediment up top and a lunette window down. Across the sunken forecourt, we are trying to maintain a conversation between the new building and the old.

CJ: But the fact is that the voided pediment of Herculean size makes one think of those other associations...

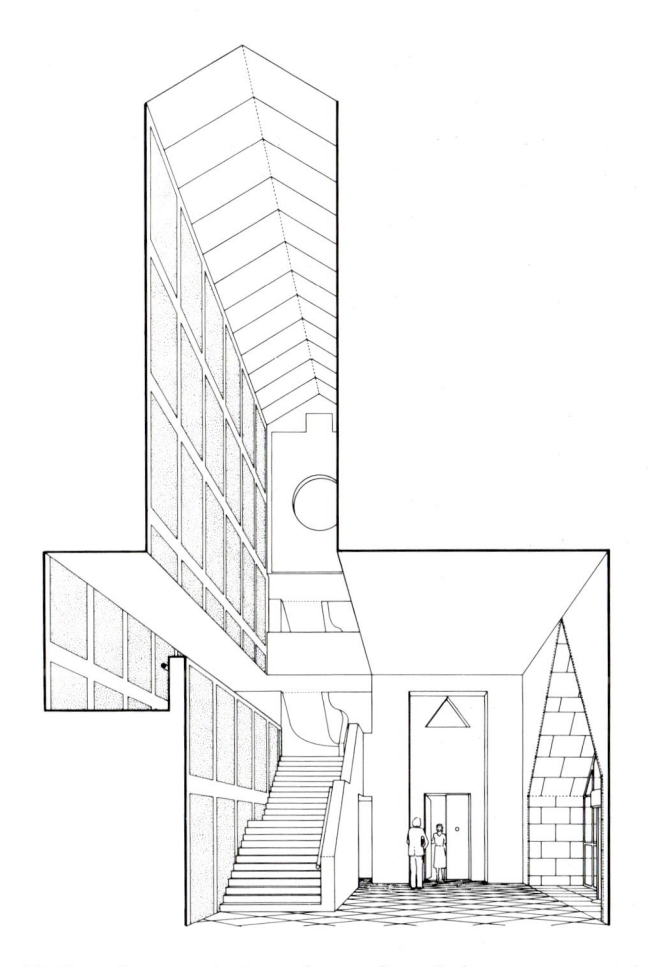

*London, Clore Gallery,
Turner Collection,
Tate Gallery
(with Michael Wilford),
1980–86, perspective
of the entrance to
the reading room*

JS: Yes, the association of a tomb and then a memorial; also you go down into those sorts of places. Maybe all museums are like tombs — secure vaults containing things of great value.

CJ: But, coming back to the problem some people will have with your allusions — they'll certainly have a problem with that wonderful corner which erodes the grid just at the point where bricks usually get supported. Above this corner the visual support falls away and the bricks hang in space,

259

which is a provocation not only to the Renaissance but the modern movement and, indeed, the normal bystander who thinks that bricks should be supported. It's also an affront to Vitruvius... who said that things should look as if they're solid and can stand up.

JS: One may become a little anxious as to how that wall is held up and gets round the corner, which is a way of emphasizing the bay window below as a major element of the interior overlooking the garden.

CJ: But, there's again a new rule here... you could have lowered the wall eight inches or so and had a transition with a frame on it — just as around the voided pediment entrance there could have been a moulding which would have been a classical thing. The fact is, you consistently cut your rhythms.

JS: All these cuts — Summerson uses the reference to scissors — expose the reality of the construction. This building is not made of solid stone or structural brickwork as are the Tate and the lodge; here the external surface is not a structural expression — the materials are all veneers onto an inarticulate concrete structure. One is trying to indicate that these veneered surfaces are not structural — hence the scissoring of walls in strategic places.

CJ: Let's call it a philosophy of the expressed veneer. You express the veneer by showing it hang in tension or by eroding it, which is a kind of grammar or rule.

JS: I think when using traditional materials in an untraditional way you have to make explicit that they are applied. Here there's a kind of abstract slashing and cutting which can only mean that these materials and symbols are not as substantial as they appear.

CJ: Yes, but architects don't have to tell the truth all the time. There's still a residual modernist thing in you that wants to tell the observer the truth.

JS: I wouldn't deny that.

CJ: You're quite didactic, like a schoolteacher who is using the scissors method and the ways of disjunction to get in his lesson.

JS: I dislike equally pasticherie and revivalism and I'm puritanical enough to want to make it clear that the building, familiar though it may look, is in fact made in a different way. How can one get back to using traditional materials like stone and brick and stucco in a way that is not false? Because one still wants to use traditional materials for contextual, urban and monumental reasons.

CJ: If we generalize and conclude, there are a series of new rules here which are exciting and stimulating and which push the history of contextualism a stage further. This is the most advanced building on that level I know of in the world and very provocative and enjoyable it is. Though, at first glance, one can experience it as being quite ugly and the tensions and disjunctions as overpowering, I wonder what you have to say to those people who will feel that it doesn't conform to any of their expectations.

JS: Well, I think they will have to come back a second time to see how they feel about it. It will take a year to settle down. Then I think its different way of doing things will become familiar and accepted.

James Stirling, 1960

Seven Keys to Good Architecture

For architects to create buildings as monuments to their own aesthetic feelings is a worthless occupation, always. Today we have to create practical, logical and appropriate organizations out of the problems of society — at the big level of the city and town right down to the smallest level, which is the street or individual house.

Knowing that what they make is going to be occupied by people, architects have a very heavy responsibility to society. As well, they should expect to go out and directly influence society's behaviour. Sometimes they must react against it. In any case they must regard almost everything with suspicion as being most certainly obsolete.

I regard myself as a routine functionalist. By this I mean using patterns of logic which involve producing a building solution which is relevant to the times we live in and which is inherent in the problem as it is presented — the site, the functions, the materials, the cost. But functionalism is not enough. The building must also be expressive. You ought to be able to look at it and recognize its various component parts where people are doing different things.

Styling cuts against this. It is a gimmick contrary to the whole twentieth-century concept of architecture as expressing the activity of a building. Unfortunately, too much em-

Published in Twentieth Century, *Winter 1963.*

phasis is put on the visual aspects of architecture. Society should not be concerned with appearance but with the aptness of the programmes, the relevance of the organizations and the correctness of the requirements. Also, structure, for me, is what holds the building up. I never isolate it as being important in itself.

From the programme you construct a hierarchy to decide what are the most important factors that you need to solve in terms of the organization you adopt. I never see a commission as just a building, a picture. I see it as this organization in which, through thorough understanding of the programme, I meet all, or most of, the problems. If the programme is wrong then you should try to influence it. There are even cases where you should actually turn jobs away because the programme is so incorrectly presented as to be arbitrary or artificial.

I believe that modern architecture has nothing to do with the past. You cannot compare a building of this time with that of another. To do so would be idiotic. The industrial revolution changed everything in every conceivable way. While I enjoy past architecture in itself I do not accept that you can carry it over into our time as a lesson to assist you. It lacks relevance.

This is Tomorrow

Why clutter up your building with "pieces" of sculpture when the architect can make his medium so exciting that the need for sculpture will be done away with and its very presence nullified.

Published in the catalogue of the exhibition This is Tomorrow *at the Whitechapel Gallery.*

The painting is as obsolete as the picture rail. Architecture, one of the practical arts, has, along with the popular arts deflated the position of painters, sculptors — the fine arts.

The ego maniac in the attic has at last starved himself to death.

If the fine arts cannot recover the vitality of the research artists of the twenties (who through the magazines generated a vocabulary for the practical arts), then the artist must become a consultant, just as the engineer or quantity surveyor is to the architect, though their relationship to the specialist, e.g. industrial designer or furniture maker, would be more intimate for they would be directly concerned with conception.

*Columns for the Berlin
Science Center, the
enlargement of Cornell
University and the
Library at Latina*

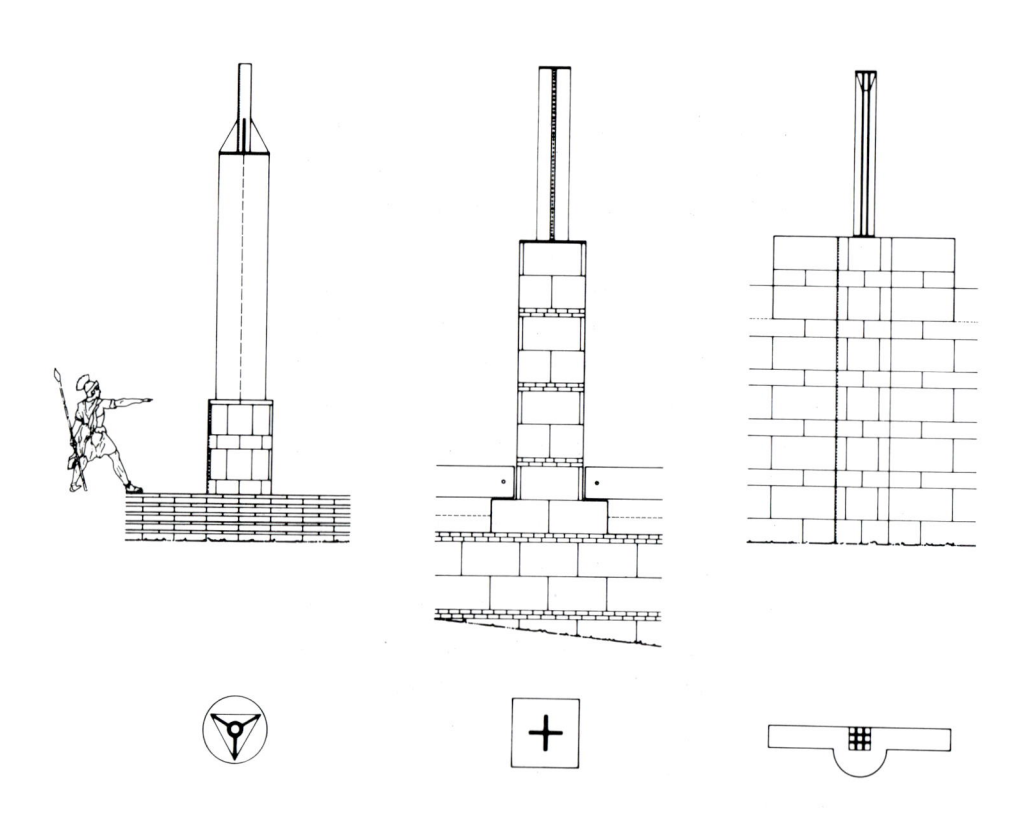

Three Loggias

Notes from a lecture, 1985.

Having always insisted that our designs emerge, as it were inevitably, from a logical analysis of the site, plus a functional interpretation of the building's requirements; hey presto. There is nevertheless the matter of "presence" and "personality", of "formalisms" and "style" in their appearance. Looking back, it is a fact that our designs have sometimes come in "series", which has led me, recently, to think that formal expression is maybe stronger than I would have liked to believe. An aesthetic style manifesting itself in "one" could be an accident and in "two" might be a coincidence, but when it reappears in "three" must surely be deliberate.

There are for instance, the three university buildings of the late fifties and early sixties — the Engineering Department at Leicester; the History Faculty at Cambridge, and the student residence at Oxford; undoubtedly variations on a theme..., another example are the three German museum projects (Düsseldorf, Cologne, Stuttgart).

I am not sure why projects come in "series" though it's a phenomenon for many architects — for instance there is Frank Lloyd Wright's "series" of concrete block houses in Los Angeles, and also Le Corbusier's early studio houses in Paris; and these architects were able to keep moving to additional "series" with all manner of "one offs" in between.

Library at Latina (with Michael Wilford), 1983, section on a reading room and detail of a skylight

Whereas with Mies van der Rohe and (to come down to my level), perhaps Richard Meier and Robert Stern, who are always consistent; indeed I might observe their projects are either all brilliantly consistent, or mainly repeats. I have to console myself with the view that our production whilst being a good deal more eclectic, is I believe more appropriate in this evolutionary phase of architecture.

I'd now like to show a final "series of three" possibly indicating an obsession with the theme of "the loggia". I was resident at the American Academy in Rome in 1982 and went with the scholars to Urbino and the Ducal Palace, though I've visited loggias before and indeed there is a loggia in our Wissenschaftszentrum project. However, it may have been the Urbino visit which compounded the obsession.

Library at Latina

We were recently asked to design a public Library in the City of Latina which was initiated by Mussolini, it was called Littoria and was sited on the Pontine marshes: which were extensively canaled and effectively drained in the thirties.

The Library is placed across the wide end of a triangular site, in the centre of town. We hope it is bold and simple in contrast to the "assortment" of adjoining buildings, and monumental — to indicate the Library's civic importance. The requirement that there should be a public park suggested the relationship of a palazzo to its garden. This garden is important as foreground to the new building and as a focal area in the city.

Flanking the Library, grass lawns slope down to form a partially sunken garden and in fine weather there will be tables and shade umbrellas outside the new café-bar. The new building may have a garden character and the loggia which links adjoining streets and overlooks the gardens will, we

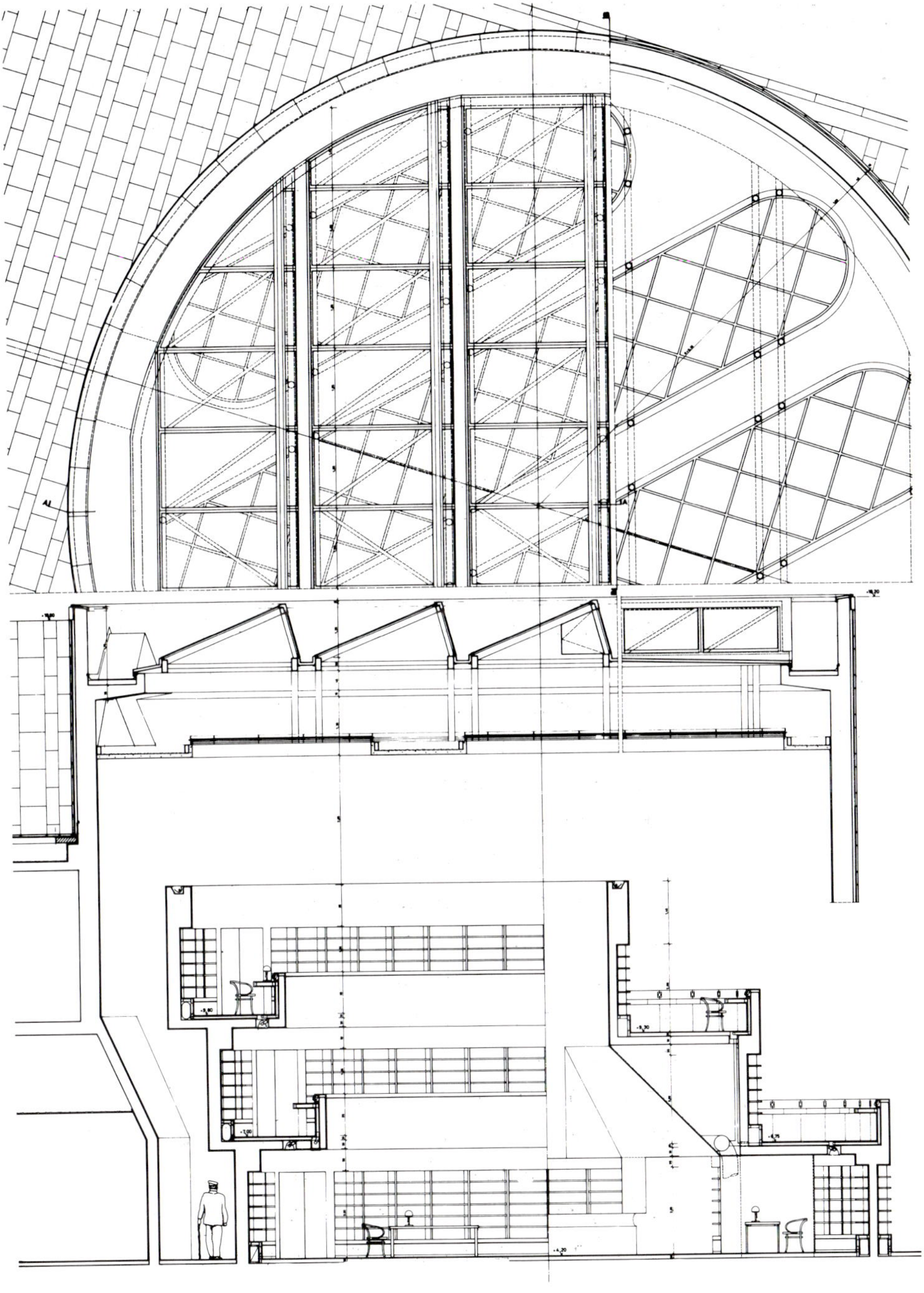

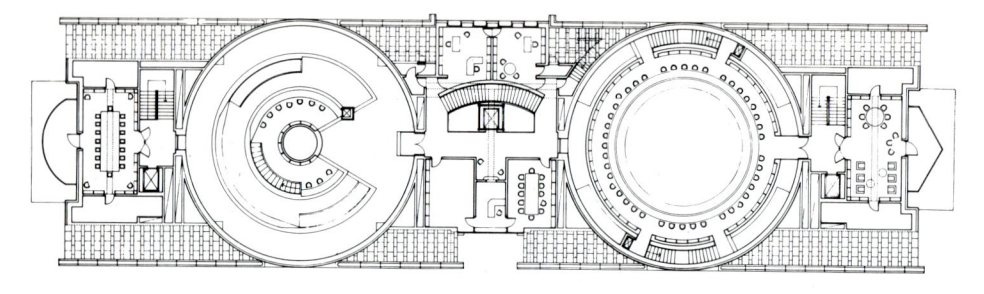

Library at Latina (with Michael Wilford), 1983, plan of the first floor

hope, be used as traditional colonnades for public promenade and informal encounters.

Cladding of walls, roofs and drums would be in alternating courses of travertine and sandstone (similar to the Staatsgalerie). The loggia roof, its trusses and supporting columns would be metallic — highly coloured and reflective, as also the metalwork to bay windows and air intake grills at gable ends.

Performing Arts Centre at Cornell

The Performing Arts Centre for Cornell University (USA) is sited on the edge of Cascadilla Gorge just off campus and the new facility will look back towards the university. Prominently sited on College Avenue it adjoins the bridge over the Gorge, reinforcing this entrance to the campus and strengthening the link between university and community. We proposed a group of buildings connected by a "loggia", the de-

Compton Verney, Opera House (with Michael Wilford), 1989, view on the loggia and the theatre

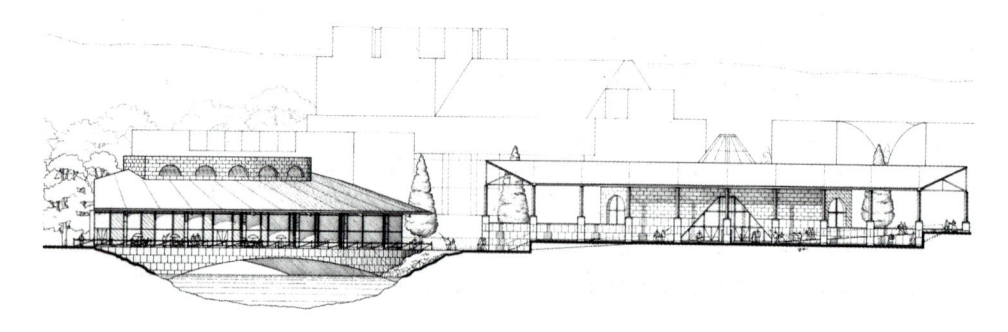

270

Compton Verney, Opera House (with Michael Wilford), 1989, general perspective of the loggia

sign of which, we hope, is appropriate to the park-like character of the Gorge.

Entry is through the loggia, a promenade approach with spectacular views towards the campus and to Lake Cayuga beyond. Part of the loggia is glass-enclosed to provide an all weather lobby leading to a central foyer.

The entrance foyer is off the centre of the loggia and connects all major spaces; encouraging student/faculty interaction between theatre, dance and film groups, and bringing them into contact with the public when there is a performance. The foyer opens to the loggia enabling audiences in intermissions to stroll in and out and take the view.

Wissenschaftszentrum in Berlin

Right now we are completing the working drawings for the Wissenschaftszentrum, which is really a Think Tank — an institute for deep thinking on matters of environment, sociology and management. The old Beaux-Arts building which somehow survived the war has to be preserved, and we will re-use it for conference facilities.

The primary requirement was for a multitude of small of-

Compton Verney,
Opera House
(with Michael Wilford),
1989, general
axonometric

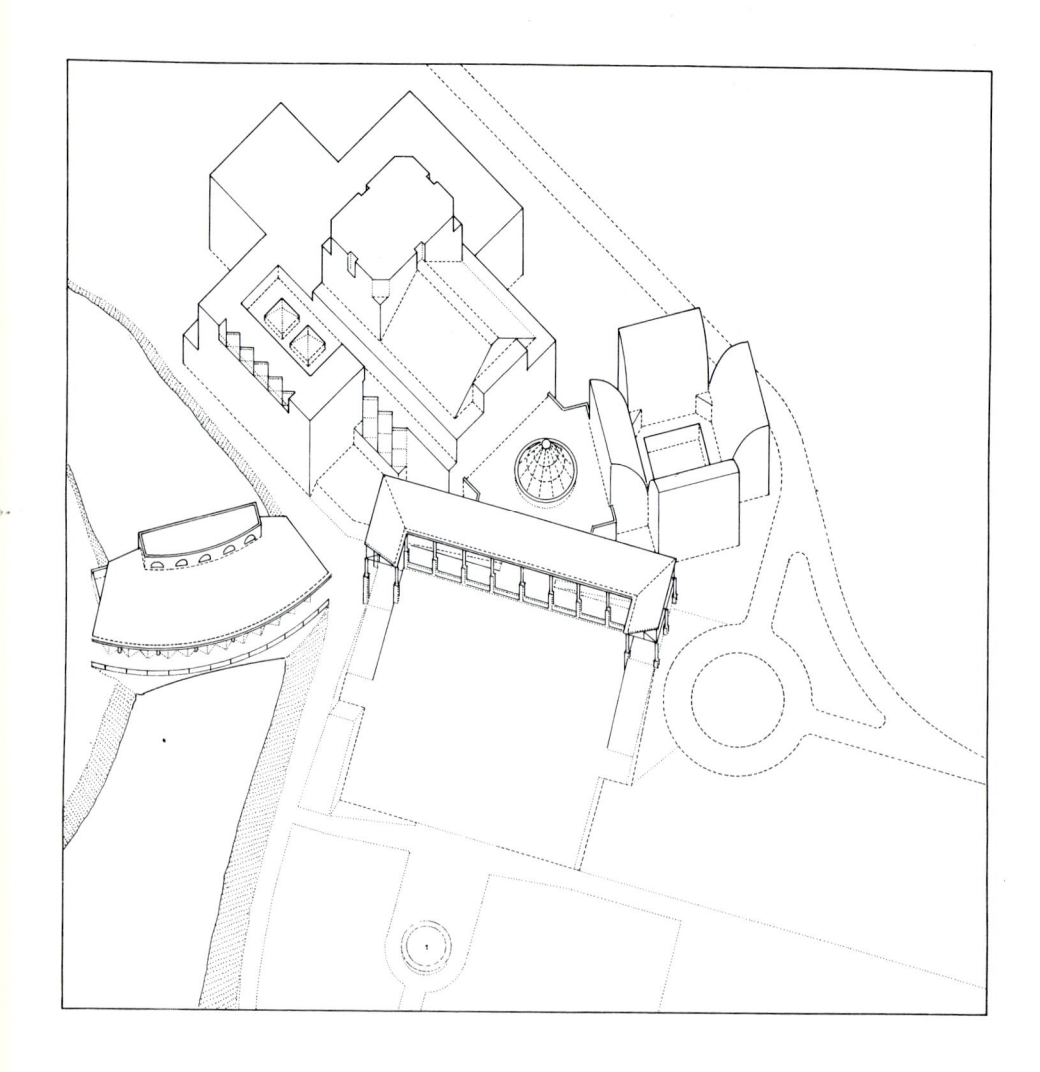

fices and we were concerned to find an architectural and environmental solution from a programme almost entirely comprised of repetitive offices. Our proposal is to use the three departments, plus the element for future expansion, plus the Library/archive to create a grouping of four or five buildings juggled together with the old building. This architectural ensemble may display familiar building types with each department having its own indentifying building. Though, as all buildings touch at every floor level the whole can function as a single complex.

The new buildings cluster around a garden and glass-roofed loggias are incorporated in the stoa and the amphitheatre buildings. There are also arcades formed within the old building and in the end of the cruciform building. We hope to make a friendly unbureaucratic place — the opposite of an "institutional" environment; it is perhaps more akin to a college or university precinct than an office building.

James Stirling, 1976

Master Class: Comments on Teaching at Düsseldorf

The ultimate teaching achievement must be a "Master Class". This seems to be given to those who professionally can go no further (and maybe on the edge of going over the top). It would give the Architect a cultural status similar to a great musician, sculptor or opera singer (which I would like to have been — if not an architect).

Architects seldom have this possibility though Louis Kahn had something similar in Philadelphia. Outside the US one can think of Van Eyck, Gardella, Ludwig Leo and others who perhaps should have a Master Class, and if the institutions had promoted Classes for Aalto, Mies, Moretti, Scarpa, to name a few, it would have benefitted the continuity and enrichment of modern Architecture. After twenty years as visiting teacher at Yale — and before as part time critic at schools of architecture in the UK — a Master Class would be a final accomplishment for me.

At the Kunstakademie there exists a special situation as teachers include Kasper, Ungers and sometimes Hollein. So my scenario for the "International Master Class" at Düsseldorf would be as follows: the students would be graduates of some years experience, highly selected for their design potential. Twice a year each would complete a complex design problem. The projects would be chosen by the stu-

Published in Aedes Gallery catalogue, July 1987.

dents who would stay in the Academy for two or three years. The subjects could be a competition, a real building, a theoretical study, etc. There would be no teaching of history or structure, only the Art of Architecture would be taught. There would be no marks or exams and except for admittance selection no administration — none would be necessary.

For a day a fortnight — though not to an agreed schedule — (it's impossible to agree mutual dates), Kasper would come from Aachen, Ungers from Cologne, Hollein from Vienna and myself from London.

So each student would be reviewed every two weeks by each teacher (I would ask all students to sit around and listen to the criticism and hopefully take part in the discussion). They would receive on different days independent criticism from the visiting teachers — and very likely they would receive differing and possible contrary advice; about which they would have to make up their own minds to select and reject according to what they thought appropriate to themselves and their project.

This would require a particular discipline; they would have to be mature and confident enough to cope with the ideas and personalities of the teachers and able to draw from a rich feast of advice (over eating could be a problem). Sometimes the teachers visits might coincide and there could be a joint review.

At the Kunstakademie there is the possibility for this unique Master Class to come into existence, as there may be no other department of Architecture anywhere which has such a group of leading Architects teaching such a small number of students.

However, the reality is less idealistic as each teacher has his own group of students and a typical day for me has been described by Marlies Hentrup. My mini Master Class at the Kunstakademie reminds me of the thesis seminars I used to have with Colin Rowe when I was in final year at Liverpool; the only difference is the presence of the other students — perhaps the tutorial teaching method changes less than Architecture itself; although the projects have changed, the subjects students choose nowadays avoid the overly social; mass housing, hospitals and schools are seldom proposed — instinctively it's felt their Architectural content is at a minimum. The style of the fifties may be of interest to some but it's not related to the programmes of the fifties and team work does not seem to be of much interest. Public buildings in the urban context are today's favoured projects, — libraries, theatres, town halls, museums, concert halls etc.

It is this dealing with a different subject per student which sustains my interest, as compared to the Yale involvement where all students were working on the same project.

As always the design ability of the students varies too much, and one has to resist better students becoming favourites.

So why do I teach — and always abroad? Firstly the UK schools are not able to comparably finance a Professorship; and Düsseldorf is one hour in the aeroplane — and it gets me out of the office, which is necessary partly as every weekend is spent in the office. But really it's because some of the students have ways and ideas which are so startling and unexpected that they make me stop and think. I may have a better responding facility but they can start with something so fresh, even naïve, that it's an eye opener, and they can end with something so pure and uncompromised that it's uplifting. So the teaching situation remains for me a give and take process.

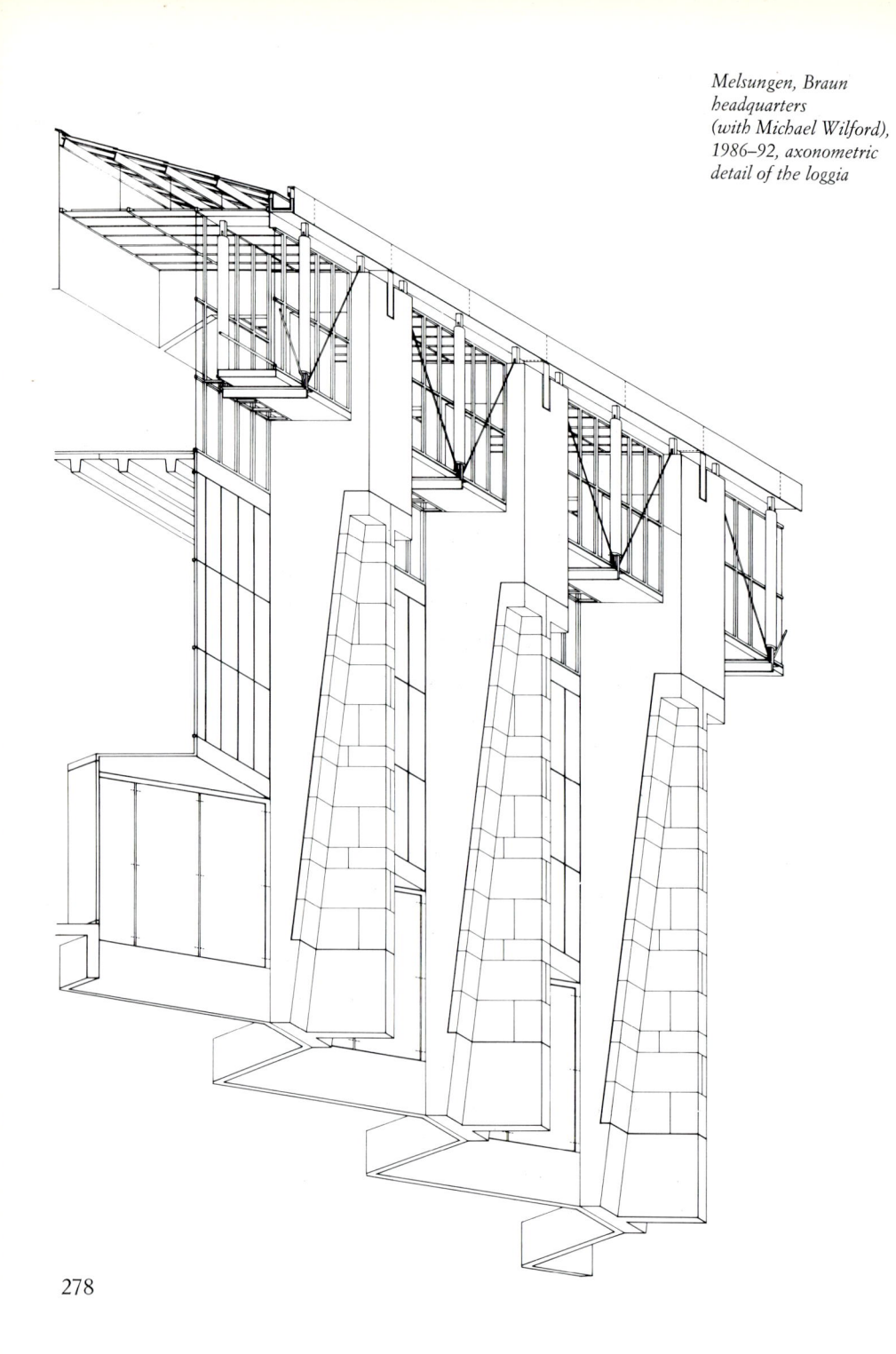

*Melsungen, Braun
headquarters
(with Michael Wilford),
1986–92, axonometric
detail of the loggia*

Building into Landscape
Content into Form

With our Braun headquarters, one architectural theme of the project is the spacial integration of large-scale buildings into an environment of rural character. The buildings are situated in an area where two river valleys meet. A small hill, the Buschberg, lies in the centre of this area like a traffic island, preventing direct view into the site when approached from the direction of Melsungen. We are trying to use the natural features of the landscape architecturally and make them a stronger experience by specific shaping and positioning of the buildings.

Published in Aedes Gallery catalogue on Melsungen, 1991.

How is it, that after all these donkey's years, I intend to speak about a cause that was won and lost so long ago?

I have always felt that what I have to say is of no particular interest or value to contemporary architects, whose convictions, intellectual manner and habits of thought I do not share. The absence of shared assumptions makes any attempt at exhortation irrelevant, any preaching ineffective.

Further it would be unfair to hold the architects directly responsible for the crippling damage they inflict upon society by disrupting, gutting and devastating the environment; pounding, crushing and pulverising our towns, or incrediblising them with looming terminal lumpen-architecture.

The Circulation Wall cuts into the valley perpendicular to its axis. The curved profile of the terrain is emphasized by the strong horizontality of the wall. This building creates a feeling of "inside" and "outside" *geist* — bearing witness to the social experience that conditions their choice. The factory. It serves as a vertical circulation building between the various levels of the multi-storey carpark and directs the user by means of natural light to the main horizontal circulation building, the timber bridge...

While deluding themselves that they are expressing their own daring personalities, they are in fact only giving expression to the Zeitgeist — bearing witness to the social experience that conditions their choice.

There are times when man extends his hold over the surrounding chaos, and rationality is at the root of his activity. Reason is now the intellectual force that guides him.

At these stages of social development, the universe is seen as a consistent, reliable order, whose manifestations are open to rational enquiry. The very clarity of the composition sustains the conviction of ultimate perfectibility, legibility and interrelation, and the belief that reason, guided by experiment, can ultimately discover order in what appears to be arbitrariness and chaos.

...the timber bridge is a connector between the northern part of the site with the Administration Building, the southern area where gangways lead to various parts of the factory, and the exits from the multi-storey carpark. The structure consists of a three-dimensional system of timber sticks whose position relative to each other is influenced by the shape of the ground below. As a result in the interior of the bridge a space is created which changes continuously. The inclination

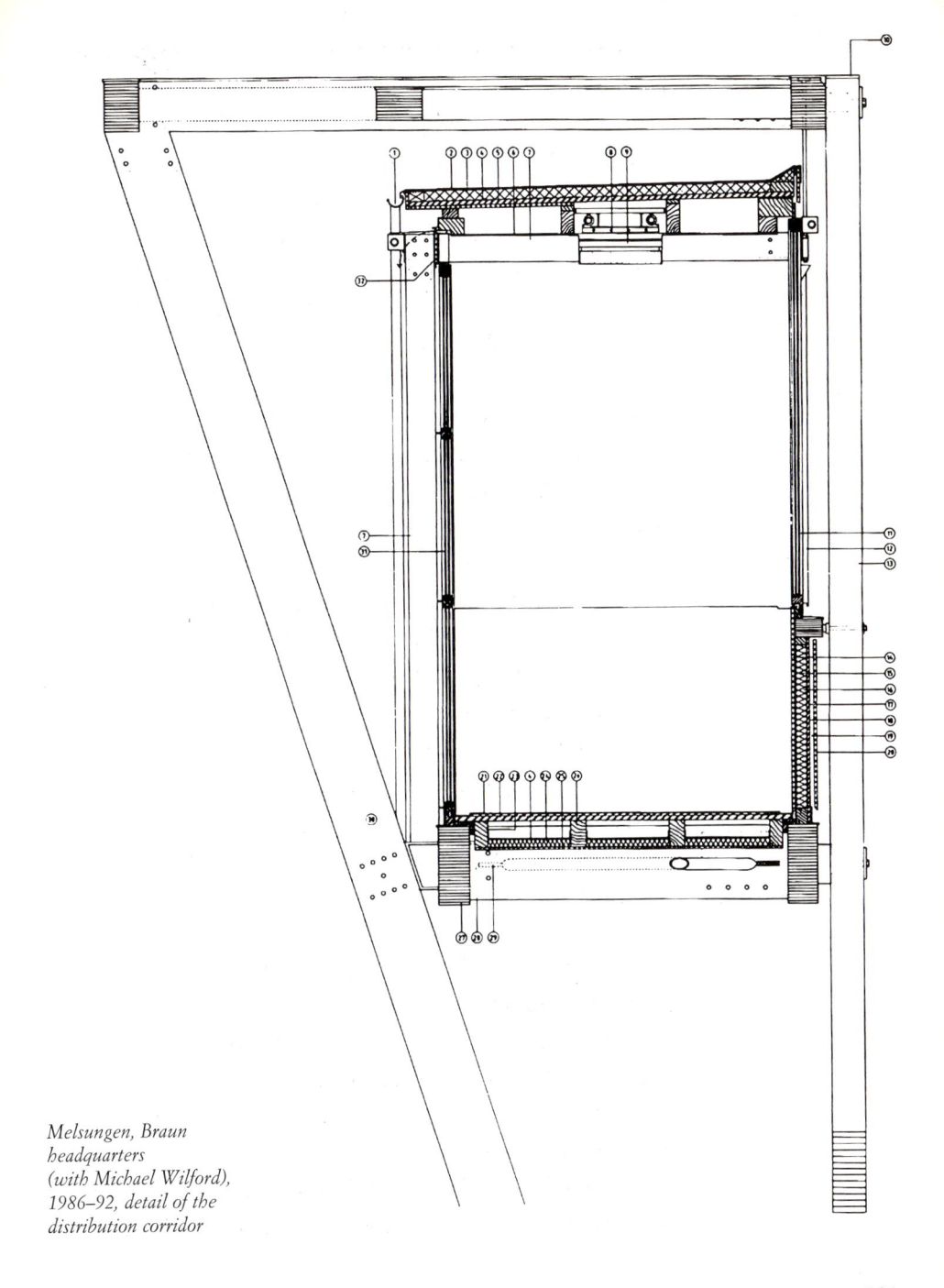

*Melsungen, Braun
headquarters
(with Michael Wilford),
1986–92, detail of the
distribution corridor*

of the back row of the timber sticks is deep in the centre of the bridge and shallow towards the ends. There is a relationship established between the increasing tendency of the building to fall over (lean against the wall) and its architectural role within the project: at the ends are the points where the building is most dependent on being supported by the building behind, and that is also the point one leaves the bridge. That way there is a relationship between the structural and the functional content of the building.

Instead of aiming at the manipulation of forms for the sake of sensory pleasure, art now sets itself to argue and reason through them, striving for harmony between part and the whole, searching for unity between causes and effects, observed events and inferred values.

Essentially, its comprehensible intention and the predictability of its meaning transcend subjective interpretations.

Today... a decaying, crisis-ridden society rejects the notion of continuity in favour of an ad hoc, *piecemeal engineering, improvised on the spot out of fragments of experience, out of bits and pieces, odds and ends at hand, with no relevance to an irrelevant past or an inscrutable future that may never arrive.*

The Production Building is organised vertically. High up, with views into the landscape, lies the main working area, the production floor. There are connections on various levels to the circulation routes for people, to the Goods Distribution Centre via a separate route for automatic goods transport and to the Energy Centre for ducting and energy supplies. The production of medical plastic products requires clean air conditions. Therefore there is only access to the production area via air locks. There are social rooms and changing rooms on garden level in the back. The Production Building in its final stage extends all the way along the site facing the Goods Distribution Centre in the middle of the site...

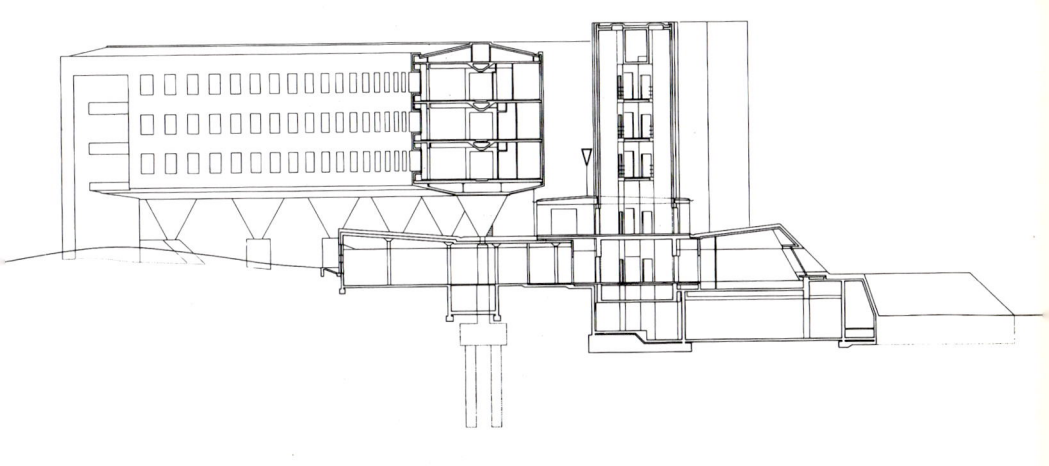

In the precarious climate of the rule of chance, on the brink of mental instability, art abandons the discipline of self-imposed restraints, and takes the form of an hysterical assault on the senses.

A cynical thought occurs: does this confusion come about because, by accepting the unfettered rule of chance, the glorification of the haphazard and the unforeseen, all the agonizing doubts and embarrassing scruples involved in the search for a rational architectural solution can be avoided?

It is perfectly possible to assume that there are innocent architects, but in an absurd world there can be no such thing as innocent architecture, since there is no art that is not part of the social fabric.

Melsungen, Braun headquarters (with Michael Wilford), 1986–92, transverse section of the administration building

If the artist reflects a world he sees as arbitrary, intractable, and at the mercy of chance, his work can only dethrone reason, and so reconcile man with a predicament that cannot be changed or improved, but must be endured.

This fatalism cannot but support a tottering order. Reason's role, on the other hand, is to appeal to universal criteria, as objective as the law of gravity, searching for orderly precision, interdependence and clarity of structure, no matter how embarrassing and troublesome this enquiry may be.

Thus, whether he realises it or not, every artist is either an apologist or a critic of society. Non-partisanship is always, in practice, support for the status quo.

...the group forming the Goods Distribution Centre serves as a semi-automatic storage facility for raw materials to the finished products, made here or elsewhere. There is a sterilization plant integrated into the flow of goods from the Production Building. The various halls form a succession of architectural spaces with different identities. A circulation building similar to the Circulation Wall connects the various halls and provides a means of orientation.

Here ends the circulation system for people terminating in social rooms on artificial ground level. The elliptical building is a large-scale element to make a transition into the landscape, similar to the Administration Building on the northern part of the site...

At this point, one can ask why, in times of ferment, confusion and disintegration, should architects, instead of rallying to the defence of sanity, open the floodgates to the wildest excesses of irrationality, unrestrained exhibitionism or institutionalised absurdity?

By rejecting reason as a guide to human enterprise, art de-

nies the universal norms, attacks systematic thought, and plunges headlong into hedonistic formalism, confining the mind in a closed circle of biological sense-impressions.

Architecture can least of all the arts be judged by what is immediately presented to the eye. Direct observation is unable to grasp and comprehend the essential interplay of visual and conceptual meaning in the absence of the ability to read plan and section, to judge the relation of load and support or of solid and void, form and content, and a vast array of social and economic factors that influence the design.

An exclusive preoccupation with those easily-measurable characteristics of form directly accessible to the senses — hard or soft, big or small, slick and up-to-date or old-fashioned — reduces art to nothing more than a branch of the fashion trade.

This is how a whirl of superficiality, and endless torrents of spurious, contrived novelty, is substituted for genuine change, development and transformation.

Melsungen, Braun headquarters (with Michael Wilford), 1986–92, general plan

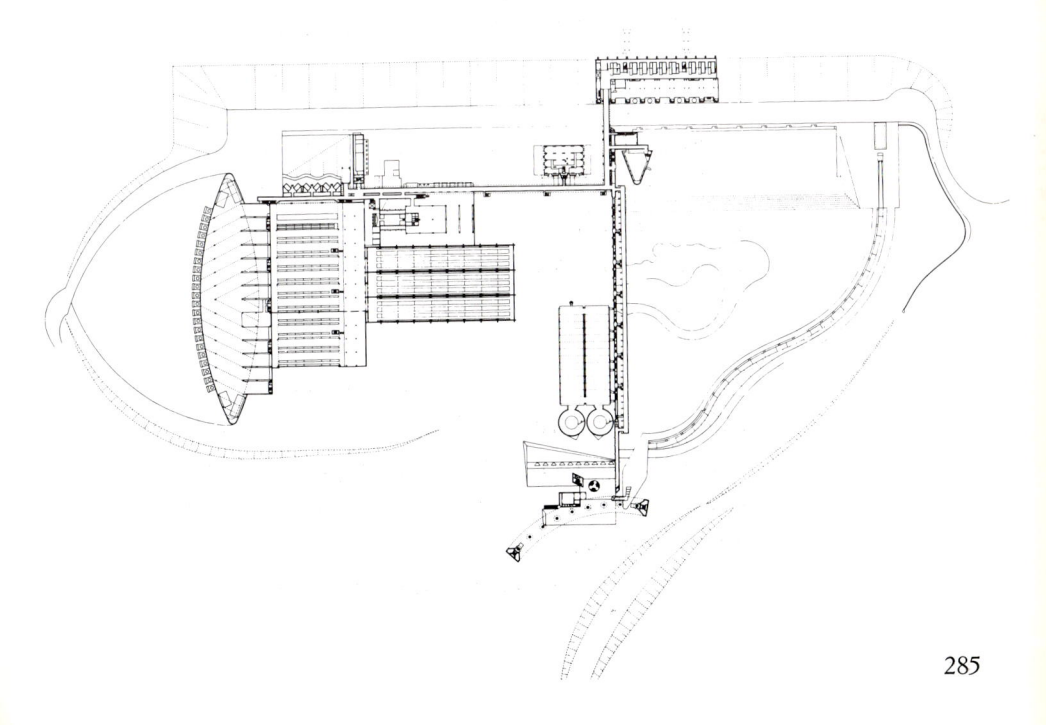

...the upper part of the Administration Building follows the shape of the little hill in front and makes it visible from a greater distance. It bridges freely over a base which is related to the internal geometry of the factory only. The upper part contains office spaces, the base is double height and contains large spaces for the central computer.

We see the stationary masquerading as progress. Not only the reliance on visual impact alone, but that mirror image, equally dear to the manipulators, the ready-made disembodied conceptual joke that echoes forever through the mental wilderness amid screams of pre-recorded laughter, shows that form without content is as sterile as content without form — the complete absence of form is only a special case of formalism.

Why do architects opt for malignant distortions and trendy obscurity? Why is architectural composition conceived today as a commotion of swarming, discordant, unrelated components, a fortuitous expression of a futile environment, apparently intended to shock and confuse, rather than to relate and assert the interdependence of the parts and the whole.

The quest for reason has been abandoned, not out of frivolity or blindness, but because society prefers not to see what it does not want to know, and rewards those artists who help to make current myths plausible, enabling us to live at ease with the sordid reality that surrounds us.

If everything is barren, illegible, and accidental, rational thought is impotent, and the philosopher's stone is to be sought in the eye of a madman. Thus we absolve ourselves of any obligation to strive for change.

Whether we realize or not, this is the content *of today's architecture, and the cause of its decay.*